The Rare Find

How does the FBI's hostage rescue team find agents for the world's toughest job? How do Hollywood casting agents size up the best talent?

There's a huge difference between elite performers and everyone else: in terms of productivity there's a five-to-one gap. No one can afford to settle for mediocrity.

Talking to the world's best, most secretive talent scouts, George Anders found that they all share an intense belief in finding high achievers who can create big successes. These are the arenas where brilliant recruiting is most vital – and in *The Rare Find* Anders reveals how the rest of us can learn the hidden 'tells' that really matter.

Pairing these frontline observations with cutting-edge research from psychiatrists, economists, recruiters and business strategists, Anders shows how anyone can hone the ability to recognize future greatness and discover tomorrow's stars.

Praise for *The Rare Find*:

'George Anders combines deep reporting, vivid storytelling, and keen analysis to help unravel the mysteries of talent. Whether you're running a large organization or managing a small team, *The Rare Find* is that rare book – a must-read'
Daniel H. Pink, author of *Drive* and *A Whole New Mind*

'George Anders is himself a rare find. A superb writer, he brings piercing intellect and persistent curiosity to examine the single most important leadership skill: finding and picking the right people. By turning his own talent upon this vital and elusive question, Anders has done a great service'
Jim Collins, author of *Good to Great*

'George Anders finds the deep truth about choosing people right. You'll never make these supremely important decisions the same way again'
Geoff Colvin, author of *Talent is Overrated*

'Quite simply, the best book on the subject I've ever read'
Daniel Coyle, author of *The Talent Code*

'Resilience, curiosity, and self-reliance are strengths that don't show up in HR hiring manuals. In *The Rare Find*, George Anders shows that they lead to fresh ways to hunt for talent. More power to him for daring to advocate that which is not obvious'
Andrew S. Grove, former chairman and CEO of Intel

ABOUT THE AUTHOR

George Anders spent two decades as a top feature writer for the *Wall Street Journal*, where he was part of a team that won a Pulitzer Prize for national reporting. He has also written for *The New York Times*, *Parade*, *Fast Company*, *Smart Money* and *Harvard Business Review*. He is the author of three previous books, including the *New York Times* bestseller *Perfect Enough*, a biography of Carly Fiorina. He lives in northern California.

THE RARE FIND

How Great Talent Stands Out

GEORGE ANDERS

PORTFOLIO
PENGUIN

PORTFOLIO PENGUIN

Published by the Penguin Group
Penguin Books Ltd, 80 Strand, London WC2R ORL, England
Penguin Group (USA) Inc., 375 Hudson Street, New York, New York 10014, USA
Penguin Group (Canada), 90 Eglinton Avenue East, Suite 700, Toronto, Ontario,
Canada M4P 2Y3 (a division of Pearson Penguin Canada Inc.)
Penguin Ireland, 25 St Stephen's Green, Dublin 2, Ireland (a division of Penguin Books Ltd)
Penguin Group (Australia), 707 Collins Street, Melbourne, Victoria 3008, Australia
(a division of Pearson Australia Group Pty Ltd)
Penguin Books India Pvt Ltd, 11 Community Centre,
Panchsheel Park, New Delhi – 110 017, India
Penguin Group (NZ), 67 Apollo Drive, Rosedale, Auckland 0632, New Zealand
(a division of Pearson New Zealand Ltd)
Penguin Books (South Africa) (Pty) Ltd, Block D, Rosebank Office Park,
181 Jan Smuts Avenue, Parktown North, Gauteng 2193, South Africa

Penguin Books Ltd, Registered Offices: 80 Strand, London WC2R ORL, England

www.penguin.com

First published in the United States of America by Portfolio/Penguin,
a member of Penguin Group (USA) Inc. 2011
First published in Great Britain by Portfolio Penguin 2011
This edition published with a new chapter on 'Becoming a Rare Find' 2012
001

Copyright © George Anders, 2011, 2012

The moral right of the author has been asserted

Printed in Great Britain by Clays Ltd, St Ives plc

A CIP catalogue record for this book is available from the British Library

ISBN: 978-0-670-92095-2

www.greenpenguin.co.uk

ALWAYS LEARNING

For Betsy, Matthew, and Peter

Contents

Introduction 1

1: Sand, Sweat—and Character 15

2: The Talent Problem 37

3: Decoding the Jagged Résumé 59

4: Where Insights Are Born 81

5: Auditions That Work 100

6: Talent That Whispers 121

7: What Can Go Right? 139

8: Lottery Tickets 159

9: Talent That Shouts 180

10: When to Say No 199

11: Picking the Boss 218

12: Fitting the Pieces Together 235

13: Becoming a Rare Find 248

Notes 274
Acknowledgments 289
Index 291

Introduction

In early 2005, Todd Carlisle began an experiment. He grabbed a note-pad and ticked off twenty factors that might distinguish between hiring great employees and picking the wrong people. His early jot-tings focused on mainstream data that big companies normally track. Where did candidates go to college? What grades did they muster? How long had they been in the workforce, and so on?

Then Carlisle started popping into executives' offices, asking them: "What else would you add?" His list got bigger. It got weirder. Carlisle didn't mind. Even when there was an outlandish, bite-your-lip quality to someone's theories, Carlisle said, "Thanks!" and logged in the suggestion. Did Eagle Scouts make better employees? How about people who ran their own businesses in childhood? Or people with the single-minded intensity to set a national record in anything, no matter how unrelated to their jobs? What about chess wizards and dodgeball enthusiasts? Carlisle was a human sponge, soaking up every question he heard.

The more the list grew, the more it intrigued people. Nobody im-portant had commissioned this project. Carlisle had dreamed up the idea on his own. Officially, he was just a new guy in human relations with a company laptop and a taupe cubicle. He carried the hazy and not-very-impressive job title of "staffing programs manager." But as

1

this affable thirty-year-old kept running around the headquarters of one of America's most famous companies, powerful people started rooting for him.

One of the company's billionaire cofounders wanted to help out, too. He had emigrated from Russia at age six, settling into a new home in Maryland. By age nine, he was tinkering with a Commodore 64 personal computer that his father had given him as a birthday present. As the two men chatted, Carlisle wondered whether the best employees might have discovered computers at a very early age. That was worth researching, too.

Eventually, Carlisle's list topped out at three hundred factors. He had rounded up every business practice, folk saying, and crackpot theory he could find. His company was less than ten years old, yet it already employed nearly five thousand people. By hiring so aggressively from all corners of the world, the company had created a rare cauldron of provocative ideas and remarkable people. It was Carlisle's great fortune to be working there—at Google—at just the right time to carry out his project.

Many of Carlisle's factors focused on the life paths of computer engineers, because they were such a huge part of Google's workforce. But his list was so long and so diverse that it had a universal quality, too. If people in any high-achievement field were to compile their own lists, a lot of the same factors would pop up, too.

It was time to test all the theories. Thanks to Google's data-centric culture, Carlisle had no trouble organizing a massive online canvassing of the company's workforce. Employees raced through census-style surveys, chronicling their habits and accomplishments. Former lemonade-stand operators checked off one box. Marathoners and patent holders checked off others. Even the dodgeball players got their moment. Meanwhile, existing Google databases documented which employees were regarded as superstars, strong performers, and laggards.

All that Carlisle needed to do (with suitable privacy precautions) was to connect these enormous databases, shake them together, and see what patterns emerged.

Within a few months, Carlisle had his answers. On the question of childhood familiarity with computers, Google cofounder Sergey Brin turned out to be right. People who grew up as early adopters of technology tended to be unusually creative adults in new, uncharted realms. Most other supposed markers of success turned out to be mirages. When all the number-crunching was done, several dozen factors—including a few real oddities—emerged as ones that could help predict candidates' chances.

The biggest impact of Carlisle's experiment, however, transcended any single hiring shortcut. What Google learned was that it had been looking at candidates' résumés far too narrowly.

Fast-growing Google had started out by focusing inordinately on candidates' education, grade-point averages, and even SAT scores. The thinking was that high-IQ people would do best at Google, and that the best way of gauging brainpower was to look at candidates' classroom record. Google ended up with lots of Ph.D. holders from Stanford, MIT, Caltech, and top Ivy League schools. But by the time Carlisle got to work, there was lingering unease that some of these geniuses weren't quite as effective as Google had hoped. Even more important, company insiders worried that they might be turning away a lot of talented people whose true abilities surpassed their academic credentials.

"Take the wide view" became the overriding lesson of Carlisle's experiment. Transcripts and scores alone weren't the full measure of a candidate. There was room at Google for people whose grades had faltered because they were working thirty hours a week to pay for college. There was room for highly competitive people who had chased an athletic dream when they were younger—and now were applying that same relentless energy to professional goals. There was room, especially in nonengineering fields, for people who weren't great students, but who had been running businesses, tutoring, volunteering, and otherwise being civic leaders from their teenage days onward.

Such candidates would stay invisible if Google rigidly scanned résumés the traditional way, from top to bottom. As many as 75,000 résumés a week streamed into Google's offices. So many candidates chased so few openings that if reviewers didn't see some "Wow!" factor right away, it was time to hit the "Reject" button. The best hope of spotting these hidden winners, Carlisle came to believe, was to steal a quick peek at the bottom of the résumé. That's where he might find out that someone had competed in four Alaska marathons . . . or had made it into the *Guinness Book of World Records* . . . or had published three software manuals by age twenty-five. For the right job, those weren't peripheral details. They might be powerful insights into someone's character or on-the-job potential.

So Carlisle stopped reading résumés the usual way.

He became known as the man who analyzed résumés "upside down." Now, when Carlisle pulls up a résumé on his laptop—which tends to happen dozens of times a day—he begins by tapping the "Page Down" key a couple times until he reaches the final entries. Then he scrutinizes the loose ends of candidates' bios. "I want to know their stories," Carlisle explained to me one morning. "I want to know what these people are all about." In a moment, he might scroll back to the top and start hunting for the classic markers of competence: work history, education, credentials, and the like. But first, he wants to see if some special, rare attribute could point the way to greatness.

This is a book about people with the audacity to do what Carlisle did—to read résumés upside down—and why their approaches are so important to America's future. Over the past thirty years, I have been interviewing hundreds of people who wrestle with the same challenges that Google faced. They may be working at army bases, ad agencies, investment banks, Hollywood studios, big industrial companies, medical schools, corporate boardrooms, college admissions offices, speakers' bureaus, or nanny agencies. No matter what their calling, they all are consumed by the same few questions: "How do we spot rare talent? How do we know it's real? How do we avoid walking right past some of the best candidates we will ever see, without even recognizing our oversights?"

Those questions have been tantalizing and tormenting managers for a long time. But here's the fascinating twist. Over the past few decades, we as a society have made talent spotting vastly more sophisticated than it ever was before. Personal hunches have yielded to an endless stream of manuals and seminars. Online job boards offer thousands of candidates—now! If we want elaborate dossiers on candidates, we can gather facts (and video) by the gigabyte. If we want to rank candidates by any formula we choose, countless software programs will sort everyone in an instant. The tools at our disposal are more powerful than ever. Yet the results have hardly improved since the days of mimeograph machines and *The Jack Benny Show*.

In fact, it's arguable now that our ability to identify great people has deteriorated. We have created so much data that we're drowning in it. We scrutinize people so exhaustively for signs of proven competence that we may be losing the ability to do anything else. All we see are past credentials. Trying to forecast what people might achieve is a bigger mystery than ever. As a result, executives shy away from the mavericks, the late bloomers, the overachievers with the underdog past, or the inexperienced newcomers with the amazing potential. We are so afraid of making a mistake that we have lost the courage to do anything spectacularly right.

Such timidity is bad news at any stage of the economic cycle. But it's especially unfortunate now, when the United States and its major trading partners are shaking off the horrors of a financial collapse and getting ready to grow again. All sorts of new business opportunities are there to be seized. Organizations with the courage to hire great people and turn them loose will capture the rewards of a new era. Gun-shy outfits will let the moment slip away.

In 2010, business strategist Marc Effron surveyed a group of 1,800 human resources managers at big companies. He asked if they thought they were winning the war for talent. Only 18 percent of respondents said yes. All the rest felt they were either losing ground or stuck in an endless struggle where they weren't making headway.

Look at how far back in history we now turn to find inspiration. In politics, it's Abraham Lincoln's cabinet choices that are legendary. In military circles, it's George Marshall's ability in the 1930s to find the up-and-coming commanders who could help him win World War II. In sports, Vince Lombardi has been dead for forty years, but the way he built the Green Bay Packers into a championship team is still admired. Modern presidents, generals, and football coaches don't evoke nearly the same awe.

There are 208,000 full-time recruiters in the United States today, working everywhere from General Electric to a three-person firm specializing in pulp-mill operators. The ones I've met—and I've met a lot of recruiters over the years—tend to be likable, diligent, well-connected people. They reliably find competent candidates for their clients. Often they go one step further and produce what the business community likes to call "A-level players."

But when it comes to recognizing the first stirrings of genius, conventional talent spotters might as well be blindfolded. In pop music, one of the biggest recording labels in the country briefly signed teen sensation Taylor Swift to contracts very early in her career, but let her go because it didn't seem worth spending more than $15,000 a year for exclusive rights to her work. In baseball, a host of future

All-Star players went undrafted through the first thirty rounds of the sport's annual amateur draft, as teams burned up more than nine hundred picks on other players, most of whom would never play an inning of major league baseball. And in book publishing, at least four houses had a chance to buy the rights to J. K. Rowling's first Harry Potter novel for less than $5,000. All but one of them said no.

Of course, in each of those cases, someone did break away from the pack. Someone did take a chance on the unlikely prospects: the Swifts, Rowlings, and all their counterparts in other fields.

This book will show how the savviest talent judges practice their art. One chapter will explain how the U.S. Army finds soldiers good enough to be in Special Forces, without asking them to fire a single bullet. Battle-tested assessors can learn much more by watching candidates trudging forward on a long road march that isn't going well. That's when soldiers show their character.

Another chapter will journey to an elite basketball tournament in South Carolina. There, dozens of top coaches and scouts watch the game in a radically different way from what the casual fan might see. It hardly matters which team wins or who scores the most points. Something as mundane as what happens during a coach's timeout can reveal more about players' prospects for advancement.

Do some of these same concepts apply to the art of picking chief executive officers of giant major corporations? Yes, they do. In the same way that a handful of obscure, statistics-driven researchers transformed the ways that baseball talent is evaluated—the *Moneyball* effect—a trio of bookish, fastidious researchers are putting some remarkable new ideas to the test in picking CEOs. In effect, they, too, are reading résumés upside down. They are downplaying the factors that fascinate everyone else. That way, they can concentrate instead on small-grain details about CEO candidates that may have huge predictive power.

Fundamentally, everyone is trying to solve the same problem.

Each field has its own lingo, its own customs, and its own history. But the specific stories that fill this book all fit together as part of a bigger mosaic. There's an art to clearing away the clutter and focusing on what matters most. It is simple and it is transferable. It just requires the courage to take a different approach. The chapters that follow will show how rare finds occur—and what can be done to improve one's chances of capturing them.

The upshot: Great talent isn't hard to find if you know how to look. Opportunities to learn from mentors, from well-run organizations, and from our own decisions (wise or foolish) are everywhere. We can debate forever what exactly defines great talent. Some people regard it as a God-given gift; others see talent as something built up via hard work and disciplined training. Either way, the ability to pick the right people isn't out of reach for anyone.

I've been poking at various aspects of the people puzzle for nearly thirty years, both as a business-book author and as a feature writer with *The Wall Street Journal, Fast Company* magazine, and other national publications. In college I quizzed admissions directors about how they culled through 10,000 applicants and decided which 1,600 belonged at Stanford, Harvard, or Princeton. Later, covering finance for *The Wall Street Journal*, I learned how hard it is to identify the shrewdest stock-market investors in the world. All the same, the hunt for investment geniuses is so intense that it has become a minor industry in its own right.

I explored America's top teaching hospitals in my mid-thirties, hearing from famous physicians how they sized up young doctors. Another flurry of stories introduced me to the ways that giant foundations decide which social crusaders have the clarity and courage to deserve major grants. At the height of the dot-com boom, one of Silicon Valley's top venture capital firms let me become an embedded reporter, watching its partners as they tried to figure out which scruffy dreamers might be capable of launching the next Amazon.com.

As this collection of articles grew, I began to see patterns. Venture capitalists didn't work in the same quarters as doctors or philanthropists, but to a surprising degree, they all talked the same language. The best ones shared key habits. The less capable ones kept making similar mistakes. Before long even the busiest experts started carving out larger chunks of time to talk about how they sized up candidates. This was their life's work. I became their confidant, interrogator, skeptic, and chronicler of a remarkable craft. Eventually my interest intensified to the point that I pushed aside all other commitments. For the past two-and-a-half years, I have been crisscrossing the United States, gathering the research that became this book.

Many of this book's examples are drawn from watching experts in action, talking with their associates, and bringing current-day decisions to life. But there is also an important role for reconstructing historic decisions with the help of memoirs, biographies, old memos, and videotapes. Key examples come from three broad areas:

- the public-performance worlds of sports, arts, and entertainment
- high-stakes aspects of business, particularly finance and the information economy
- "heroic professions" of public service: soldiering, teaching, government, and medicine.

In these fields, experts don't just screen a few more candidates, ask tougher questions in the interview, or conduct more reference checks. They aren't merely paging through a well-thumbed personnel manual. They pick people and build teams in a profoundly different way. In some cases, it is as if they take the usual rulebook on hiring and hurl it into an incinerator. It was easy to see *how* they operated, but it took a while to understand *why*.

The answer popped into focus one afternoon over coffee with a longtime friend in advertising. We were chatting about what made his best salespeople successful, when Tony cut to the quick. "The reason that you're talking to me, along with all these other people," Tony said, "is because there's a huge difference between our very best performers and everyone else. If you take a hard look at productivity, you're seeing what easily amounts to a 300 percent difference. In fact, it's probably a five-to-one gap."

Where else was I encountering some version of that five-to-one test?

The answer: everywhere.

Sports coaches were constantly looking for that "impact player" who could transform an average team into a championship contender. Venture capitalists kept hunting for the entrepreneurs who could create the next Apple, Amazon, or Google. My most intriguing medical example, former surgery chief John Cameron at Johns Hopkins School of Medicine, didn't spend his career merely hunting for fine young surgeons; he was trying to identify people who could become department chairmen at top teaching hospitals, where their breakthroughs would transform disease care for the world. And the part of the FBI that interested me most was the elite Hostage Rescue Team, which found and developed agents who could handle the bureau's toughest tasks.

In all these fields, the gap between good and great turns out to be huge. Leaders can't ignore it. It isn't enough to figure out which candidates are competent and then move them along safe, predictable paths. That's a recipe for lackluster results. If talent spotters want to create a great organization, they must aim higher. They need to think constantly about how to find people with breakthrough potential, even if that's a chancier proposition that involves constantly navigating through ambiguity. The key question stops being: "Are you good enough to belong here?" Instead, it becomes: "Is there a chance you could become spectacular?"

Once this five-to-one standard enters the picture, it changes everything. Traditional thinking about risk gets turned inside out. Bad hires aren't the only peril. Now the gravest mistakes may involve a failure to hire someone great. Instead of constantly worrying about what can go wrong, talent-spotting specialists often need to think about what could go right.

The process of evaluating somebody becomes transformed, too. Traditional yardsticks of past achievement (test scores, academic degrees, or chin-ups) become preludes rather than the main event. Great selection now centers on the uncertain but far more fruitful realms of assessing what the future will be like and how well or poorly someone's growth will mesh with an organization's evolving needs. As a Silicon Valley engineering chief once told me: "We don't just care what you can do today; what we really want to know is what you can learn tomorrow."

In fields where capable people all perform at about the same level, there's no need to obsess about finding such a spark. It may not even exist. But in fields where the five-to-one test applies, talent-spotting experts are constantly hunting for that rare glimmer. They form theories about it in private, debate those ideas with their peers, and recalibrate their methods, again and again. It's their great pursuit.

If this book had been written a generation or two ago, it would have placed talent on a higher but much narrower pedestal. Historically Western societies have regarded great ability as a freakish gift from the gods. That created both an exaggerated respect—and also a certain degree of distaste—for spectacular performers. They were seen as prodigies from another planet, able to compute cube roots in their head or play Mozart sonatas at age four, but not necessarily adaptable to complex organizations. Most managers didn't need or want such people. The few that did simply turned them loose in some esoteric field, charged the rest of the world to see these stars perform—and hoped that it wouldn't all end in tears.

For much of the twentieth century, the United States in particular tried to assess regular workplace talent as if it were no more complicated than a problem in metallurgy. Engineers knew how to size up the hardness of steel or the melting point of various brass alloys. Shouldn't it be possible to assess human talent just as quickly, precisely—and permanently? Endless batteries of tests were developed that purported to do just that. IQ tests gained favor in the 1920s and remained a workplace standard for many decades beyond. The military tested more than 10 million people during World War II and used those scores to help determine who should be a cook and who should be an espionage agent.

Those tests were better than no placement system at all, or a system that relied on the prejudices of unsophisticated assessors. But they all assumed that talent was such a standard, unchangeable aspect of someone's identity that it could be identified effectively by a single pencil-and-paper test.

That's not the way we think about talent today. Pioneering work by psychologists such as K. Anders Ericsson of Florida State University has led us to regard talent as much more malleable and much more accessible. People get really good at something because they practice hard and have excellent mentors or reinforcing peer groups. Right now, at least, the nurture camp is vastly in the ascendancy. Nature's role now appears far smaller. Some of Ericsson's acolytes have even gone so far as to suggest that anyone can become quite talented in the field of their choosing, simply by mastering the art of working diligently at the hard stuff. (This is known as "deliberate practice.")

As a result, there's vastly more energy and anxiety these days about talent's role in our mainstream world. Big companies such as AT&T, Pfizer, and Deloitte & Touche now have "chief talent officers." In some cases, lively titles are merely an effort to make long-established parts of the human-relations department seem more exciting. But there's also a recognition that even fields such as law and accounting need to be thinking about concepts such as the five-to-one standard. In these old-line professions, credentials and quiet competence used to rule. Now a Darwinian struggle for survival is making constant innovation a necessity, not a choice.

In the chapters that follow, this book will introduce several crucial new terms to help break down the overall talent-spotting challenge into more manageable pieces. An early section of the book will look at situations involving "the jagged résumé." These involve people whose background to date appears to teeter on the edge between success and failure. Such people can do spectacular work in the right settings, where their strengths are invaluable and their flaws don't matter. They also are the people most likely to be shunted out of consideration in conventional hiring systems, because of some perceived shortcoming. Some of the most talent-rich organizations in the world achieve greatness by knowing exactly what kinds of jagged résumés are right for them. This section will show how such discernment takes shape.

The middle of the book introduces the notion of "talent that whispers." It will show how to track down the obscure, out-of-the-way candidates that most scouting systems overlook. Finally, the closing chapters of the book examine "talent that shouts." This is the realm of spectacular but brash candidates that can make or destroy a program. Sizing up such people involves getting a grip on issues of loyalty, motivation, and willingness to sacrifice on behalf of a greater good.

Running throughout the book is the recognition that rare talent often emerges in unexpected ways. That creates exquisite challenges on both sides of the table—for scouts as well as candidates. Assessors need a hard-nosed optimism that lets them bet on unproven potential. They can't wait for rock-solid confirmation of their hunches; they need to say "Yes" on the strength of their belief that today's flickers of promise could ignite greatness. Such convictions tend to be based on a keen eye for powerful but hard-to-quantify success markers such as unstoppable resilience. That particular virtue that is almost invisible in traditional résumés yet so highly prized in domain after domain. Other favorites include creativity, self-reliance, efficiency, judgment, or a nonstop desire to improve.

For candidates, being recognized as a rare find has always required a willingness to defy standard career paths. That's never easy, but as this book's final chapter will show, new paths are starting to open up. If mainstream hiring channels are inhospitable, get to know the behind-the-scenes players who control the "hidden" job market. Build networks of people who recognize your unique strengths and can become your advocates. Make up for any apparent gaps in your résumé by establishing yourself as a stunningly quick learner. And learn how to build a public portfolio of your work that can help employers find you.

Success may be difficult at first, but over time it becomes contagious. After all, who are the most discerning talent scouts? Time and again, they are people who, early in their careers, were nearly shunted to the sidelines themselves before someone recognized their uncommon potential. For the rest of their careers they repay the favor, opening doors for other unlikely heroes, too.

1: Sand, Sweat—and Character

Of all the military equipment at Camp Mackall, nothing is more piti-ful than trailer 2K9395. Oil stains and rust patches have devoured the trailer's cargo bed. A rusted axle droops awkwardly from the frame's left side. The left wheel has vanished, and the remaining right wheel is a flat-tired disgrace. This trailer joined the Army in June 1967, bound for service in Vietnam. Where it has been since is a mystery; even the supply-depot clerks don't know. Judging by ap-pearances, this contraption has been rotting for decades at this Army outpost in the North Carolina pinelands.

For Dan Fagan, the trailer is perfect.

He is a tall, broad-shouldered sergeant in the Army Special Forces. A combat engineer by training, Fagan can build bridges in a hurry and blow them up even faster. After years of overseas deployments, he has come to Camp Mackall for three years. In this job, he helps screen about three hundred soldiers a month, all of whom hope to join the elite Special Forces, also known as the Green Berets. By the time Fagan sees candidates, they have withstood days of physical tests aimed at culling out the weak. The survivors have completed all-night marches through swamps. They have slithered safely from one rope to another, twenty-five feet off the ground. They have

15

proven themselves stronger and tougher than the average soldier. That's a good start, but it's not enough.

It is time to see how these candidates perform in messy, arduous team exercises that approximate some of the stresses of battle. There's a way to do this without firing a single bullet. On this particular morning, unprepared soldiers will be thrust in front of the Army's worst-kept trailers, to see who can propel these eight-hundred-pound wrecks, by hand, to a faraway destination. The mission is both simple and devilish. Success requires a rare blend of brains, muscle, and an ability to recover from constant, small mistakes along the way. Fagan's job is to hover near a small cluster of candidates, seeing everything and saying almost nothing. He will judge their work. He is the watchman.

The encounter begins at 5:30 A.M. in a forest clearing. Fagan singles out a skinny soldier with a high-pitched voice, telling him to lead a team of sixteen soldiers that will drag two of these trailers along two-and-a-half miles of sandy roads. If the trailer's unwheeled edge ever drags along the ground, the mission fails.

In the predawn darkness, the only way for soldiers to see is with tiny halogen headlamps that wrap around each soldier's cranium. Erratic illumination creates the feeling that the soldiers control only a patch of scrubby soil, while the wider countryside is another story entirely. Soldiers struggle to discern the outlines of 2K9395 and other one-wheeled trailers. Next to each trailer is a weird assortment of equipment: some poles, some cotton lashings, and a long coil of rope. Fagan's team leader gazes at the pile in bewilderment. Can this gear help make the trailer more roadworthy? Are some supplies just a useless distraction? It could take half an hour to know for sure. Fagan won't provide a clue. Instead, he demands a rapid plan for getting a patched-up trailer on the road.

"You have five minutes," Fagan declares.

Pressure. Pressure. How do you handle pressure?

Racing to make sense of the task, the leader creates a hurried sketch of crisscrossing poles and oddly draped rope. He dashes around, sharing his drawing with teammates who strain to fit everything in place. It's soon apparent that the diagram badly distorts the parts' actual dimensions. The sketch is a mirage. It's bogus. As rank-and-file soldiers press for clarification or design changes, the leader briefly panics.

"Just lash the f——ing poles to the f——ing brackets!" he declares. "Push harder!" Soon, three soldiers are hurling their entire body weight at a two-and-a-half-inch-diameter pipe that needs to slip into an opening where zero inches were budgeted. Somehow they wedge it in, bending the heavy metal frame of the trailer in the process. The leader gazes at the spectacle, slack-jawed for a moment. It's obvious that his design can't be right. It can't even be remotely on track. Yet it is the best he could devise. "That's f——ing good enough," he declares. "Let's f——ing get going." Profanity splatters his speech as if he were trapped in a locker-room version of Simon Says, cursing for credibility.

A few feet away, Fagan watches with quiet amusement. He has spent most of his Special Forces career in Pacific Rim nations and Afghanistan. He speaks passable Korean, Russian, and eight other languages. He can do all kinds of things that these candidates can't. Working at Camp Mackall is a sabbatical of sorts—a chance to rest up for a few years stateside before returning to overseas action. Yet it's also his opportunity to help pick men who might one day fight alongside him. So he takes his role in assessing candidates very seriously.

For more than two years, Fagan tells me, he has monitored trailer-building squads. No matter what the teams try—and he has seen nearly thirty designs to date—it's almost impossible to come up with a configuration that functions smoothly. "There are about a half-dozen designs that barely work," he says. "They're all mediocre. But you can get them to the finish line in three or four hours if you push hard enough." Then he grins. "There are also some awful designs," he says. Pick one of those, and pushing an eight-hundred-pound trailer through sand becomes a hellish ordeal that never ends. Soldiers may collapse with blisters, twisted ankles, and separated shoulders before they reach the halfway point of the two-and-a-half-mile exercise. They may not make it by nightfall.

Fagan takes one more look at the team's design. "Their plan is a mess," he whispers. "But that's all right. In fact, it's good. They will realize it soon enough. And then we'll learn a lot about them."

It takes only fifty meters for Fagan to be proven right. A few soldiers can't find any handhold that lets them push their trailer through the sand. They hover uselessly on the periphery. Others discover that the trailer is terrifyingly unstable. They grab it for a moment, then sway and fall. At any given moment, only two or three soldiers are productively pushing each trailer. The rest keep tumbling into the sand as if an invisible genie is yanking them off balance.

"Request permission to adjust the poles," the team leader tells Fagan.

"You can't make any adjustments until you have gone one hundred meters," Fagan replies.

Minutes later, the team reaches its allowed adjustment point. Now rank-and-file soldiers get to work, tugging poles into better positions. The team leader jogs back and forth between the two trailers under his supervision, taking note of each team's best ideas. He relays suggestions between crews. Two new versions of the trailer-pulling system emerge. They are weirdly asymmetrical and imperfectly lashed together. But at last soldiers have created three or four excellent pushing positions. It's now possible to balance the trailer's weight more effectively. The teams resume pushing, with noticeably better results.

"I am open to suggestions," the team leader tells his men. "If one of you guys is f——ing smarter than me, which is not out of the question, go ahead and speak up."

It's hardly inspirational leadership. But it's a big improvement over the quagmire at the start. As dawn takes hold, Fagan jots down notes on which soldiers impress him, and which don't. At the top of his list are men who broach good ideas for design improvements, as well as those who consistently push hard, rotating through the toughest positions on the contraption. In the middle of the pack is the group leader, who finds his rhythm after an awful start. ("He isn't great, but he isn't horrible," Fagan decides.) At the bottom of Fagan's scorecard are the whiners and the fakers. No matter how much they grunt with each labored step, Fagan can spot their soft-fingered grips and their sham grimaces. He wants them gone.

As the trailer teams trudge on, I ask Fagan if a full-fledged Special Forces soldier would ever spend hours on such a primitive task. "Yes," he says. "I've done it." He recalls an overseas deployment where he needed to move ammunition crates along down a narrow mountain trail. He didn't have access to any Army helicopters or transport planes. There weren't any jeeps or other motorized vehicles that could safely navigate the twisting path. All the transportation techniques of a modern-day soldier were unavailable. "We did have mules," he says. So if he was willing to think like a nineteenth-century soldier—piecing together a primitive carrying system with ropes, poles, and canvas lashing strips—he could get the ammunition to its destination. To many soldiers, that would have been preposterous. To Fagan, that was his kind of warfare. Within a few hours, he had improvised his way to success: roping up the mules, loading them with ammunition crates, and safely transporting them and their cargo to a new Army outpost.

While Fagan's group inches along, other Special Forces sergeants keep vigil on six more teams trying to propel their trailers, too. Each team amounts to a study in stress—and the candidates' performance varies dramatically. There's no longer a hazy commonality to all the sweating young men in the green camouflage uniforms. Even an untrained outsider can sense a chasm forming between soldiers who thrive in this sort of setting and others who come unglued.

A half-mile ahead of Fagan's group, a young, West Point–trained captain has figured out an ingenious design that balances the rickety trailers as much as possible. His team will finish the course in less than two hours, faster than anyone else. Special Forces examiners will make note of his cunning. He's a keeper. But a quarter-mile behind Fagan, a different team takes a wrong turn near a landmark known as Big Muddy Lake. They waste half an hour on this detour; they emerge demoralized and incapable of keeping pace with anyone else. Special Forces assessors put black marks next to the name of an assistant team leader who couldn't navigate. Poor grades are in store, too, for team members whose will to finish was sapped by the setback. Two laggards will be gone from the program within forty-eight hours.

Walking alongside the trailer-pushing soldiers in the hot North Carolina sun is tedious, unpleasant work for the Special Forces assessors. There's no way of predicting when the next revealing moment will occur. Soldiers can trudge through the sand for hours without doing anything out of the ordinary. Yet Special Forces assessors regard their duty as an honor. For them, moment-by-moment observation is a crucial part, maybe even the essence, of how Army Special Forces ensures it is selecting the right new soldiers.

Their vigilance provides what every organization wants: accurate early assessments of who has the right stuff—and who doesn't.

Camp Mackall's rituals aren't just a fascinating glimpse into an American subculture; they also provide a useful starting point for thinking about talent selection. Any system for picking the right people needs to be more than just a thousand disconnected habits.

Success means building on a few central principles. Step back from the details of Special Forces' methods, and it's possible to discern three big ideas that can apply almost anywhere. They are as follows:

Look for the hidden virtues. One of the most overlooked strengths in America today can be expressed in one word: resilience. It's invisible on most résumés. It's hard to spot in a brief interview. Yet in profession after profession, resilience turns out to be absolutely crucial in differentiating between people who do vastly better than expected—and those who turn out to be severe disappointments. When Army Special Forces assessors ask soldiers to show what they can do in the nightmarish circumstances of the predawn trailer push, they are turning the spotlight—at last—on soldiers' ability to bounce back from adversity.

Who else cares about hidden virtues such as resilience, ingenuity, curiosity, and compassion? Try Teach For America, which has overhauled the way it sizes up candidates for teaching in some of America's most beleaguered schools. Or look at the ways some Silicon Valley companies seek out engineers who are natural-born tinkerers, regardless of whether they ever finished college. Chapters 2 through 5 will show how standout companies pull ahead by seeing the hidden strengths—and discounting the supposed flaws—of unusual candidates with "jagged résumés."

Find your unlikely stars by noticing what others don't see. The best assessors in any field are constantly learning something new about their subjects. Within Special Forces, there's an art to appraising something as mundane as a soldier's demeanor in the midst of a long march. Are his rucksack straps tidy, or are they splayed all over, like an octopus's tentacles? Do his eyes scan the horizon? Has his face begun to glaze over? Details count, not because one minor factor holds the key to everything, but because many small impressions will add up to a decisive, accurate judgment. Special Forces use an inordinate amount of experienced talent to size up the rawest candidates. That costs money in the short term; it saves untold lives and national resources in the long run.

Who else looks in unexpected places? Chapters 6 through 8 will explain the art of finding "talent that whispers," the overlooked prospects that go on to greatness. The middle chapters of the book also will underscore the importance of sweating the small stuff. Watch the scouts at a youth basketball tournament when a time-out is called. Casual fans may look away, but people in the business grab their notepads. They see which players run over to the huddle and which dawdle; who pats a teammate on the shoulder and who stays aloof. All these small gestures provide clues about motivation and team ethos. Those are the traits that later will play a huge role in deciding which players soar to stardom and which never make the most of their gifts. Similarly, watch the best executive recruiters as they size up a potential chief executive. They aren't just evaluating the candidate's charisma and vision. They are paying close heed to the minor habits that can reveal a lot, both good and bad, about character.

Push your best candidates to grow even stronger. At Camp Mackall, ambitious candidates are constantly challenged with tests of valor. They engage. They lock in. The winners start pushing themselves harder and farther than if they were simply shunted through a sorting system. That means candidates' potential for growth—one of the most vital and elusive factors in any selection system—is no longer a mystery. It's obvious. Motivation reveals itself as the selection process plays out. What's more, successful candidates start building peer-to-peer bonds that will drive them forward for their entire careers.

What other outfits make a point of challenging, not coddling, their brightest prospects? Try one of the most famous talent-spotting systems in corporate America, General Electric's Corporate Audit Staff program. It is a multiyear gauntlet designed to be a selection/initiation hybrid. Candidates may spend six months in Brazil, working around the clock on leasing deals—and then be rocketed off to Australia on short notice to learn the mining business. Such progressions draw the most dedicated into a fast-paced career in corporate finance while discarding those who can't keep pace. Or consider the classic internship-residency-fellowship training cycle for doctors, in which each step on the ladder involves both selection and a deeper initiation into the healer's life. Such examples will be showcased in chapters 9 to 11, which look at "talent that shouts."

The interplay between broad rules and specific examples is endless and rich. It's possible to learn from a vast assortment of fields, so long as each discipline's unique habits are seen as metaphors, rather than as literal role models. No one in their right mind would transfer the sweaty road tests of an Army program into civilian life. It's amusing but wildly inappropriate to imagine picking investment bankers by sending them on ten-mile marches with seventy-pound rucksacks on their backs. No one would size up computer programmers by seeing how skillfully they could push a broken jeep trailer. And no one would assess actors, teachers, or architects by running them through a ropes course.

Yet the process of drawing comparisons from one talent-picking program to another needn't be jarring at all. Our everyday speech is packed with allusions to other fields, often in such familiar language that we glide past the original context. We warn ourselves about *prima donnas* without thinking of opera; we prize *home run hitters* without thinking of baseball; we appreciate managers willing to *slug it out* with the competition without thinking of boxing.

In fact, the extreme physical tests of its Special Forces candidates are seen as metaphors within the Army itself. The reason that rope climbs, multimile marches, and the like have become so prominent in Special Forces selection isn't because military leadership regards those as exact matches with everyday soldiering. Rather, these tests help gauge the abstract virtues—perseverance, motivation, judgment, etc.—that matter in almost any calling. The score sheets for tallying each candidate's performance go far beyond a stopwatch analysis of how quickly each candidate finishes. What the raters want are clues about candidates' character.

To understand why, it helps to take a moment to review Special Forces' history and identity. From its inception in 1952, Special Forces has focused on high-skill, high-ingenuity jobs that require a few well-placed soldiers. Its standard fighting unit is a shockingly tiny group of twelve men. They operate at the edges of regular warfare: training guerrillas to fight unfriendly governments, conducting sabotage and reconnaissance behind enemy lines, helping friendly governments bolster their internal defense, and so on. Fast-paced commando raids can be part of the mix, but that isn't the single-minded focus of Special Forces, in the way that Army Rangers or Navy SEALS are defined by high-intensity action. Some of Special Forces' most successful missions may involve months of diplomacy with indigenous peoples in out-of-the-way parts of the world before any military action takes place.

Because Special Forces represents the outermost reach of American military force, there's an inherent unpredictability about the way its soldiers may be used. That puts a huge premium on finding soldiers with the adaptability, stoicism, and stamina to make a go of almost anything.

Two former World War II officers, Aaron Bank and Russell Volckmann, infused this spirit into Special Forces at its founding. Bank, a multilingual adventurer, had parachuted into occupied France in 1943 and spent months organizing French resistance fighters so they could ambush German convoys, blow up bridges, and the like. In 1945, he recruited seventy German prisoners of war to form Operation Iron Cross, a plot to seize and kill Adolf Hitler if the Fuehrer fled Berlin in the war's final days. The plan was never invoked. Nonetheless, its precision and daring won admiration at the highest military levels. Volckmann was an Army officer who got trapped in the Philippines after the Japanese invasion of 1942. He turned that dire fate to his advantage, organizing at least 15,000 Filipino guerrillas to undermine Japanese control.

Both men regarded unconventional warfare as their way of life. They saw the creation of Army Special Forces as a way of keeping wily, unorthodox operations strong in the American repertoire, whether this was needed in Cold War situations or some other scenario no one had anticipated yet.

Vietnam was the most controversial chapter in Special Forces history. Green Berets swarmed into villages along the Ho Chi Minh Trail in the 1960s, hoping to train residents to stop Communist incursions. Early enthusiasm for such missions gave way to the frustrations and distrust associated with the eventual failure of U.S. involvement in Southeast Asia. Redemption came in Panama in 1989, where Special Forces soldiers helped topple dictator Manuel Noriega; in El Salvador in the 1990s, where Special Forces shaped a successful campaign against violent insurgents; and the early days of the Afghanistan war in 2001–02, when Special Forces soldiers worked with Northern Alliance allies to dislodge the Taliban from power in a matter of weeks.

Anna Simons, a Harvard-trained anthropologist who spent more than a year observing Special Forces soldiers during training exercises, declared that the most important strength of these soldiers was what she called "mettle." In her 1997 book, *The Company They Keep*, she singled out Special Forces soldiers for being able to function effectively without guidance, tolerate stress, make adjustments— and still act with stunning decisiveness when the situation called for it. In sum, she wrote, mettle is "being able to deal confidently with the unknown."

Dick Couch, a former Navy SEAL, came to a similar conclusion in his 2007 book about Army Special Forces, *Chosen Soldier*. As he put it: "Special Forces training is all about finding talented men who have adaptive, creative minds. . . . Physical toughness is a requisite; mental agility is essential."

Within Camp Mackall, one nighttime test has long been prized for its insights into candidates' overall merit. The test is called Land Nav; it involves a sprawling, multihour search in which hundreds of candidates try to track down a series of tiny markers in a vast stretch of forest. The soldiers' only tools are a five-color map, a compass, and a protractor. Markers are scattered in such a way that each candidate's quest is different. If everything goes right, a skilled soldier might complete the task in eight or nine hours. For most candidates, all sorts of mishaps lie ahead.

When I first heard about Land Nav, it sounded like an anachronism. Modern satellite technology has become so good, and so pervasive, that it's rare for any soldier or civilian to attempt serious navigation with tools that date back to the days of General Grant. Old-fashioned map-reading skills might have been essential for the Special Forces soldier of the 1970s. Now active soldiers refer to map-and-compass technique as a lost art. In a combat or reconnaissance zone, traditional navigation is valued mostly as an emergency backup skill, used only when equipment fails or batteries are unavailable. It was tempting to argue the matter with Don King, the Army major who runs Special Forces selection, but he waved me off with a smirk.

"Come see for yourself," he said. "We start at one A.M. We'll let you travel with a couple of the cadre"—the longtime sergeants who serve as frontline assessors of each new candidate. "If you can stay awake, you'll see a lot."

A few hours later, I am sitting in the back of a parked pickup truck, in total darkness, just a few feet away from Sergeant First Class Greg DuBois. He peers through night-vision goggles, gazing nearly a mile down a wide gravel road. Candidates have been told to maneuver stealthily through the forest, as if this were a genuine combat exercise. They have agreed to obey nearly a dozen rules: don't walk on roads for more than a few steps; don't use your flashlight for more than a momentary map check; don't navigate with a buddy; keep a good grip on your rifle, and so on. All the rules sound straightforward and easy to follow at the start of the exercise.

Now some of the candidates are lost and behind schedule. Others are unnerved by the forest's harsh conditions. This is nasty terrain. On dry land, exposed tree roots and stump holes abound. Frogs, rabbits, and the occasional snake interrupt the stillness with eerie sounds. At chest and eye level, walls of brambles are so thick that they can't be brushed aside. Getting through means accepting constant scratches on arms, hands, and any other exposed skin. The lowest stretches of land are filled with smelly, waist-high water. As candidates realize how hard the course is, some are tempted to cheat.

"Candidate!" Sergeant DuBois shouts.

He has spotted a soldier walking for more than three hundred meters along the middle of a gravel road. "Candidate! What is that under your feet?"

"It's a road, sir," the soldier mumbles.

"Are you supposed to be walking on a road?" DuBois asks.

"No sir."

DuBois writes down the candidate's uniform number, makes a note in his assessment book, and sends the candidate back into the woods. A single infraction may weaken a candidate's chances slightly but most likely won't eliminate him, DuBois explains. If candidates are caught repeatedly walking on roads or using flashlights, however, that sends Special Forces assessors two warning signs. First, these soldiers aren't capable of learning a complex task despite several days of instruction. (Whatever the value of land navigation in its own right, it also is a handy proxy for anything involving precise work and careful judgment.) That's worrisome enough, but the second danger sign is even worse. When these soldiers get stuck in a stressful situation and don't think anyone is watching, they undermine the rules.

What's at stake? As one officer puts it, men who make it into the Green Berets are likely to end up on overseas deployments with faint supervision and a lot of open-ended responsibility. They may be given $50,000 to buy months of supplies in whatever local markets they can find. There will be little formal accounting of how that money is spent. All that Special Forces leadership can hope for is that these soldiers will do the right thing when no one is looking. Keeping track of who cheats, and who doesn't, at 4 A.M. on a gravel road at Camp Mackall is an early clue toward making that assessment.

As infractions pile up, I'm astonished to see how fiercely the Special Forces assessors rip into each violator. It's as if they've spotted the first cancerous sign of laziness or selfishness—and now must blast it away so it never returns. I hear shouts: "Candidate, get off my road!" There's vengeance in assessors' voices when they describe each caught candidate as "a road kill." These sergeants don't see themselves as small-time cops running a routine speed trap. Instead, the assessors peer into the darkness for hours because they believe they are guarding Special Forces' culture from the small bad habits that can slowly destroy a team's effectiveness.

They may well be right.

At other times, Special Forces selectors want deeper insight into candidates' tenacity. It's easy to sound tough in formation, shouting out classic military call-and-response slogans. What the Army is looking for, though, is how soldiers hold up on long deployments that aren't turning out to be as much fun as anyone hoped. Do they absorb criticism, press on, and complete the job as best they can? Or do they come unglued, in some mix of anger, self-pity, and despair that means they won't finish the job? There will be overnight vigils in cold mountain passes, waiting to intercept bad guys who may not show up. There will be multiday marches on limited rations in tough terrain. Local allies will be assiduously courted for weeks, only to prove fickle. Special Forces duty consists of extreme soldiering, and the best soldiers find ways to press on with stoic resolve.

At Camp Mackall, examiners say, the best way to test tenacity is also the simplest: See how candidates hold up during extended marches with little sleep. Soldiers on those marches get plenty of high-calorie meals; they carry lots of water; they receive regular checkups with medics who can bandage up blisters and the like. There's nothing tortuous about any single twenty-minute segment. But the marches keep coming. They're long. They occur on short notice. Often the finish line isn't divulged. Even when a target is announced, that may be a trick. The real end will turn out to be miles farther. Everything is structured to be a test of willpower.

I had expected to see the weakest soldiers in obvious pain, collapsing as their bodies failed them. But breakdowns didn't happen that way. The laggards betrayed their fate chiefly in their eyes. They took on the glassy stare of daydreamers who had decided it was all just too much. They didn't want to be at Camp Mackall anymore. They slowed down, falling behind the rest of their platoon. Special Forces assessors provided three warnings, telling the stragglers they needed to pick up the pace or risk flunking out. Most of the time, the warnings were futile. Candidates made momentary efforts to catch up to their peers, and then faded behind once more. When it was finally time to pull them off the course and give them a ride back to the barracks in an Army truck, the dropouts looked relieved.

Physical tests—all designed to assess personal character.

I asked Brian Shanahan, a Special Forces sergeant working as a frontline assessor, whether tenacity really was a mental rather than physical attribute. He responded with two stories. Years ago, one of the most stubborn soldiers to go through Special Forces selection broke his foot with two days to go—and still finished the entire program, including a thirty-mile hike on the last day. It wasn't until he limped off the course that he got X-rayed and fitted for a cast. Once he healed, Special Forces proudly brought him back for advanced training. He became a model of warrior grit.

At the other end of the spectrum, Shanahan once came across a soldier walking along a trail while wearing only his Army shirt, rucksack boots—and underpants. Shanahan asked him: "Candidate, where is the rest of your uniform?" The reply, delivered with weird serenity: "My pants won't fit over my boots."

In Shanahan's words, "He had lost his mind. He was still moving around, but he had completely lost track of what he was trying to accomplish. There was nothing to do but take him off the course."

Tenacity and mental toughness are so crucial for Special Forces that Camp Mackall tests for them almost daily. One of the most gut-wrenching reviews is known as the Log Drill. Candidates attempt calisthenics in groups of eleven to fourteen, maneuvering a 1,200-pound telephone pole all the time. Candidates are expected to hoist the pole together over their heads . . . lower it partway . . . bring it back up . . . and repeat the gyrations as many times as their assessing sergeants demand. It's an exercise where the strongest candidates struggle to do mediocre work and the weaker ones perform miserably. The pole is too big, too unwieldy and too unfamiliar for anyone to maneuver it properly.

Breaks come only when soldiers are told to put the pole down—at which point they must crank off twenty or more pushups. By this time, everyone's pectorals and triceps are exhausted. No one can muster more than a dozen or so legitimate pushups. After that, the soldiers writhe like seals. Backs arch in the weirdest ways, in desperate efforts to ease body weight away from wounded muscles. The assessing sergeants snap out critiques: "What kind of pushup is that?" "Is that the best you can do, candidate?"

Yet most candidates make it to the end. Afterward, I ask some soldiers how they did it. All the finishers say they recognized the exercise as a mental challenge and found some way to bolster their spirits. "I've done worse than this" is a common refrain. "This sucks so bad that it's humorous" is another. Some soldiers talk bluntly about identifying a weaker candidate, vowing to outlast the other guy no matter how bad things get. Most candidates come to the Special Forces wanting to be surrounded by other soldiers who care as much as they do. As attrition sets in, the soldiers who survive take pride in uniting as a new group of winners. They earn the right to be in the brotherhood.

It isn't just a selection process. It's an initiation ritual, too.

As much as Special Forces assessors appear in charge, there are moments when fate acts unexpectedly. I see that one afternoon when aspiring soldiers split into teams of sixteen and are told to carry an assortment of heavily weighted ammunition crates for two-and-a-half miles. This is a variant of the Special Forces' standard march/endurance test. The assessors informally size up the teams, muttering about a squad that finished dead last in the previous exercise. Its soldiers are crabby and dispirited. Two of them look utterly drained; others are openly cynical about their teammates. "This is a team ready to implode," one of the Special Forces assessors tells me. "Walk with them for a bit. It probably won't take long for you to see something spectacular."

When I join, team members are wrapping up an awkwardly brief rest break, cut short by their inability to finish the last job on time. Phillip Enoch, the sergeant overseeing this group, taps a broad-faced young Texan with wire-frame glasses and close-cropped hair and tells him: "You're the new team leader."

No fanfare. No speeches. But within fifteen minutes, both Enoch and I are watching this commander with fascination. He is calm, friendly, and confident. He addresses everyone as "Gentlemen!" He recognizes right away that his men are tired, so he adds a few rest breaks at the outset. Then, when a long stretch of flat, smooth road opens up, he turns to the group and declares: "Gentlemen! We've got a chance to make some good time here. You're moving well and we need to keep going. We'll go with half the rest breaks for a bit." His team absorbs the message and accelerates a little. The laggards still struggle, but for the first time all day, they aren't getting worse.

Toward the end of the march, it is clear this team will finish the march a few minutes inside its allotted time. I turn to Enoch and ask: "Who impresses you on this team?" His answer: "To be honest, the team leader. He surprised me. He's confident. He's thinking of everything. He's told them when to refill their water containers without us having to remind him. He's given them stretching exercises to keep their grips strong. He doesn't have a great team. But he's getting the most he can out of them."

Later that day, I chat with the team leader over a break. He grew up in Levelland, Texas, a cotton-farming town near the New Mexico border. The son of an Army recruiter, he earned a college degree in history and then commanded regular Army soldiers in Iraq. The more time he spent in Iraq, the more he saw Special Forces as the military's most effective presence. By his own admission, he wasn't the physically strongest soldier at Camp Mackall. But he showed a shrewd grasp of what was needed to clear each selection hurdle. If he passed all the tests, he said, he hoped someday to run a twelve-man Special Forces team overseas that could train hundreds of indigenous soldiers, too. That would be the best of both worlds, combining the intensity of small-scale command with the impact of mass leadership.

A few days later, all the drills were done. It was time for Special Forces officers to huddle inside a bare-bones Camp Mackall trailer, discussing the fate of each candidate. Of the 397 soldiers who started that month's selection cycle, about 190 had failed to reach the finish line. Soldiers who arrived out of shape were long gone; they were tagged as "bums." Also sent packing were the ones with mid-course injuries, burnout, weird phobias, anger issues, lawless pasts, or poor aptitude-test scores. A few more borderline candidates would be weeded out in case-by-case review. What remained were the keepers.

Anyone driving through Camp Mackall at the moment when selection decisions were announced would hear a brief roar from the mess-house tent, about fifteen seconds of applause—and then silence. Some two hundred soldiers, 51 percent of the class, had earned the right to continue. There would be substantial further attrition in the months ahead, as soldiers embarked on eighteen months of training. For now, though, the soldiers had made it. Regardless of how excited, exhausted, relieved, or triumphant the soldiers felt about this moment of passage, the unwritten code of being a Special Forces soldier said that moments like this were celebrated briefly and quietly. Years from now, there might be secret missions that couldn't ever be discussed with outsiders, no matter how well they went. Older Green Berets talked about being "quiet professionals." Moments like this taught new initiates what that meant.

Every few years, Army statisticians analyze candidates' records to see if there is an easier way of identifying winners, without churning up so many thousands of hours of assessors' time. Brigadier General Bennet Sacolick, head of the Special Warfare Center in Fort Bragg, North Carolina, has pored over those studies as much as anyone. His answer: "There is no shortcut."

The Army knows the minimum fitness levels and aptitude-test scores needed for candidates to have a realistic chance of making the cut, Sacolick explains. Beyond those levels, jacking up the standards doesn't yield better Green Berets. The Special Forces' finest warriors aren't necessarily pushup champions. Nor do they need to have been straight-A students in school. To discover who belongs, Sacolick says, there's no alternative but to start with a large pool of contenders—and then take the full measure of each soldier through stress-packed tests that involve far more than just traversing sandy roads.

Because Camp Mackall's rigors date back to the earliest days of Special Forces selection in the 1950s, it would be easy to make the place into a living museum of Army testing: a sweating, grunting tribute to what always has been and always will be. Any organization with a long history runs the risk of falling too in love with its own past. The peril, of course, is that if old habits never budge, selectors become blind to their organization's evolving needs, as well as to the constant societal changes that redefine candidates' skills, potential, and inner motivations.

How does fresh thinking keep coming into the mix at Camp Mackall—or any organization that remains in the talent hunt for many decades? Army leadership can drive some high-level change. But the fastest, nimblest reforms come from bringing in a different selection commander every few years, particularly when the new boss's ideas are shaped by recent battle-zone experience. That repotting works better than relying constantly on a headquarters perspective. The push toward constant modernization becomes even more effective if frontline assessors are rotated in the same fashion, with newcomers allowed to help fine-tune the system, too.

Don King, the major who took over Special Forces selection in 2009, set to work on retooling the program right away. In formal meetings, he explained his agenda to me using the safe, abstract words of "professionalism" and "standardization." But whenever he walked or drove along the roads where candidates were being assessed, it was clear that he wasn't just another boss with a PowerPoint presentation. He was someone who lived and breathed the Special Forces ethos. King went through Special Forces selection himself in 1991, and he has thought a lot about the lessons from that volatile experience. He was an individual-event star, rattling off pushups, marching quickly, and beating everyone else in the two-mile run. Then came the team events. He and three teammates got caught in a blizzard, trying to haul "The Sandman"—a stretcher filled with more than two hundred pounds of sandbags, in a simulation of what would be involved if a downed pilot needed to be tugged to safety. It took desperate improvisation involving a poncho-liner cover to keep the sandbags from becoming so moisture-laden that they would become unbearably heavy. Only with the help of stronger partners did he get the Sandman to the finish line on time.

In dozens of deployments over the next two decades, King's running prowess never made much difference away from training grounds. But his ability to think like a soldier and work in a team has been constantly tested. So when he came back to Camp Mackall to run the selection program in 2009, he and his command team decided to make land navigation and team events a much more prominent part of selection, while spending less time grinding down soldiers in solo tests of strength to see who would collapse.

"You want to apply stressors to the candidates," King explains. "You want to see how they hold up with little sleep and one task after another. But you don't want to break them, just to prove that you can do it. We don't learn anything that way. And we end up knocking out some candidates from the Army entirely—with broken bones or heatstroke—who could have been good soldiers somewhere else."

In King's version of Camp Mackall, the most profound stresses often are psychological. He doesn't rely on physical ordeals such as pushup marathons that won't stop until five men drop out. But he rattles soldiers' sense of routine by upending schedules and never giving a clear sense of what comes next. Even soldiers trying the program for a second time find they can't predict the next day's agenda. That matches the constant uncertainties of being on deployment, King says. It also gives him more insight into the "racehorse" personalities of soldiers who thrive on predictable excitement but become so moody or hostile during long waits that they can be detrimental to the force.

Under King's command, the frat-house hazing of a generation ago is largely gone. The assessors don't shout as much, and they no longer spit in anyone's face. Old-timers grumble that the Army has gone soft, bowing to the gentler norms of modern-day society. Not so, King says. "We may think we're being tough by yelling at candidates," he explains. "But actually we may provide a sudden burst of motivation. A candidate about to give up will decide that he's not going to let that red-faced sergeant drive him out. That's not what we want.

"There won't be a screaming sergeant when that soldier is stuck alone on a tough deployment. There may not be anyone. We need to see what that candidate can do, all by himself, to stay motivated in tough times."

2: The Talent Problem

"What is wind?"

Two decades ago, that sly question was meant to be Teach For America's code-cracker. TFA's recruiters stormed onto college campuses in the early 1990s with a tantalizing proposition for college seniors: "Do something exciting and socially meaningful. Help fix America's most troubled public schools." Earlier generations embraced the Peace Corps as a way to do brave work in faraway places. Now young idealists could make their mark in inner-city Los Angeles, the Rio Grande Valley of Texas, or some similar locale. The old guard had failed. It was time for someone new to create a brighter future for America's most overlooked children.

Across the country, students at elite schools clamored for a chance to try. TFA sounded better than medical school, law school, or a cushy stint at Goldman Sachs. On campuses such as Harvard, Princeton, Berkeley, and Georgetown, TFA was besieged with applicants. Low pay and harsh working conditions only made the job more alluring. TFA's change-the-world rhetoric was so powerful that it concealed a terrifying problem. No one inside the organization fully knew what it took to be a great teacher. TFA's recruits would get only a few weeks of training before being hurled into America's toughest schools. For TFA to build any enduring credibility, its recruits had to succeed in these high-risk postings. That meant TFA needed to get its hiring decisions right in a hurry—or else risk collapse.

So when TFA's recruiters asked: "What is wind?" they didn't want textbook definitions involving air molecules in motion. They wanted responses that soared like a kite into fresh areas of knowledge. This was a call for aspiring poets who could evoke Rilke's elegies about terrifying angels. It was an invitation for musicians who could spin connections between Bob Dylan and a dozen other artists. Dullards might flub the question. Tomorrow's stars would respond with verbal arpeggios that dashed into the mysteries of solar wind, the jet stream, the voyages of Magellan, or anything unexpected. This question could reveal the sparkle that TFA regarded as the hallmark of great teachers.

It wasn't until seven or eight years later that TFA began having second thoughts. By 1999, TFA had sent thousands of recruits into the chalkboard jungle, with decidedly mixed results. There was an inconsistency about this teaching corps that undermined TFA's hopes of revolutionizing the American educational system. Some of TFA's recruits worked magic in their classrooms, putting up with broken windows, missing textbooks, and old-line resistance to change. Others faltered grievously when too many things went wrong. They snapped at their students. They bickered with their principals. They counted the days to the end of the school year, and some didn't make it to the end. Hundreds of TFA's recruits dropped out of their teaching jobs before their formal two-year commitment was finished. A few quit after just one week.

TFA's selection system was out of kilter.

By relying so much on screening systems that looked for charisma, such as the iconic "wind" question, TFA had lost track of what defined great educators in grades kindergarten through twelve. TFA's leaders, starting with founder Wendy Kopp (a 1989 Princeton graduate), were so close to their own college experience that they still saw the rest of the world through the eyes of bright undergraduates. So in TFA's early years, they ended up pinpointing the sorts of students who dazzled in late-evening bull sessions in the dorms. TFA's questions might have been appropriate for identifying tomorrow's leaders in politics, journalism, or other adult-to-adult environments. But at this stage, TFA hadn't yet solved the talent puzzle for teachers.

Over the next decade, TFA got a fresh grip. The fast-growing non-profit tore apart its old, instinctive model for picking talent. A lot of what TFA thought it knew about great teachers' character and background turned out to be wrong. It was time to confront the indisputable evidence of teachers' on-the-job performance. Years of difficult rebuilding ensued. At the end, TFA had reoriented its approach to talent in ways that allowed it to move forward far more than before.

Travel through the United States, and it's easy to find frustrated talent assessors in field after field. Sports teams squander first-round draft picks on "can't miss" athletes who turn out to be horrendous busts. Corporate boards spend millions in signing bonuses for hot-shot new executives, only to write even bigger severance checks a few years later to get rid of costly disappointments. The discount bins at Costco and Sam's Club are packed with creations by authors, singers, and movie stars who were supposed to attract big fan bases and somehow never did.

It's tempting for cynics to say that talent is an unsolvable mystery. William Goldman, the Hollywood screenwriter, famously declared in the early 1980s that when it comes to gauging a movie's audience appeal ahead of time, "Nobody knows anything." Richard Caves, a Harvard professor of political economy, dressed up this idea in his 2001 book *Creative Industries*, which surveys more than twenty different fields. Caves declared that all these areas are defined by "pervasive uncertainty" and "symmetrical ignorance." And Joe Posnanski, a gifted writer for *Sports Illustrated*, wrote a hilarious retrospective piece in early 2010 about the pro football draft of a decade earlier. With the benefit of hindsight, experts' bombastic old talent proclamations turned out to be a parade of foolishness. Posnanski's wry conclusion: "Mistakes get made."

What's maddening is that talent scouts aren't just trying hard; they keep redoubling their efforts in the hope that more of the same will work out better. Assessors now may screen fifty or more people for a top business job, six hundred for a hard-to-cast movie role, and literally thousands for a top sports pick. These aren't perfunctory efforts to pad a spreadsheet with a few more names. We live in an era when information about any serious candidate—in whatever digitized form you want—can be rounded up by the gigabyte. The process is exhaustive and exhausting. Sometimes it even seems futile. In spite of everyone's hard work, mismatches, blind spots, and false hopes are endless.

That's the real talent problem in America. It's not that we don't know enough about candidates. Today's dossiers on serious contenders for a CEO's job frequently surpass what the U.S. Senate knew about Supreme Court nominees a few decades ago. It's not that there are too few talented people to fill crucial openings. This is a country in which talent proliferates. It isn't even that competition for the most capable people is unbearably intense. Many great talent discoveries of recent years involved overlooked prospects such as author J. K. Rowling and baseball pitcher Mariano Rivera, who attracted almost no interest from anyone at the time. The real problem is that even some of the most diligent, ambitious organizations have built talent-scouting systems that don't work.

Peter Drucker, the legendary business-strategy scholar, spent much of his career studying the ways that organizations hire. His advice always flowed from the same starting point. Before you do anything else, he wrote, "*Think through the assignment.*" That sounds painfully simple. It seems so obvious that many leaders dash past that step. They prefer to get started right away on the high-stakes drama of grilling candidates and slotting them into a scoring system. Yet Drucker was right.

The chief blunder zone for talent searches comes at the very beginning, when it's time to think broadly and clearly about context. Put simply: "What is this job all about?" If that question isn't properly resolved at the start, mission myopia ensues. And then the risk of trouble later on becomes catastrophically higher. As behavioral economist Dan Ariely noted in his book *Predictably Irrational*, "Most people don't know what they want until they see it in context. . . . Like an airplane pilot landing in the dark, we want runway lights on either side of us, guiding us to the place where we can touch down our wheels." Sticking with Ariely's metaphor for a moment, high-profile talent mistakes generally amount to a case of heroically aiming for the wrong runway.

Such errors happen in one of three ways. The talent-hunting framework can become unduly narrow or superficial, with assessors mesmerized by a few showy traits that are exciting to evaluate but aren't really at the heart of success. In such cases, the wrong people keep being hired. Other times, quests become so hazy that there's no clear sense of priorities. That's when hiring decisions are tinged by desperation, a dispiriting randomness, and Oprah-size paychecks for people who ultimately deliver YouTube-quality performance. Finally, there's a special circle in hell for quests that become frozen in time. Yesterday's formulas for success begin to sputter as jobs and society change. When that occurs, the best people stop being hired. Unless organizations have the courage to retool, such mismatches can transform a widely admired talent magnet into an insular, arrogant outfit that repels greatness.

The perils of superficiality and narrowness are most obvious in professional sports. There, some teams keep putting the wrong sorts of players into their starting lineups, creating costly shambles that play out in public display. In the period from 2003 to 2008, sportswriters and economists grew fascinated by the talent carnage of the New York Knicks' basketball team. Despite spending as much as $126 million a year on player salaries, more than any other squad in the thirty-team National Basketball Association, the Knicks compiled one of the league's worst won-lost records.

Sports economists David J. Berri and Martin J. Schmidt picked apart the Knicks' team-building failures in their book *Stumbling on Wins*. Their conclusion: the Knicks placed way too much emphasis on a single objective: acquiring players with high scoring averages. This fixation meant that the Knicks ignored faults such as weak rebounding, mediocre defense, and torrents of missed shots as these stars laboriously jacked up their point totals. The league's best teams did it differently. They cherished the less glamorous virtues of accurate shooting, good defense, and strong rebounding. The farther the Knicks pursued this misguided strategy, the more their losses kept mounting.

What made the Knicks' stumbles so eye-catching was the team's unwillingness to back down in the face of bad news. Berri and Schmidt suggest that the Knicks' general manager at the time, Isiah Thomas, didn't see low-accuracy scorers as problems. During a long career with the Detroit Pistons, Thomas made a tolerable but hardly impressive 45 percent of his field-goal attempts—and won a place in the Basketball Hall of Fame anyway. He was acclaimed as a tough competitor, an inspiring team leader, and a high scorer. During the Pistons' best years, when the team won two NBA championships, Thomas was surrounded by other, less-heralded players whose accurate shooting, tough defense, or strong rebounding helped the team win. As the Knicks' general manager, that balanced formula eluded Thomas. Instead, he cloned the biggest flaw in his own playing style to fill the Knicks' roster. The team's owners couldn't see anything wrong, either. More than three years into Thomas's tenure, in the midst of another losing season, James Dolan, chairman of Madison Square Garden, which owned the Knicks, was asked how matters stood. His response: "We have created a great foundation for building this franchise." Only in 2008 did the Knicks retrench, forcing out Thomas and embarking on an entirely new approach to player selection.

When narrowness and superficiality infect the talent-picking process, shaking loose of those problems can be devilishly hard. As business strategist Jim Collins wrote in *How the Mighty Fall*, troubled organizations have a hard time owning up to their shortcomings. Leaders make a lot of pronouncements and don't seek out new information. Data loses its power to persuade, both in terms of cold, hard numbers and in terms of up-to-date, anecdotal reports from the field. People shield those in power from grim facts, Collins wrote, "fearful of penalty and criticism for shining light on the harsh realities." Meanwhile, power concentrates in the hands of self-promoters who aren't really interested in fixing anything. For them, it's easier to blame other people or outside factors for everything that goes wrong.

Mismatched time horizons also help perpetuate close-minded, glib approaches to talent. The key tests are quick and easy to run. The consequences are remote. As a result, flawed tests keep being administered, week after week, because there's too long a gap between the momentary euphoria of having found "winning" candidates and the distant nausea of realizing that those picks have gone sour once again.

Consider the software industry's long reliance on asking computer-programming candidates to solve rapid-fire brainteasers. Microsoft, for example, used to ask candidates how many golf balls could you fit inside a Boeing 747?* For any recruiter, such puzzlers are

---

* A passable estimate is 500,000. There are about 33,000 cubic feet of space inside a 747, and each cubic foot can hold about 150 golf balls.

delightful power trips. Interviewers know the answers, candidates don't, and anyone hoping to get a job will scramble feverishly to please. Yet such riddles backfire in the same way that Teach For America's "wind question" proved faulty. Such puzzles focus too tightly on quick-wittedness; they overlook other traits that are far more crucial to success.

By 2008, most of the top software companies had shaken free of puzzle mania in favor of longer, more nuanced interviewing themes that assessed people's ability to make complex programs come together. As engineers at Facebook explained to me, hair-trigger math skills alone are only a modest part of the picture. Ingenuity, stamina, and an adherence to standards are at least as important. In chapter 5, we'll learn about a clever Facebook technique that requires candidates to submit as much as forty hours' worth of their programming for inspection. Thanks to automated evaluation systems, Facebook assessors can quickly discover far more about a candidate's chances of succeeding on the job than any math riddle can provide.

When organizations become hazy about what they want from high-talent jobs, different penalties arise: short-lived, inconsistent—and expensive—hires. Mark Mayerson, a Canadian film director, bumped into this one time when visiting an animation studio with a troubled reputation. As Mayerson walked past artists' cubicles, he was flabbergasted by brilliant drawings thumbtacked to various artists' walls. Talent was bountiful; the studio just couldn't deploy anyone properly. Over time, Mayerson came to describe this as "the talent differential." In well-run animation shops, he explained, most good work ends up in finished movies, television shows, and commercials. In badly run shops, projects suffer through so many delays and changes of direction that nothing works out very well. The gaps between what people want to accomplish and what they are able to do becomes huge.

Failings associated with hazy talent strategies are especially costly on Wall Street. Boris Groysberg, a Harvard Business School professor, has spent years following the ways that top Wall Street firms hire their stock-research analysts. These analysts are the fact-filled, highly opinionated experts who advise big-time money managers when it's time to sell Walmart stock, buy Disney, and so on. Many of them earn more than $1 million a year. They almost all work in New York City. They job-hop a lot. And at some point in the 1990s, almost anyone known as a star analyst was likely to get an offer from Salomon Brothers.

"The research group at Salomon was in constant flux," Groysberg wrote in his 2010 book *Chasing Stars*. "Control and compliance functions were weak or nonexistent, as were systems to monitor performance. Teams formed and disbanded quickly. Though the department did develop some star analysts in house, turnover among them was high." Salomon wanted a prestigious research department, but it lacked any enduring way of setting itself apart from more than twenty competitors. Without a defining culture, Salomon's only way of replacing or retaining talent was to pay more than all its competitors. Even that didn't work. In 1998, Salomon ceased to exist as an independent firm; it was sold to Citigroup.

Similarly, the rise and fall of "talent conglomerates," built by many hasty acquisitions in fields such as law, advertising, and consulting, amount to case studies in what can go wrong when there's no clarity about the work at hand. Such outfits become uneasy amalgams of a half-dozen smaller predecessor firms, all trying to coexist somehow. No one can agree on what values should be most prized in looking for additional talent. Top-flight people begin to leave, because they feel they can't do their best work anymore. These organizations usually have big enough hiring budgets that they can recruit waves of high-paid, proven stars from the outside as replacements. But these new hires often work out badly. No one can agree on how to make the most of this new talent—or whether the new hires are a good fit.

In the worst cases, talent hemorrhaging becomes so acute that the bloated enterprise disintegrates.

Talent-hunting systems also can flounder when once-brilliant approaches become frozen in time. The people running selection cling to tactics and mental models from a now-gone era, unable to adjust to changing times. In extreme cases, it can require three or four complete turnovers of top leadership before an organization is fully ready to make a fresh start.

A prime case in point is the Federal Bureau of Investigation. For decades, the FBI's ideas of what it wanted in new agents were shaped by J. Edgar Hoover's views when he took command of the agency in 1924. Hoover was driven by a desire to rise above the grubby habits and corrupt practices of local law enforcement at the time. As FBI chronicler Bryan Burrough explained in his authoritative book *Public Enemies,* Hoover "wanted young, energetic white men between twenty-five and thirty-five, with law degrees, clean, well spoken, bright, and from solid families—men like himself."

As apt as those criteria might have been in the FBI's early days, they became increasingly stifling. Hoover stayed in charge of the FBI for an astonishing forty-eight years, all the while restocking the FBI with new agents as if it were still 1924. The FBI kept seeking out physically fit lawyers or accountants, even though new types of specialty training— such as computer-science or foreign-language aptitude—were becoming more vital. Women didn't stand a chance; Hoover ousted a few pioneering female agents when he took over, and he never allowed another woman to become an agent during his long tenure. Minorities fared hardly any better. At the start of the 1970s, the 8,000-agent FBI had fewer than 150 Asian, Latino, or black agents. No matter how much the rest of America was integrating, the FBI remained a white man's bastion.

There was a grotesque quality, at times, to Hoover's preferences. The boss didn't like people with sweaty palms or red neckties. So candidates struggled to hide such failings for fear of being dinged. Physical appearance mattered greatly to Hoover, so he regularly visited the FBI's training academy to see what potential agents looked like. These ceremonial hellos and handshakes couldn't reveal much of substance, but that didn't stop Hoover from making snap judgments anyway. After one walk-by, Hoover muttered something about seeing "a pinhead" in the candidates' ranks. According to the memoirs of retired agent Joseph Schott, underlings hurriedly opened up trainees' lockers to check everyone's hat size. The upshot: three candidates with size 6 7/8 heads were kicked out.

After Hoover's death in 1972, criminal-justice experts saw the FBI as woefully out of step with its true talent needs. For undercover work alone, America required an FBI that better matched the demographics of the country. The FBI also needed more agents who could crack organized crime rings and drug cartels, and perhaps less of an emphasis on the gunplay or relentless background checks that had defined the FBI in prior eras. The bureau might even have benefited from a few agents with red ties.

For years, though, the FBI had a hard time changing its culture. The first permanent successor to Hoover, Clarence Kelley, had been with the FBI since 1940. He got rid of obvious nonsense like the hat-size fixation, but it was hard for him to stretch the FBI's concept of special-agent talent in a big way. A case in point was the FBI's reliance on iconic interviewing questions such as asking candidates what books they liked to read. Long ago, the query might have been intended to probe for curiosity and intellectual breadth. Over time, it instead became a way of perpetuating a few specific ways of looking at the world, no matter how much times were changing. Assessors who liked Robert Ludlum novels—and there were a lot of them—tended to hire new agents who liked Robert Ludlum, too. The FBI stayed deeply insular. It continued to hire mostly from the same narrow pools of people that Hoover had targeted in the 1920s.

The next director, William Webster, talked about opening up hiring and promotions to a wider range of agents. He didn't move fast enough, though, to head off discrimination suits. His successor, William Sessions, was an outsider who had trouble establishing leadership within the bureau. It wasn't until 1993, when Louis Freeh took over, that the FBI made its greatest progress in shaking free of the problematic parts of the Hoover legacy. As a longtime federal prosecutor, Freeh was able to bring decisive, fresh perspectives to the FBI. And because Freeh had been an FBI agent himself for six years early in his career, he had a deep enough understanding of FBI culture to know how to budge the organization. Perhaps most important, advancing age and retirements were extricating the FBI from its obsession with all things Hoover.

By the early 1990s, some sort of new direction at the FBI was a court-ordered necessity. Black and Latino agents had brought powerful class-action suits against the bureau, alleging widespread patterns of discrimination. Rather than let those cases go to trial, the FBI had agreed to settlements that included a commitment to overhaul its hiring practices. To drive change, Freeh recruited a team of industrial-organization psychologists, brought in from industry and academia, who could guide the FBI toward a fairer, better way of finding great agents.

Leading this transformation was Elizabeth Kolmstetter, Ph.D., an industrial and organizational psychologist from Virginia Tech. She spent much of the 1990s as the FBI's chief of personnel assessment and research. Her degree gave her credibility, but what made her effective was a quick wit, constant curiosity, and a knack for bringing people around to her way of thinking. Being one of the few women in leadership didn't fluster her; Kolmstetter's mother had broken down barriers in the 1970s as dean of faculty at Union College in Schenectady, New York. "I'm a pioneer," Kolmstetter explained, when I tracked her down years later at a different Washington-area intelligence agency. "The FBI intrigued me. I decided: 'I'll just set the way.'"

At the FBI, Kolmstetter quickly became known as the spunky outsider who dared introduce her version of Peter Drucker's famous starting question: *What is it that we actually want in these jobs?* "As it turned out, we needed people with computer-science backgrounds," Kolmstetter recalled. "We needed pilots. We needed people with foreign-language expertise." The FBI's old systems of screening candidates didn't attach any extra weight to such skills. So she and her team fixed that. Candidates who were uniquely good at what the FBI required could now get faster interviews and full recognition for their strengths.

"Not only did we create a more diverse pool of applicants," Kolmstetter said, "we met the needs of the organization." Before long, Kolmstetter and her team modernized the FBI's approach to job interviews. Gone were the old questions about favorite books, which had become pathways to cronyism. Instead, the retooled FBI spent far more time systematically inventorying candidates' expertise in crucial areas. FBI interviewers also developed standardized, preset ways of sizing up candidates' ability to reason through cases.

It was a hard adjustment for veteran FBI assessors to make, she recalled, because they were used to the feints and indirections of free-ranging interviews when they quizzed witnesses or suspects. "But job interviews are different," Kolmstetter observed. "We trained agents on this new approach. They came up to me afterward and said: 'I never thought this would work. But it's actually much better. We're very impressed with the caliber of the candidates coming in." By the time Kolmstetter left the FBI in 2000, the bureau's special-agent pool included far more experts with the right skills for the twenty-first century, and an emerging reputation as an agency where women, Latinos, African Americans, and other minorities could thrive.

In Teach For America's case, the fast-growing organization nearly became trapped in two lethal talent binds. TFA's early approach to picking teachers suffered from the narrow/superficial problem, with assessors relying far too much on the illusory value of tests that looked for classroom charisma. Those were easy tests to administer, and they appeared to be ferreting out attributes that were highly relevant. In reality, though, chasing charisma wasn't the right approach. If TFA had been more rigid, it might never have budged from this seductive but wrong-headed formula. With most of TFA's founding team still at the helm a decade later, there was no massive change of leadership to drive a wholesale change in thinking.

Nonetheless, TFA got back on track, and how it did so is instructive. Recovery started with some serious rethinking by Wendy Kopp, TFA's founder. In her autobiography, *One Day, All Children*, Kopp talked about a series of visits she made in the spring of 1999 to schools where the best TFA-selected teachers were at work. "What I realized in getting to know exceptional teachers," she wrote, "is that good teaching is not about charisma. It's not anything magical or elusive. These teachers set clear goals for their students, motivate people (in this case students and their families) to work hard toward these goals, work relentlessly to accomplish them, and constantly assess their effectiveness and improve their performance over time. As I got to know these teachers, a whole new conception of teaching formed in my head."

One of Kopp's most crucial stops was the gritty Los Angeles suburb of Compton. It's a city where the most reliable path to fame involves being either a rapper or a basketball player. Compton burst into national awareness in the late 1980s, when the legendary hip-hop group N.W.A. made its debut. The five-man group infuriated the police and delighted millions of fans with songs like "Gangsta Gangsta" and "Straight Outta Compton." When N.W.A. broke up, individual members such as Dr. Dre, Eazy-E, and Ice Cube became wildly popular solo acts. More recently, high-school basketball stars such as Tayshaun Prince and Brandon Jennings have transformed their early Compton successes into high-profile careers in the National Basketball Association.

When Wendy Kopp came to Compton, however, she called on Anthony Griffin, a first-grade teacher in his mid-thirties. Somehow, this TFA instructor had created a teaching style that sent Latino and black students' reading scores rocketing ahead. Kopp wanted to know what made him so good. To her surprise, he wasn't dynamic in the classroom at all. His teaching style was unusually calm and precise. He carried himself like a former accountant, which, in fact, he was.

Children thrived in Griffin's orderly world. When he started a writing lesson, he cranked up a small kitchen timer so that it would buzz after fifteen minutes. That was just the right amount of time to teach a new idea without stretching beyond his students' attention span. "Time management is built into my personality," Griffin later told me. Everything about him was friendly but focused. "This is my classroom," Griffin would tell students at the start of the year. "But it can become our community if we work together."

Kopp came away seeing Griffin as exactly the sort of efficient, unflappable person that TFA hadn't been seeking to date but ought to value much more highly.

Within TFA, other factors were pushing for change, too. Starting in 1994, new laws in Texas created intense focus on public-school test scores, particularly teachers' ability to boost their entire class's performance in core areas such as reading and math. Great teaching was being redefined. It wasn't so much about a teacher's "wow!" factor; what mattered now was the ability to drive broad, step-by-step gains in testable areas. That transformation took hold, nationwide, with the passage of the No Child Left Behind Act in 2001. TFA's leaders quietly let go of their original, somewhat naïve, ideas about great teaching—and got in step with the times.

Guiding TFA's redirection was Steven Farr, a program alumnus who had taught English from 1993 to 1995 in the south Texas town of Donna, ten miles from the Mexican border. Farr had been seen as a strong teacher, but had fallen short of his own goals. When he learned that 24 percent of his sophomores didn't pass the state English test one year, he burst into tears. Working at TFA as national head of training and support allowed him to redeem himself.

So Farr became the "data jock," identifying hundreds of teachers who could propel classes forward by more than one and a half grade levels—and then studying how they did it. As a 2010 feature article in *The Atlantic* recounted, Farr "observed their classes, read their lesson plans, and talked to them about their teaching beliefs." What's more, TFA admissions chief Josh Griggs told me, the organization did some "reverse engineering," pulling out these teachers' original applications so it could see, in retrospect, what was distinctive about them. Most of Farr's findings involved technique: superstar teachers set big goals; they kept trying to improve; they coaxed families into the process; they planned by working backward from the desired outcome, and so on. If TFA wanted its next crop of teachers to excel in these respects, it would just need to train them better.

But there was also one discovery about character, unearthed by the sort of reverse engineering that Griggs and his colleagues championed. Great teachers were unusually resilient. They persisted in the face of problems that crushed other candidates: students who urinated in the classroom, rooms with thirty-four students and only thirty-one desks, surly colleagues, supply shortages, and so on. Such perseverance wasn't necessarily something that could be developed by training. But TFA could look for it, right from the start.

Sure enough, resilience became the new watchword within TFA. In its 2004 Web site briefing for prospective applicants, tfa.org declared: "Because our corps members face such tremendous challenges, we seek applicants who have demonstrated determination and persistence when confronted with obstacles in the past." The language was recast a few years later, but the message remained just as strong. In 2010, tfa.org informed candidates: "Our successful corps members refuse to allow the inevitable challenges that they face to become roadblocks." In other words, work hard. Don't complain. Don't lose faith. Come back the next morning and do it again.

TFA wanted people like Emily Lewis-Lamonica. I met her in the summer of 2009, after she had finished two years of TFA service as an eighth-grade history teacher. She is a trim, blond-haired woman, about five-foot-four, with round cheeks and bright blue eyes. Many people mistake her for a junior-high student until they start talking with her. She radiates a can-do intensity, constantly rallying other people to help make their shared goals come true. As a college senior at Brown, Lewis-Lamonica had built up a 3.6 grade-point average and a strong commitment to social service. But what clinched her candidacy was an essay she wrote about her ruined track-and-field ambitions—and how she bounced back anyway.

As a college freshman, Lewis-Lamonica was one of the fastest 400-meter hurdlers Brown had ever seen. She improved even more as a sophomore, but then suffered stress fractures in her feet. The injuries destroyed her ability to run for sustained periods. She couldn't train anymore with her teammates. Instead of quitting, she crafted a safe—but lonely—indoor workout regimen. To stay in shape, she swam thousands of laps; she pedaled hundreds of miles on a stationary bike. Defying her injuries as much as she dared, Lewis-Lamonica stepped onto the track for a competitive run just twice in her junior year. In the first meet, she ran fast enough to qualify for the Ivy League championship. Two months later, when the championships arrived, she gingerly suited up for what became the last race of her college career. Barely a minute later, she crossed the finish line. Her time of 63.16 seconds in the 400-meter hurdles was the best showing by any Brown hurdler that season.

The moment Lewis-Lamonica joined TFA, her resilience was tested anew. She originally wanted to be placed in California, Texas, or New York. Instead, TFA sent her to northern Miami: her ninth-rated choice. She didn't know anyone there. Even so, she recalled, "I just told myself: 'Okay, that's where you're going to go.'" The next surprise: many of her students were recent Haitian immigrants, with limited English. They couldn't keep pace unaided. So she set up an early hours tutoring program for them. She also created a recycling program, launched a cooking club, and volunteered to coach the track team. Within months, she was helping longtime F and D students figure out how to do work that could earn them their first Bs in years.

When I chatted with Lewis-Lamonica, she was running much of TFA's West Coast recruiting for new teachers. Throughout the academic year, she would be visiting colleges in California, Oregon, and Washington, explaining TFA's program to candidates, inviting them to interviews, and then sizing them up. We talked about her methods, but after an hour or so, we both realized that the best way to understand how TFA picked teachers was to watch an assessment session in person.

So on a drizzly morning in December, we both visited the massive, blue-and-white Career Center Building at Berkeley. This would be a make-or-break chance for students wanting to join TFA's corps to show what they could do in a classroom.

At 8:15 A.M., half an hour before the applicants were due to arrive, Lewis-Lamonica and a partner begin transforming a small first-floor conference room into a simulated classroom. The two women tidy a large whiteboard on the wall so each applicant can use it to teach a five-minute sample lesson. Chairs are spread around a conference table so all the other attendees can pretend to be age-appropriate students in a classroom. There isn't any obvious warmth to the room, which is how Lewis-Lamonica wants it. Candidates need to take command of the situation as best they can. Meanwhile, Lewis-Lamonica settles into the back of the room, in a somber navy blue suit, taking notes on a laptop.

By 8:45 A.M., everyone is ready to begin. "You will take turns teaching a five-minute sample lesson," Lewis-Lamonica tells ten Berkeley seniors clustered around a conference table. "You will write your first name, your grade level, your subject, and your objective on the board. You will have one minute of prep time."

The students' eagerness is palpable. Now this imitation classroom is packed with college students trying very hard to make a good impression. On a campus known for its tattered, casual clothing, just about everyone wears some variant of a black suit. The men sport neckties; the women opt for conservative blouses. One aspiring teacher clutches paper-cutout zebras that she created as props to help teach population biology. Some have been waiting years for this moment.

First up is Danielle. She rises, walks to the front of the room, and begins a brief, ninth-grade English lesson on how to prepare a bibliography. Everyone, including Lewis-Lamonica, pretends to be back in high school. As the sample lesson unfolds, Lewis-Lamonica's initial formality and command vanishes. The no-nonsense recruiter has morphed into an eager, puzzled girl in the back of the room. Her face softens. Her eyes open wider. Everything about her projects a childlike sense of curiosity and puzzlement. Even her joints seem wired differently.

For the rest of the morning, this new girl with the floppy elbow and wiggling fingers will keep raising her hand, demanding attention. It doesn't matter whether candidates are trying to teach tenth-grade biology or first-grade arithmetic. No matter what the subject, the blond girl in the back will keep shooting her hand in the air, eager to be called upon. Whenever anything occurs to her—relevant or irrelevant—Emily's hand goes up, and she expects to be called upon right away.

There's something so cute and clumsy about this incarnation that job candidates are eager to play along. No matter what the subject, they stop in mid-sentence. "Yes, Emily," they say. "Do you have a question?"

Moments later, candidates feel as if they've stepped into an empty elevator shaft. That's because Emily, for all her eagerness, is what educators call "the off-task student." When she volunteers an answer, it's usually wrong. When she makes a suggestion, it involves marching down a road violently at odds with the lesson plan. Sometimes, in fact, her questions don't relate to the lesson plan at all. She is just free-associating on her own, sharing whatever new thought popped into her head. Call on Emily and suddenly a well-rehearsed lesson plan goes haywire.

This is the new, retooled way that TFA sizes up teaching candidates. Gone for good are the old chances to spin stories about "wind." Placing strong teachers into Compton or Miami isn't about identifying the most gifted extemporizers. What TFA wants to see now is how a teacher holds up when things start going wrong. If candidates can regroup smoothly here, that's a good sign. If they can't craft a rescue strategy in the Berkeley career center, the odds are it would be cruel to let them go any farther.

In the opening bibliography lesson, Emily is the fourth "student" to speak. Three other pseudo-students in this mock classroom have neatly responded to Danielle's prompts, volunteering useful tips about how books should be documented. Not Emily. She randomly guesses that key information is hidden in the back of the book. Danielle freezes for a moment and then recovers. "No," she declares. "It's not in the back of the book. But that was a good guess. Anyone else?" The class gets back on track. Emily is left adrift, but the overall lesson is saved. It was a decent debut.

A few minutes later, a new candidate gets stuck in a deeper predicament. She is crunching numbers on a whiteboard, trying to show how eighth graders can convert fractions into percentages, when Emily weighs in. "Isn't it called cross-multiplying?" Emily asks.

The would-be teacher gulps. That's a totally different solving technique. It works, too. But it clashes with everything she has put on the board so far. She can't accept Emily's idea; she can't reject it. For the next twenty seconds, she thrashes through her own confusion. "You could do it that way," the candidate says. "I was going to try it the simplest way. . . . Cross-multiplying is a lot quicker. We'll do it . . . next time." A tentative, questioning tone creeps into her voice. Moments later, she miscalculates some of her own on-the-board arithmetic. She is visibly relieved when her lesson time runs out and she gets to sit down again.

The "Emily moments" keep coming. Questions from this chatty, befuddled girl terrify some of the candidates. Others achieve some sort of détente, keeping Emily at bay but not really knowing what to do with her. No one has yet figured out how to round up this straggler and smoothly bring her back into the flow of the class.

Then a stocky student, Lali, transports the room back to first grade, for an exercise in sorting out coins' values. This time, the candidate teacher is friendly, confident, and in charge. Lali looks as if she has been teaching for years. When Emily excitedly offers to buy a fifteen-cent trinket with two dimes, Lali doesn't miss a beat. "If you give two dimes, that's twenty cents. You'll get back a nickel. That's five cents. So it will be as if you only gave them fifteen cents." Emily smiles. She's been brought into the lesson and treated warmly. Now Emily is ready to let the class proceed.

By the time the 2009–10 academic year is over, TFA recruiters will have auditioned a record 46,359 applicants, competing for just 4,500 openings. As selectors narrow down the candidate pool, they will enjoy a pickiness that outsiders find breath-taking. Some 18 percent of Harvard's graduating class will apply; most of those students won't get in. A future Fulbright scholar will be turned down. A Duke senior will tell *The New York Times* that getting into the teaching corps is just as hard as "being accepted to an Ivy League grad school."

Does all that intense jockeying for a few slots mean that TFA is able to find extraordinary teachers? Dozens of academic studies keep tackling that issue; no two scholars completely agree. Traditionalists say that they are more comfortable with the classic belief that top teachers develop slowly, through years of training. TFA's defenders counter that by selecting only the most promising candidates, they have been able to launch teachers successfully into classrooms with only a few weeks of intensive training. Often these newcomers can achieve gains in their classrooms that match those of longtime teachers—and exceed what traditional first-year teachers with years of conventional training can do.

Focusing on candidates' resilience has made a huge difference, but it isn't the last big insight that TFA ever expects to have, admissions chief Josh Griggs told me. For example, TFA is starting to look at students' college transcripts differently. Now that perseverance is a key factor, TFA prizes students who struggled in their first year of college and then gradually earned higher grades, year after year. Those strivers may be stronger teachers than other candidates whose elite high-school educations left them so well prepared for college that they never strained to earn As.

There is a broader lesson in TFA's newfound willingness to keep retooling its hiring system. The best experts in any field constantly stretch their horizons so they can do something new. That is how they stay sharp. Nobel laureates do this; great composers do this—and so do the savviest judges of human potential. They refuse to become so habit-bound that familiar customs unthinkingly turn into ruts. Instead, they keep analyzing their own track records, looking for new opportunities and unexpected misfires. Doing so helps turn agility and continual improvement into a way of life.

As Griggs puts it, "We're constantly learning more about what it takes to make a great teacher. I'm sure that five years from now, we'll decide that the methods we're using now are too simplistic. We'll have something even better."

3: Decoding the Jagged Résumé

Alan Kay was a child prodigy who couldn't find his direction in college. He majored in mathematics and molecular biology at the University of Colorado, while dabbling in English and anthropology on the side. Instead of studying, he often poured his energies into jazz guitar performances in local nightclubs. His transcript ended up as a weird amalgam of As, Ds, and Fs.

Ed Catmull spent most of high school thinking he wanted to become a great animator like Walt Disney. Belatedly, he realized that while his drawing skills were quite strong, they weren't quite Disney class. He regrouped in college, studying physics and hoping to become a legendary scientist like Albert Einstein. That didn't work out either. He made it as far as a junior-level job on Boeing's engineering team, only to be sacked in a mass layoff. At age twenty-five, he needed a third destiny.

Jim Clark was thrown out of high school for taunting one of his English teachers. He ended up in the Navy for a few years, but he didn't like that either. Eventually someone noticed his formidable math skills and steered him toward an overdue college education. At Tulane and the University of New Orleans, he earned degrees in physics. His grades were top-notch. So was his reputation for defiance.

All three men tried to stake out careers in computer science at about the same time. In each case, their candidacy files ended up on the desk of a small, skinny man in his early forties. He was an Eagle Scout and former Army intelligence officer working in Salt Lake City. It would have been easy for him to say "No" to any of these high-potential drifters. But he didn't. Instead, David C. Evans invited all three to become part of his inner circle of graduate students at the University of Utah. In the years to come, Kay, Catmull, Clark—and many more of Evans's protégés—dazzled the world with their contributions to modern-day computing.

Evans is one of the most intriguing figures in the computer revolution of the past half-century. He did well as a researcher and co-founder of a company making flight-simulator software. But his landmark impact came from his ability to spot unrecognized genius in other people. During his time at the University of Utah, he filled his graduate programs with the young engineers and scientists who later created the Pixar movie studio, a pioneering Internet-browser company, Photoshop editing software, and more. As *The New York Times* declared in Evans's 1998 obituary, Evans discovered and groomed "an extraordinary group of graduate students who went on to groundbreaking careers in computing."

Practically all of Evans's selections required him to make sense of what amounted to "jagged résumés." That term doesn't appear in standard human-resources manuals. But it's a familiar concept for top assessors in fields ranging from commerce to medicine, sports, high finance, and philanthropy. Knowing what to do when a jagged-résumé candidate enters the picture is the single biggest differentiator between leaders with a gift for picking winners—and those who keep wrong-footing themselves. This skill is so crucial that the next three chapters of this book will focus on how the best talent spotters find their bearings in such situations, how they develop strategies they can trust, and how they screen candidates.

First a few words of definition. Whenever a search for talent begins, it's customary to draw up a list of all the desired traits that a winning candidate should have. As business writer John Byrne observed in his book *The Headhunters*, these specifications sometimes become so long and lofty that they verge on absurdity. Nevertheless, as candidates come in, standard protocol calls for dividing résumés into two piles. People whose background and credentials largely fit expectations become serious contenders for the job. People who come up short are shunted aside.

That's a perfectly logical system, with a grievous flaw. The most intriguing candidates often don't fit into either pile. Parts of their résumés sparkle with fascinating strengths. There's something about their drive, their ingenuity, or their unusual background that hints at one-in-a-million promise. And yet, there are flaws. Run these candidates through the master checklist, and there will be embarrassing blank spots for some of the seemingly crucial requirements. By some yardsticks, such contenders may seem just plain wrong for the job. These are the candidates who don't have smooth, well-rounded credentials to date. They show up with a tantalizing, jarring combination of promise and pitfalls. They are the jagged résumés.

The cautious answer in such situations is to shunt such candidacies into a third pile: the "maybes." That way, no one needs to make a decision for a while. Such candidates aren't instantly rejected. But too often they aren't ever seriously considered, either. They hover on the edges until the business at hand is done, much like a theatrical understudy who keeps waiting backstage in case the star suddenly has a heart attack. The "maybe" category is actually nothing more than a face-saving fiction. It's a way of saying no slowly, by inertia. Only later do some of those evasive judgments demand a second look—when last year's "maybes" become someone else's superstars. That's when there's no escaping the uncomfortable question: "What did we miss?"

The best assessors thrive on analyzing the middle of the pile. Even if there's just one overlooked winner in each stack of fifty "maybes," they find him or her. They widen the talent pool without ever lowering their standards to the point that they tarnish their reputations with a flurry of poor hires. In their hands, the jagged résumés aren't so hard to decode after all. The next three chapters will showcase their most powerful methods, as follows:

Compromise on experience; don't compromise on character. At the University of Utah, David Evans succeeded by opening the doors to people whose bright minds and constant hunger to be working on the frontiers of knowledge made them standouts, regardless of their erratic transcripts and work history. His method focused on people's potential to rise beyond what they have done to date. This chapter will show how other great assessors in high tech, finance, sports, and commerce achieve breakthroughs with similar methods. The key requirement: being willing to embrace unconventional views of what skills are truly needed in each specific field.

Your own career is a template; use it. For an eerie set of reasons, many leaders treat their own life experiences as off-limits when it comes time to evaluate candidates. There's a school of thought that calls for assessments to be as neutral as possible. Wrong! As chapter 4 will show, the best insights into candidates' potential come from leaders whose own life experiences speak to the traits they are seeking. That's how venture capitalists score some of their biggest coups; it's how discoveries are made in fields ranging from music to medicine.

Rely on auditions to see *why* people achieve the results they do. Who tries hard? Who works well with others? Who recovers quickly from a setback? Conversely, who cuts corners? Who turns brittle under pressure? Who ultimately doesn't care? When great assessors watch a candidate in action, they aren't just looking for a momentary flash of brilliance. They are hunting for dozens of small clues that show how and why someone succeeds. That's where character is revealed. Chapter 5 will show how experts in sports, aviation, finance, and law enforcement extract special insights from auditions that the rest of us don't even see.

These three principles clear the way for efficient, accurate assessment of candidates who seem baffling to anyone else. Everything learned about a newcomer is matched against deeply held knowledge of what strengths are crucial for the job at hand—and what deficits don't matter. After all, these leaders aren't hunting for an all-purpose manager, athlete, author, or inventor. Their quests are far more specific. A basketball coach may hunt for a backcourt dynamo who can energize a team of slow-moving shooters. A theater director may want someone who can play Hamlet's father with a sense of impotent rage. Corporate board directors may want a hard-nosed CEO who can revive a dying business even if it means harsh measures along the way. In all these cases, leaders are looking for people uniquely right for the job at hand. It doesn't matter how ill suited such a person might be for something else.

When experts decode jagged résumés, they start by tightening up their "must-have" lists to a few crucial criteria. Often these factors barely register in competitors' minds. The process of getting to know candidates is defined far more by questions involving "why" and "how"—and less about "what" or "when." The payoff: the mysteries of motivation, fit, and potential become much clearer.

Warren Buffett, the Nebraska tycoon, is famous for saying that great investing doesn't require extraordinary intelligence; it calls for an extraordinary temperament. His point is that financial success often comes down to simple virtues: an ability to stay calm in a crisis; the patience to do nothing at times; the willingness to absorb new information; the confidence to stick with a plan. All those precepts sound easy. Yet when markets behave erratically, the vast majority of investors succumb to the frenzies, too. Unable to calm their emotions, they act in ways that ultimately become self-destructive to their portfolios no matter how smart they may have been in the past.

Most Wall Street bosses love to cite Buffett's maxim in casual conversation, only to ignore it when hiring investment experts. At big mutual funds or investment boutiques, it seems safer to recruit proven brainpower, year after year. So such outfits seek top business school graduates at Harvard, Wharton, and the like. Temperament is supposed to sort itself out later.

In the early 1980s, Chicago commodity trader Richard Dennis tested Buffett's proposition with a remarkable hiring experiment that has been tracked in books and newspaper articles ever since. Today it is seen—rightly—as a spectacular affirmation of the importance of temperament in the world of high-stakes investing.

Dennis's experiment began as a call to all comers, asking for people eager to learn to be futures traders. He and his partner, Bill Eckhardt, selected a motley bunch that included a bartender, a backgammon champion, a pianist, and an air force pilot. There wasn't a single traditional trader in the bunch. Dennis and Eckhardt taught these neophytes how to trade and then turned them loose on the Chicago futures markets with the freedom to invest as much as $1 million apiece of the firm's capital.

Dennis jokingly called these protégés his "Turtles." ("We are going to grow traders just like they grow turtles in Singapore," he told a friend.) If the experiment had gone badly, Dennis and Eckhardt would have lost many millions of dollars of their own funds. But the experiment didn't misfire. Instead, Dennis's offbeat collection of understudies generated more than $150 million in profits by the late 1980s, when the training program was disbanded.* Since then, the best have soared to even greater heights as independent traders. The

---

* Dennis and Eckhardt got 80 percent of those winnings, amounting to at least $120 million. The apprentice traders collected 20 percent, for incentive fees totaling at least $30 million.

more these Turtles thrive over time, the more their savvy begs an answer to the question: *What in the world did Richard Dennis do right?*

For a while, Dennis thought he had merely shown that commodity trading was a lot easier than everyone else believed. Follow a few simple rules, he contended, and you can be a multimillionaire, too. Dennis and Eckhardt had shared their formulas in brief training sessions with the Turtles before actual trading started, and Dennis was smug enough to think that those chalkboard talks were the key. As Dennis told the *Wall Street Journal*'s Stanley Angrist in 1989, "Trading was even more teachable than I imagined."

Later Dennis changed his mind. All the Turtles had enjoyed identical instruction. As time played out, however, the individual Turtles' results weren't remotely similar. The most skillful ones made as much as 290 percent on their money in their best years, without ever getting stuck in the cascades of bad risks that create catastrophically bad years. They became known as investors who could beat the market averages, big time, over a quarter century of trading. By contrast, some other Turtles couldn't sustain success. A few good years were followed by disasters. Career frustrations became so severe that some Turtles eventually dropped out of the investment business altogether. Some other success factor was at play, and all the clues pointed toward temperament.

Dennis's trading rules might be simple. Being able to abide by them in the midst of market turbulence wasn't easy at all. A few people could stay the course. Most others became prisoners of their own emotions. Hope led them to stick with losing positions too long, fear left them paralyzed in turbulent situations where great traders made bold bets, and greed made them take profits way too soon, before their best investments had fully played out. Such people lacked the temperament to be great traders.

In a 2009 panel discussion at a Chicago futures conference, Dennis said he had come to believe that the Turtle experiment succeeded to a significant degree because he and Eckhardt picked people who were disciplined enough to keep trading the right way, no matter what the temptations were to stray. That turns out to be a surprisingly rare gift.

Former Turtle Liz Cheval told me she believes that people's brains are hardwired to take profits quickly on winning investments, while sticking with losers for a long time in hopes of a recovery that will vindicate their initial judgment. Such tendencies are anathema to Dennis's approach. He wanted traders who could do the opposite: abandon small losers in a hurry so they could reload quickly. His formulas called for traders who could seize on a big market move and ride it for maximum profit, no matter how tempting it seemed to cash out early. That was how Dennis himself had built a $200 million trading fortune after starting with a $400 bankroll as a college student in the early 1970s.

"Rich always talked about doing the difficult thing," Cheval recalled. "You had to start feeling comfortable doing something that felt so wrong."

When Dennis and Eckhardt picked their Turtles in 1983 and 1984, they affected great insouciance about people's backgrounds. Some two thousand people answered small newspaper ads that said, in essence, "Traders Wanted." Barely two dozen got jobs—and these weren't the ones with deep knowledge of finance or proven success in the commodities pits. Instead, the Chicago traders made room for a security guard, a tractor salesman, and a designer of Dungeons & Dragons board games.* But whimsy alone wasn't guiding the process.

Dennis and Eckhardt did a great deal of quick filtering by looking for people who approached life analytically. Even simple true-false

---

* Some commodities traders believe Dennis was inspired at least in part by the 1983 movie *Trading Places*. In that film, two elderly, snooty investors take comedian Eddie Murphy into their trading business on a dare, to see if an uneducated homeless person can learn to make millions in Chicago's commodity exchanges. Murphy, of course, does just fine. Dennis has maintained in media interviews that the similarities are coincidental.

questions proved fruitful. "Would you rather be lucky or smart?" Dennis asked the candidates. Those who picked "lucky" were shown the door. Trading futures wasn't gambling, in Dennis's eyes. It was a systematic attempt to make the most of small edges in the marketplace. While not every investment would work out, good traders over time should reliably have the odds in their favor. Dennis wanted math majors, card counters in casinos, and other people with deep analytic skills who believed that "smart" was the right choice.

Dennis also asked candidates to respond to the aphorism "Most of your trades should be profitable." That is a cautious trader's watchword. It can be the basis of quite reasonable investment strategies. It wasn't Dennis's way. He wanted traders who could be at peace with the idea of attacking and retreating, again and again, until the chance to make a killing arrived. People who preferred tamer approaches didn't belong in his shop. Other interview questions reinforced his hunt for people who could become "unaddicted" from what he and Eckhardt regarded as a wrong-headed approach to risk.

In a 2007 book about Dennis's protégés, *The Complete Turtle Trader,* author Michael W. Covel concluded that Dennis chose newcomers with the "emotional and psychological makeup" necessary to succeed as big-time traders. By and large, the results bore out Dennis's judgment. When the *Wall Street Journal* reported the Turtles' first four years of trading results in September 1989, the group's average annual return was about 40 percent. The three best Turtles each topped 100 percent. Even allowing for overall rising markets, Dennis's Turtles were dashing ahead of typical independent commodities traders or stock market averages.

More than two decades later, former Turtles Jerry Parker, Liz Cheval, Jim DiMaria, Tom Shanks, Paul Rabar, and Howard Seidler have established themselves in the enduring ranks of America's top commodities traders. Some, in fact, have fared better than Dennis himself, who strayed from his own rules at times. Little wonder. As one former Turtle acknowledged, even if Dennis's rules had been published in a full-page newspaper ad, few people could have stuck to them, "because psychologically it was so difficult." Dennis's ultimate vindication came in the Turtles' success. When other people saw a ragtag group of amateurs, Dennis discerned the raw material of top-flight traders.

It's hard to imagine other professional investors testing temperament in such a flamboyant way. Few bosses could toss as much as $1 million apiece into the hands of a dozen neophytes to see what happened. Few would want that latitude. At most financial organizations, experience does matter. Technical skills do matter. So does team harmony. No one is ready to brush all those traditional factors aside.

Yet the idea that temperament counts—just as much as mainstream credentials—has independently become part of the way that some top hedge-fund investors now think about talent. Two prominent examples involve SAC Capital in Greenwich, Connecticut, and Tiger Management Corp. in New York. Both firms have used board-certified psychiatrists to size up and coach incoming talent. As SAC's longtime in-house psychiatrist, the late Ari Kiev, told me, the idea is to see who is best suited to making good decisions in chaotic markets.

"You have to ask the tough questions that people are afraid of," Kiev explained. He focused most intently on candidates' reactions when prior market picks proved disastrous. Even the best investors may do worse than the market averages with 40 percent of their picks, he explained. Failure, to some degree, is a fact of life. How investors work through those disappointments was what fascinated him.

"The best candidates are constantly trying to figure out why they went off the path," Kiev added. "They're introspective. They remember every detail. The ones who don't learn much have hazy memories. They tend to blame external factors. They sound intellectually honest, but they aren't. Their excuses are plentiful." In Kiev's view, the difference between rebounders and evaders is "hardwired into people. If you're inquiring well, you should be able to get at it."

Other SAC executives endorsed Kiev's approach. Jason Karp, who ran SAC Capital's research department from 2005 to 2008, said he drew on Kiev's assessments or methods for at least forty hires. "I definitely wanted Ari to screen candidates," Karp recalled. Because of Kiev's assessments, Karp said, "I was willing to hire people whose careers had imploded once, if I was confident that they had learned lessons that would keep them from ever making such mistakes again."

In the corporate world, plenty of people have tried to stretch in some direction that hasn't worked out. Some of those setbacks turn out to be hidden strengths, rather than shortcomings. There's something about having been snubbed early that propels certain people to greater success, no matter how much they achieve. The hardiest plants draw strength from harsh environments. The most durable civilizations come of age in hard times. Even individual careers can benefit from the gritty work required to recover from a career stumble.

Something similar happens in the world of sports, entertainment, and public performance. People tagged early as "not suitable" because they don't conform to some standard for size, vocal quality, good looks, or the like—but who press on anyway and start making significant headway—can turn out to be some of the most underrated prospects. Most scouts see only the unfixable flaw. Mavericks spot what's right in such a jagged résumé, allowing them to reap the rewards of signing a superstar that no one else recognized.

A delightful case in point involves the college baseball career of Tim Lincecum. In the spring of 2006, as a junior at the University of Washington, Lincecum overpowered college opponents. He posted a commanding 1.94 earned run average, striking out 199 batters in just 125 innings. No other college pitcher rivaled his results. Yet when pro scouts came to see him, their favorable impressions of his actual pitching were tempered by what they regarded as an unfixable shortcoming.

By baseball standards, Lincecum was too short. He was listed at five foot eleven and 170 pounds on Washington's roster; friends joked that he was actually five foot ten and weighed no more than 160, soaking wet. Sportswriters called him Seabiscuit, after the undersized racehorse that did so well in the 1930s. Most scouts regarded him as a chancy prospect, too likely to injure his throwing arm by trying to match the performance of bigger, stronger opponents.

So when the amateur draft began in May 2006, the team with the first pick, the Kansas City Royals, opted for a six foot five pitcher from Tennessee. The next team to pick, the Colorado Rockies, chose a six foot seven pitcher from Lincecum's own Pac-10 conference, with a much less impressive 3.35 earned run average. (The Rockies' choice wasn't nearly as dominating, but he was undeniably bigger.) In the following six selections, four more pitchers were chosen, averaging six foot three. Everyone wanted height. No one wanted Lincecum.

Eventually it was the San Francisco Giants' turn. The Giants' top scout, Dick Tidrow, had seen Lincecum pitch during the college season and had worried briefly whether a pitcher that small could hold up as a major-league starter. Lincecum relied on an unusually long stride and a lot of upper-body torque to generate the power needed for a 98 mph fastball. But as Tidrow watched Lincecum's motion, the Giants' scout came to believe that Lincecum's pitching mechanics were sound and didn't put his throwing arm at undue risk.

Wanting more insight, Tidrow had lingered on the Washington campus for an extra day, so he could watch Lincecum practice twenty-four hours after a game. A pitcher who was straining his arm would warm up gingerly, needing to let damaged muscles and ligaments heal for a day or two. To Tidrow's surprise, Lincecum exuberantly launched into long-toss catch—tossing a baseball 250 feet, back and forth, to a teammate—as if there hadn't been a game the day before.

On draft day, when it became clear that no one else was picking Lincecum, the Giants jumped at the chance. "This guy's going to be a big-league pitcher for a long while," Tidrow declared. "We were kind of shocked that he was still there" and available to be picked as the tenth choice in the draft.

Two years later, in 2008, Lincecum won a Cy Young Award as the National League's best pitcher. He repeated that feat in 2009, and then won two games for the Giants in the 2010 World Series. Ironically, most of the taller, stockier pitchers picked ahead of Lincecum in the 2006 baseball draft ended up with arm trouble of one sort or another. Some missed entire seasons. None came close to Lincecum's performance.

In *Good to Great*, Jim Collins argued that great talent selection transcends formulaic efforts to pick out the best résumés. Collins found that the standout companies he studied were far from dogmatic about their recruits' schooling, specialized knowledge, or work experience. In their eyes, extra credentials and experience could be acquired over time. In fact, these companies were unusually likely to make allowances for limited track records if they felt a candidate had great potential. What mattered most, Collins wrote, were "character attributes" such as work ethic, basic intelligence, and dedication to fulfilling commitments. Those are powerful labels—and they point toward a whole new round of insights. To achieve the full payoff, though, it's necessary to explore these succinct phrases much more closely.

Take something as universal (and idiosyncratic) as "work ethic." That's a cherished value at almost any top-tier organization. Ask leaders at Goldman Sachs, Walmart, the Mayo Clinic, NASA, the New England Patriots or Google if they are looking for candidates with a first-rate, world-class work ethic, and the answer will be a resounding: "Yes!" Now press further for examples of what exactly the term "work ethic" means at each organization. On Wall Street, it's the sudden determination to get to Cleveland in a snowstorm, no matter how badly transportation is snarled, so that a key client meeting can happen on time. In medicine, it's a mid-career willingness to spend weekends and evenings staying abreast of new research findings, instead of coasting on knowledge gained twenty years ago. And so on.

Everyone's definition of "work ethic" calls for slightly different virtues. Some jobs call for people who can summon up extraordinary stamina and ingenuity in a crisis. Others require orderly souls who are totally comfortable with the tireless preparation for a challenge that may be months or years away. The work ethics of a great doctor and a great football player aren't the same. Solving the talent puzzle means looking for exactly the right ethos that's vital for a particular job—rather than trying to match candidates to a long list of universal virtues that might or might not be especially relevant.

All these nuances came to life a few years ago, in Silicon Valley, when I started chatting with Bob Dobkin. He is a legendary semiconductor designer who has hired more than five hundred inventors over the years, either directly or through his lieutenants. Dobkin oversees the technical side of one of Silicon Valley's most profitable companies, Linear Technology. If you have ever stepped on a digital scale, or taken a flash picture with a cellular phone, you have used a machine with a Linear-designed microchip inside it. The company makes more than 7,500 kinds of chips that amplify signals, modulate power, and perform other sorts of electronic wizardry.

Dobkin wants engineers with ingenuity, persistence, and passion. So does everyone else in Silicon Valley. If he defined his quest that loosely, he would always be competing for talent with more than two hundred other major technical companies within a forty-minute drive of his headquarters in Milpitas, California. Try to hire the same people everyone else wants—without any differentiators—and you soon discover that conformity is a tax. In that case, Dobkin's payroll would be defined by limited loyalty, high costs, and frequent turnover.

But Linear doesn't work quite the way other technical companies do. Dobkin knows that. In fact, he knows it well enough to be able to keep tapping into an unusual pool of inventors who are just right for his company, even if they wouldn't fit in especially well anywhere else. Once engineers join Linear, they rarely leave.

Most of Dobkin's competitors practice "big engineering," with hundreds of people working on the same massive project for years. By contrast, Dobkin and his inventors still make their living by being champions of "small engineering." They usually work solo or in small groups. They may spend a year designing a specialized chip that will sell for as little as 23 cents apiece. If it takes a hundred breakthroughs for Apple, Ford Motor, or the like to create an amazing new product, the engineers at Linear are the ones who solve the last few stumpers at the end of the list. They don't build entire devices; they simply come up with elegant solutions to problems involving electrical signals.

Practically everyone at Linear regards this work as the analog version of old-fashioned craftsmanship. "Designing one of our chips is like writing poetry," Dobkin says. Another colleague compares the work to high-end woodworking, creating beautiful cabinets and chairs. A third talks about the way you can look at someone else's chip design and tell—just by the way the pieces are put together—who created it. Each inventor has his own, signature style. "It's like listening to Oscar Peterson or Bill Evans playing the same jazz piece," Linear engineer Robert Reay told me. "Without looking at the label, you can tell who's at the piano."

In that sort of proud, prickly culture, Dobkin wants engineers who love to tinker. Linear's research building looks like a wild corporate skunk works, full of one-man labs in which engineers solder prototypes together. All day long, engineers pick apart designs that almost worked—and put them back together a little differently to see if they can come up with a better solution. Many people would find that work exhausting. It involves constant brushes with failure, and an endless hunt for new ideas. The engineers that Linear picks can't imagine doing anything more fun in their working lives.

At campus job fairs, Dobkin and his lieutenants look for people who fiddle with gadgets. Linear's booths at those events look more like a chapter meeting of a "home-brew" electronics club than a serious corporate outpost. That's fine. Intrigued candidates quickly strike up conversations with Linear's hosting engineers. People who walk by probably weren't right for the chip company anyway.

Dobkin learns more about his tinkerers in interviews. The best engineers start young, he finds. So he likes to hear about their early electronic pranks and explorations. One of Linear's top patent holders rigged up capacitors at age thirteen, so that when his younger sister pressed an innocent-looking button on the kitchen table, she got the shock of her life. Another prolific inventor tore apart an Apple computer as a teenager, trying to squeeze in a speech-synthesizer chip where none belonged. He ruined the machine, but learned a lot about circuits.

Those are Linear's kind of people. They daydream about circuits. They build things in their spare time. They range from Ph.D. holders to engineers with ragged college transcripts, if they finished college at all. That's hardly a deterrent to hiring them. When they are working solo on a devilishly hard new design, nothing can tear them away.

All of the methods described so far share a common payoff. They allow assessors to commit more confidently to a forward-looking view of what a candidate might become. Sizing up a candidate's capacity to learn and grow is usually the hardest part of an assessment. Some organizations don't even try to hazard a guess. They simply hire people whose current skills are sufficient. Only when organizations have the courage to make judgments about potential do the odds of landing an eventual superstar increase.

This willingness to bet on the future can be seen with particular clarity in the story of David Evans and his gathering of computer-graphics geniuses. When Evans arrived at the University of Utah in 1965, he had no choice but to focus his attention on the future. All he received at the start was a title (chairman of the new computer science department, population one), as well as a small office, an $18,000-a-year salary, and the freedom to dream. He was a forty-one-year-old newcomer on a campus where no one knew what a computer department should do. It wasn't clear what other professors should join the department, what sorts of courses should be offered—or what kinds of students Utah might want.

"We won't ever be big enough to do everything," Evans told an early confidant. "So we're going to do one thing well."

To build a plan, Evans started by pondering what he didn't like about computers. These new machines were proving to be ferocious number crunchers, all right. They processed data faster than anyone could fathom. But they were annoyingly hard to use. Information display techniques were so primitive that almost every problem had to be "solved" with a tidal wave of numbers. There wasn't yet a good way of creating computer-generated images that could let users *visualize* information.

Even in the 1960s, military pilots were pressing for realistic flight simulators with constantly changing views that could approximate a tough landing. It was possible to imagine draftsmen wanting to rotate a computerized version of an intricate part in three dimensions. Similarly, chemists might yearn to do something similar with a molecular model. And for whimsy's sake alone, it would be nice to show a computerized version of light sparkling on everyday objects such as a shiny teapot.

Opportunities abounded. Evans just needed the right sorts of students and junior faculty members to exploit the situation. The first people to join Evans's team were technically capable folks already at the university, who thought computers sounded interesting. They published modest papers and moved on. They didn't sense an epic opportunity. Clearly, if Evans wanted to wow the world, he needed to draw in zestier souls.

Within two years, Evans had begun finding his pioneers. He wanted Ivan Sutherland—an intellectual gypsy on the East Coast—to join him as part of Utah's faculty. Sutherland was famous for starting countless projects and finishing none of them. He came to work in sandals; his appetites included lawn volleyball during the daytime and risqué movies in the evening. He had already made brief stops at Carnegie Mellon, Caltech, MIT, Harvard, and the Defense Department's Advanced Research Projects Agency. No one could contain him for long. But Sutherland was a genius. His Ph.D. dissertation at MIT spelled out a revolutionary new technology called Sketchpad, which would allow computer users to manipulate full-fledged images on their screens. Even though Sketchpad wasn't fully working yet, it was an eye-catching breakthrough. Month after month, Evans kept urging Sutherland to come to Utah, join the faculty, and help launch a commercial company that would incorporate some of Sketchpad's best ideas. By 1968, Evans had his man.

Meanwhile, Alan Kay had wandered onto campus one autumn with a girlfriend, a college degree, and some hazy ideas about finding temporary work in Utah's computer lab. In the autumn of 1966, Kay had just graduated from the University of Colorado and didn't feel like getting a respectable job just yet. Evans invited him in for a chat—and quickly pegged him as an unfocused whiz kid who ought to be in graduate school, parked in front of a big, thrilling challenge.

"I remember walking into Dave's office," Kay later told me. "Here was this guy who was forty years old and looked thirty. Research papers were stacked all over the place. Dave pushed a copy of Sutherland's Sketchpad thesis into my hands and said: 'Read this tonight. Tell me what you think of it.' It was a completely different way of thinking about everything." A month later, Evans accepted Kay as a graduate student, shrugging off the newcomer's spotty grades. By the time Kay left Utah, he had mapped out a futuristic sense of notebook-sized computers that would engage users mostly via their graphics-dominated screens. A decade later, Kay would build the early graphics interfaces that inspired Apple's Macintosh computers. In Kay's words, that meeting with Evans "pretty much set up the rest of my career."

A pattern was forming. Evans began focusing on bright, restless young researchers eager to tackle challenges no one had ever confronted before. Even if they were hazy about what problems they wanted to solve, they needed an underlying hunger to be pioneers. Evans wasn't picky about how they acquired some technical grounding: an undergraduate degree in math, physics, or engineering would suffice. Computer science was a hot new field with explosive growth. It was fine to make up the rules as people went along. So Evans shrugged off bumpy transcripts, erratic hygiene, or a tendency to start the day at 11 A.M. As long as bright people wanted to stretch the boundaries of human knowledge, he could point them in the right direction.

Soon a second wave of searchers arrived at Utah. Physics major John Warnock had tried a few years at IBM, but that was too stifling. Evans brought him in as a graduate student and turned him loose on the "hidden surface problem," which involved finding a way for computers to calculate how a three-dimensional object's visible surface would keep changing as viewers saw it from different angles. Warnock's elegant solution won him a Ph.D. in less than three years;

it also launched him on a career in computer graphics that led to his founding of Adobe Systems, maker of Photoshop, PostScript, and Acrobat software.

Two more itchy physics majors, Ed Catmull and Jim Clark, followed soon afterward. Catmull was a former Mormon missionary; Clark was an atheist and a hell-raiser. Intellectually, though, they traveled a similar path to Utah. "I wanted to be out on the frontier," Catmull told me over lunch in 2009, as he recalled his time at Utah. "Staying in physics was going to involve a long wait to get there." As one of Evans's graduate students, Catmull tackled the mystery of why early computer graphics had so much trouble rendering smooth edges on boxes, airplane wings, and the like. The culprit wasn't easy to find, but once Catmull got it, he opened the way for vastly more realistic imagery. In the process, Catmull developed such an intense interest in computer-based animation that he later helped create Pixar Studios.

"I had concluded that physics was a dead end," Clark told me in 2009. At Utah he, too, tackled the challenges of three-dimensional design of smooth surfaces, earning his Ph.D. in 1974. A decade later, Clark founded Silicon Graphics, the mastermind behind the virtual-reality dinosaurs of the movie *Jurassic Park*. In the 1990s, Clark teamed up with a young Midwesterner, Marc Andreessen, to start Netscape Communications, which became a groundbreaking Internet browser company.

When the Utah idea machine was performing at its peak, Evans's second son, Peter, was a freshly minted college graduate who helped his father sort out corporate recruiting. "My dad looked at people very differently," Peter Evans recalled in a 1996 interview with an oral historian. "He hired a lot of people that happened to fail history, or fail music theory, or whatever else. Some of them you might even call scary. It didn't matter to him that they weren't polished in some areas that weren't important to their job performance. What he really cared about was what they liked to do."

The more Evans packed his Utah computer science department with intriguing people, the more they accomplished. Everyone had ideas. Everyone jostled for a chance to help create the future. The third floor of the Merrill Engineering Building became a nonstop proving ground for innovation. "You felt empowered," Clark later recalled. "You saw how simple the best solutions could be. You felt: 'Hey, I can do this, too!'"

Decades later, former students recall Evans's lab as a surprisingly safe place to try out new ideas. Evans was a constantly sunny, slightly vague personality. He liked his students' new ideas. He seldom tried to micromanage how they went about their research. Occasionally he would ask a brief, audacious question about what might come next. Those queries usually took the form of: "Have you considered . . . ?" Evans knew how searchers' minds worked. As long as he pointed them toward giant, heroic quests, his kinds of students would fire up all the internal motivation needed. The best ideas would flourish; the weaker ones would quietly fail on their own.

Evans could stay in the background. His restless, ambitious students would keep the department humming.

All the same, there was a cunning side to Evans's easy-going methods. After a few years, Evans brought in a gifted Utah nature photographer, Mike Milocheck, to run a small photo development lab. Instead of situating Milocheck's lab in a back corner, Evans made sure it was in the most-trafficked corridor. Milocheck was also encouraged to post his most intriguing photo prints quite prominently, right outside his lab. That way, everyone walking through the department could see their colleagues' latest breakthroughs. Before long, the researchers' unstated goal was to create work that would be admired by their peers as hallway masterpieces.

Evans regarded his research lab as a launching pad, not a destination. He told several of his students that graduate school wasn't a great place to spend a big chunk of their lives. They should pick an important thesis topic, get the work done, earn a Ph.D., and then move on. In the mid-1970s, Evans took his own advice. The flight-simulator company that he and Ivan Sutherland had set up, Evans & Sutherland, was commanding so much of his time that he resigned as computer science department chairman, and then a few years later stepped down entirely from the active faculty. Later in life, his own health betrayed him. Just at the point when outsiders appreciated the depth of talent that he had attracted to Utah, he was stricken with Alzheimer's disease and wasn't able to explain much about how he did it. Fortunately, vast amounts of his working papers are archived at the university, and dozens of his students retain keen memories of his methods.

Utah's computer science department remained an important center of discovery after David Evans left, but it never quite matched its preeminence during his era. As author Robert Rivlin wrote in his 1984 book, *The Algorithmic Image*, "Virtually every modern concept in computer graphics either had its origin or received significant further development at the University of Utah in the late 1960s and early 1970s."

The most powerful legacy of Evans's talent spotting is in his students' careers. Ed Catmull, for example, has won five Academy Awards for his contributions in developing computerized film animation. Pixar movies such as *Toy Story, Finding Nemo*, and *The Incredibles* have delighted hundreds of millions of people and redefined the ways that animated stories are told.

Beyond that, Catmull said, his own approach to hiring people has been shaped by what he learned from David Evans. And that sense of exuberantly racing ahead on the frontier has never disappeared. "I came out of the University of Utah thinking that we would be able to do full-length, computer-animated movies in about ten years," Catmull recalled. "I was wrong. It took us about twenty years. But we never lost faith, and we did it anyway."

4: Where Insights Are Born

Each year, about 42,000 college students apply to America's medical schools, hoping to win a place in the next year's entering class. Less than half will make it. Sorting out this avalanche of candidates is not just a mathematical ordeal; it's also a fascinating test of priorities.

If medical schools wanted, they could focus entirely on the candidates who rung up the best grades and scores at the most demanding colleges. Students with mostly As in chemistry, biology, and other science classes would get in; students with B-plus averages or worse would be shooed away. Cutoffs for MCAT* scores could be even more absolute. Getting into medical school would be like passing a tough civil-service screening. Everyone on one side of the threshold would be treated as equally suitable; everyone on the other site would be regarded as insufficiently qualified.

But America's medical schools don't do that. They periodically dip into parts of the candidate pool that the rigid, civil-service approach wouldn't touch. Schools will take a chance on the student with erratic grades who published a landmark research paper before graduation. They will open their doors to the student with ragged MCAT scores and a powerful personal history of overcoming adversity. And

* Medical College Admissions Test.

81

to make room for such jagged-résumé prospects, schools will sometimes say no to candidates whose fine grades and scores are undercut by troublingly weak recommendations, essays, or other parts of the picture. Charts published each year by the American Association of Medical Colleges show that for the vast majority of medical school applicants, grades and scores aren't the sole determinant of their candidacy's fate. Whether the students get in or not will depend on a more subjective sense of which candidates ought to become doctors.

Here's the really intriguing twist. The most prestigious medical schools—Johns Hopkins, Harvard, Stanford, and the like—are also among the ones most willing to break away from a formulaic approach. It would be easiest for them to focus entirely on students with 3.9 grade points and 95th percentile MCAT scores. Instead, they go out of their way to practice the medical-school equivalent of reading the résumé upside down.

Johns Hopkins in particular has been famous for taking at least a few offbeat candidates that it calls "broken arrows." They are applicants who have poured tremendous energy into wildly different career choices, before deciding late in the game that what they really wanted was the chance to become a top-flight doctor. One such applicant, Pat O'Neill, spent four years as an NFL punter. Another tried his hand at being an Alaska fisherman. Others briefly made their mark as fighter pilots, Olympic-caliber rowers, submarine commanders, or concert pianists. Most of them applied to Hopkins with decent—but not spectacular—grades and scores. For them to win a place at this renowned medical school, something about their career zigzags needed to go beyond being an irrelevant oddity. There had to be a particular spark that Hopkins saw in such applicants.

Looking for the answer, I ended up one morning in the office of James Weiss, the associate dean at Hopkins who oversees medical school admissions. He is a wiry man in his late sixties with a shy smile and a kind word for almost everyone he mentions. He also happens to be one of America's top cardiologists, a job that requires superb diagnostic skills. When Dr. Weiss sees patients, much of his job involves fitting many disparate clues into a coherent picture. So, with a twinkle in his eye, he decided to introduce me to the Hopkins way of thinking, one clue at a time.

"When I was a senior in college," Dr. Weiss began, "I was told that I was completely unqualified to go to medical school." It was the early 1960s. Weiss had spent much of his teenage years believing that he wanted to be a concert oboist. He had trained extensively with one of America's top oboe players, Ray Still of the Chicago Symphony Orchestra. As an undergraduate at Harvard, Weiss had poured his energies into his music major. And then, partway through senior year, Weiss realized he had started down the wrong track. He didn't want to sit in orchestra pits the rest of his life. He wanted to be a doctor.

It took a year of premed science classes as a graduate student at Harvard before Weiss got into medical school. But from that point onward, everything clicked. He graduated from Yale Medical School and won residencies at Michigan and then Hopkins. He published influential research papers. He won a prestigious fellowship with the National Institutes of Health. He took charge of Hopkins's Heart Station as well as the echocardiography lab, working with colleagues to develop cardiac care standards that benefited many thousands of patients each year. The more his own career prospered, the more he thought about the fate of other late bloomers who were ready to devote their lives to great patient care, if they just got the chance. America needed such doctors, he believed. So did Hopkins. When he took charge of the admissions effort in 1999, part of his ambition was to pay more attention to the full human dimensions of each candidate, beyond what grades and scores revealed.

There was an archetype in Dr. Weiss's mind—and he wanted me

to understand it. "A physician has to be incredibly patient and forgiving of the sick," he said. "There's a lot of altruism involved here. Collegiality is crucial. You can't just look out for yourself." The entire tone of a 120-person med school class—arrogant or humble; selfish or caring—can be set by the personalities of a few crucial students. Salting each cohort with the right role models was, Dr. Weiss believed, a vital part of his job. As he explained: "We'll get applicants who may not have the greatest MCAT scores. But they will be fabulous classmates. These are the future doctors who will lead us."

Medicine's best new leaders tend to be candidates who had already made a mark outside the classroom, Dr. Weiss found. They brought a seriousness of purpose to Hopkins. Their ability to stay on task and keep their composure during tough times helped inspire classmates, too. When I asked Dr. Weiss and H. Franklin Herlong, a former Hopkins dean of student affairs, for examples, the illustrations were endless. One year, inspiration came from a coal miner's son who had taken care of his dying father during college. Another year it came from a former fighter pilot. All told, 45 percent of Hopkins's entering class these days arrives with at least a year of postcollege work experience.

One of the most memorable "broken arrow" applicants was Mary Schuler Cutler, who applied to Hopkins Medical School eight years after finishing college, with a résumé dominated by her work as a Chicago police detective. Her college transcript was thin on science classes, but she had made up the gap by taking evening classes during her police years. Hopkins admissions officers pegged her as a winner, and they were doubly vindicated. As a medical student, she calmed younger classmates during their panicky moments, telling them, "I've never been so sure of anything in my life." And after graduating from medical school, Cutler emerged as a standout resident in psychiatry. Her background on the Chicago police force turned out to be a valuable asset, providing her with unique perspectives on the ways that mental illness is understood and misunderstood in society. Dr. Weiss's assessment: "She will undoubtedly end up on the faculty."

Months after that chat with Dr. Weiss, what lingered most prominently in my mind was his certainty that Mary Schuler Cutler would do well. To him, she wasn't a high-risk applicant at all. Her unconventional background didn't fluster him. The fact that she needed to take catch-up science courses after getting her college degree in Latin American studies wasn't a basis for concern either. He *knew* how those sorts of candidates could work out. After all, he had been one himself.

With a different sort of doctor running the admissions program, Hopkins might never open its doors to so many jagged-résumé candidates. Even if it periodically tried taking candidates with offbeat backgrounds, the odds of repeatedly picking winners would be far smaller. What made the difference was having an admissions chief with an unusually good sense—honed by his own life experiences—of what kinds of nontraditional candidates could succeed at Hopkins.

Look around more widely, and the same pattern holds again and again in jagged-résumé assessment. The assessors who do the best job of sizing up such candidates are the ones whose own life experiences speak to the traits they are seeking. Start with intense, unforgettable personal knowledge, and the offbeat candidate isn't so offbeat anymore. It's much easier to identify commonly overlooked strengths that could prove crucial over time. It's also much clearer which flaws matter and which ones don't.

To revisit a few examples from the previous chapter:

- Why did David Evans place such a high value on restless explorers when he built the University of Utah's legendary graphics team? He was one himself. He was an Army scout in World War II; a pioneer in developing easy-to-use computers at Bendix in the

1950s, and an observant Mormon who chose to live in Berkeley, California, in the early 1960s. As an academic leader, Evans was ready to stock Utah with his kind of people.

- Why did Richard Dennis hunt for commodities traders with wildly eclectic backgrounds? It helps to know that Dennis was a philosophy major as a DePaul undergraduate, transfixed by the writings of Locke and Hume. His intellectual coming of age involved a classical exploration of the way human beliefs are formed, rather than a lot of worrying about soybean prices' next move. Commodity trading for him began as a minor hobby. Only when he realized how freakishly good he was at trading did he turn it into a career. As a result, there was a lot of room in Dennis's world for people who accidentally figured out markets by getting good at something else.

- Why was baseball scout Dick Tidrow uniquely willing to see the potential in a pitcher less than six feet tall? There's a vital clue in Tidrow's own career. He was a big, strong pitcher, standing six foot four, who played for thirteen years in the major leagues, with middling results. In 1978, Tidrow made the New York Yankees' starting rotation during their run to the World Series, as did Ron Guidry, a wisp of a man at five foot eleven and 161 pounds. Tidrow contributed just seven wins that season. Guidry was the best pitcher in baseball, with a won-loss record of 25–3. Tidrow came out of that season with the poise and humility to realize that great pitchers didn't need to tower over their opponents. Sometimes it's the small guy who dominates.

- Finally, what made Bob Dobkin so confident that childhood tinkerers could excel as semiconductor designers? By now, the answer should be obvious. Dobkin—who went on to earn more than forty patents as an adult—was a hell-raiser extraordinaire as a child. At age ten he created a contraption that electrified the family's outdoor garbage bins, so that neighborhood dogs couldn't prowl for scraps. At age fourteen he made another gizmo that commandeered a local diner's intercom system, so that he could boom out insults to the cooks and waitresses. Decades later, Dobkin couldn't help giggling about all his long-ago mischief. But he had a serious point to make, too. "You can always learn more equations as an adult," he said. "We can teach that. But you can't learn to be an inventor if it isn't in your blood."

If assessors all felt comfortable drawing insights from their own lives, this wouldn't be a controversial chapter. What's more, organizations' ability to make sense of jagged résumés would be far more advanced than it is. But the sorry truth is that hiring norms in recent decades keep leaving less room for individual perspectives. In big organizations especially, the notion of hunting for talent in quirky ways evokes shudders. Formulaic conformity feels safer. In this rearranged world, hiring becomes a labored exercise in not making mistakes, rather than an ambitious hunt for greatness.

Consider this admonition from a popular management primer on hiring: Lou Adler's *Hire with Your Head*. The author's number one precept is as follows: "Remain objective throughout the interviewing process, fighting the impact of first impressions, biases, intuitions, prejudices and preconceived notions of success. This way, all information collected during the interview is both relevant and unbiased."

That's a fine way to pick out a lawn mower. It's not a great way to choose people.

What gets lost in such straitjacketed systems is any ability to gauge candidates' motivation, drive, or potential. Shut down experts' intuitions drawn from personal notions of success—and Mary Schuler Cutler never gets offered a spot at Johns Hopkins. David Evans never welcomes the restless spirits at Utah who later help create Pixar, the Apple Macintosh, Netscape, and Adobe. Dick Tidrow never urges the Giants to take a chance on the not-so-tall pitcher with the powerful fastball. Hiring becomes driven by a mechanical emphasis on credentials, formulas, and prior work history. Payrolls become filled with unobjectionable souls that are consistently a little above average. There's no room for transformative geniuses who can breathe new life into a place.

How did individual insight become so endangered? Why do so many people think it's safer to rely on formulas that miss the best candidates?

The answers start in the late nineteenth century, when two of the most important professions—medicine and law—were booming in a frightening, chaotic way. Thousands of poorly trained characters were proclaiming themselves to be doctors. Self-styled lawyers were rampant as well. Outraged reformers pushed for minimum standards in both fields, to be enforced either by state medical boards (starting in 1878) or the American Bar Association (formed in 1891).

At first, this new system of licensing accomplished a lot. It spelled out mandatory amounts of training, as well as tough certification exams. Most of the charlatans disappeared. Professional training became much more systematic and higher quality. Citizens could be confident that someone who claimed to be a doctor really had earned that distinction. Licensing ensured that all practitioners met a minimum standard. It wasn't a mechanism for identifying or rewarding greatness, but that limitation seemed tolerable. The nation's most urgent need at the time was guaranteed competency.

If medico-legal licensing was good, then why not shake up dozens of other professions the same way? From the early 1900s onward, licensing mania swept through America. In Texas, for example, the pharmacists got licensed in 1907, with nurses, barbers, podiatrists, and optometrists following soon afterward. In the Great Depression, civil engineers, architects, and morticians entered the ranks of licensed professionals. Then teachers, psychologists, marriage counselors, and lie-detector specialists joined the fold during the first few decades after World War II. Today, state licenses in Texas define at least forty professions.

The more competency-based testing caught on—with its streamlined, check-the-box approach to assessing people—the more such systems overwhelmed more imaginative ways of hunting for talent. The experts who developed licensing systems weren't solving all the challenges of getting the best people into the right jobs. Yet these specialists mastered a sparser set of tasks. They designed good credential-checking systems and kept improving them. They brought the same diligence to standardized tests and cautious, depersonalized interview questions.

Even ambitious corporations came to believe that people should be graded from a distance—according to a few, all-purpose scorecards—rather than sized up individually, in terms of the task at hand. In his book *Talent on Demand*, Wharton business school professor Peter Cappelli notes that while companies cared a lot about character in the 1950s, they generally thought the best way to gauge it was through formulaic personality tests. By 1954, 63 percent of large companies used standardized personality tests for hiring decisions. Some companies even created lifetime ledgers of an employee's test scores, which could be carried from job to job, like a passport. This lockstep approach seemed scientific and satisfactory. Besides, everyone was doing it.

Over time, the failings of this approach became clear. Most of the fast-growth, high-excitement fields in America couldn't be sustained by using depersonalized templates that focused strictly on competence or a mechanical assessment of character. In 1981, economist Sherwin Rosen tallied up a wide list of fields—sports, arts, show business, even the teaching of economics—and discovered that in each one, "relatively small numbers of people earn enormous amounts of money and dominate the activities in which they engage." Success in such arenas required either being one of these high achievers, or stockpiling such talent in an organization. The United

States, Rosen declared, was entering a new era defined by "the economics of superstars."

It wasn't obvious how to find such people. Their prowess was obvious after the fact. But when tomorrow's superstars were getting started, they didn't necessarily stand out relative to their peers, at least as gauged by the traditional checklist approaches in favor at the time.

Rosen threw up his hands at what he called "the elusive quality of box-office appeal." But even if he hadn't figured out in 1981 why some talented people did so well, he urged others to see what they could learn. Over time, insights did emerge. They just tended not to come from traditional sources.

If any field lives and dies by its practitioners' ability to harness past insights in judging unpredictable talent, it's the brand of venture capital practiced along Silicon Valley's Sand Hill Road. Each year, thousands of entrepreneurs stream toward these financiers' offices, pitching exciting visions of what tomorrow's technology could be. They arrive by Porsche, bicycle, or Segway. Some have engineering Ph.D.s from the likes of MIT and Stanford; others are college dropouts. They all share a zealot's insistence that their ideas will work.

Sustaining this theater of wild dreams is the knowledge that even though most visitors are sadly mistaken, every few months one of them will turn out to be spectacularly right. Venture capitalists routinely scan hundreds of ideas for each one they actually fund. To them, that's tolerable. The payoff from investing in the next Apple, Google, or Facebook can be a thousand to one. Even if the most dazzling opportunities arise only a few times a decade, their allure is so huge that it justifies all sorts of missteps and time-wasters along the way.

Over time, I got to know three of the earliest investors in Google. In the late 1990s, all of them warmed up to the search-engine company and its founders for different reasons. Hearing their stories, it struck me that they weren't so much judging a business plan as they were listening for a melody that they had heard before. Once they recognized similarities to a previous high point in their lives, they were ready—in fact, quite eager—to write a check on behalf of what might be just a tiny dream of a company.

The first backer was Ram Shriram, an Indian immigrant who had helped run a series of software companies. He was well connected with Stanford University's computer science department, and he let it be known in 1998 that he would like to invest in any promising start-ups that graduate students were building. When he got an invitation to meet Google founders Larry Page and Sergey Brin, Shriram was impressed with the power and accuracy of their search engine. But what he remembered most vividly years later were the two men's family stories.

Both Page and Brin had grown up in academic households. Their fathers were university researchers; so were their mothers. That resonated perfectly with Shriram, who was brought up by his academic researcher mother. "I like young entrepreneurs whose parents are teachers or professors," Shriram told me. "That generates kids with great curiosity. They want to push the envelope. They gravitate to interesting, unsettled issues."

Two of the next investors were venture capitalists John Doerr and Michael Moritz in 1998. Doerr by then was famous for backing the Netscape Web browser business and Amazon's online retailing. Moritz was the first venture investor in Yahoo!'s Internet portal. Both drew inspiration from similar, but slightly different defining events much earlier in their careers.

For Doerr, everything tied back to the start of his high-tech career, selling Intel microchips as a young man in his twenties. He was a spectacularly successful salesman, with the maturity to realize that it wasn't just his own boyish good looks that won the orders. Intel at that point in the late 1970s was in the midst of a revolutionary reshaping of the computer industry. It was almost as if an entire new continent of economic might was forming before his eyes, with Intel in the middle. When everything lined up just right—as it did with Intel—the chance to create thousand-to-one wealth was right there in front of him.

For the rest of his career, Doerr hunted for those moments. He found one in 1982, backing a trio of brash Stanford researchers who were building advanced workstation computers. Their success with Sun Microsystems transformed Doerr into a venture-capital kingpin, with uniquely good insights about next-generation companies that arose in Sun's ecosystem. In 1993, he did it again by backing Netscape Communications' Internet browser, opening the door to the entire dot-com boom. From that point on, Doerr looked for entrepreneurs so audacious that they could launch a new industry out of nothing. Google's founders fit that test.

For other venture capitalists, key insights came even earlier in their lives. Sequoia Capital partner Michael Moritz spent his late twenties as a *Time* magazine journalist, eventually gaining inside access to write a book about Apple and its founder, Steve Jobs. That helped Moritz form a lasting view of what entrepreneurs acted like—including the importance of jarring traits that left other people squeamish. Entrepreneurs weren't just visionaries to Moritz. As Moritz told me, "They have this incredible need to do what they're doing. They can't think of anything else they want to do." No matter if that made them cranky, obstinate, arrogant zealots. In fact, such flaws often made it possible for them to chase their business dreams so relentlessly.

"So many breadcrumbs from Apple are strewn across the path of my life," Moritz declared in 2010. He judged the most ambitious entrepreneurs by whether they had a bit of Steve Jobs's spark. Most didn't, or were faking it. On the rare occasions that Moritz found a match, he pounced. It didn't matter if these entrepreneurs' eccentricities rubbed other financiers the wrong way. Moritz believed more

Steve Jobses were coming to Silicon Valley. When he backed the founders of Yahoo! and Google, he was proven right in gigantic style.

Each potential investor, looking at Google, heard a different melody. But the company's earliest backers each found something that sounded just right. If other venture capitalists couldn't connect Page's and Brin's project to anything magical in their lives, the chance to make an epic investment could slip out of their awareness before they even knew what they missed.

In music, of course, the imagery of matching past melodies isn't a metaphor; it's the literal truth. Sam Phillips, the founder of Sun Records in the 1950s, won lasting fame as the man who provided some of the first recording contracts for the likes of Elvis Presley, Johnny Cash, Howlin' Wolf, B. B. King, and many others. His label succeeded by blurring the boundaries between what at the time were sharply different tastes for "white" music and "black" music.

Late in life, Phillips tried to explain how he, the son of a white Alabama cotton farmer, developed an ear for the music he made famous. It all went back to black musicians he heard in the 1930s on his family farm, he said. There was a blind man making up songs about molasses and pancakes; there was a broken-backed shoeshine man tapping out rhythms on his knee. Phillips remembered odd details with great vividness. "It was impossible in those days not to hear and grow to love all the . . . music that uplifted people—blues, country, gospel—all of it," Phillips told an interviewer in 1999.

Even in elite colleges' admissions offices, a genteel version of pattern-matching across the generations is constantly taking place. As *New York Times* education reporter Jacques Steinberg pointed out in his book *The Gatekeepers*, each college admissions officer comes with her or his own life story. There are Latino strivers who worked their way up from difficult beginnings. There are bookish souls from small towns in the Upper Midwest. There are people who loved math contests in high school, and people who couldn't wait until the Friday night football game. Each one, Steinberg wrote, draws on that past in assessing students' applications.

By and large, that's good. Schools such as Harvard, Yale, and the like are overwhelmed each year by more bright applicants than they can possibly accept. So universities dream of enrolling a dazzling human bouquet of future scientists, political leaders, social activists, CEOs, comedians, Pulitzer Prize winners, and healers. The schools all hope to identify teenagers who will succeed at life. No one can predict destinies with 100 percent accuracy. But the assessors with the best shot of getting it right—or at least with enough confidence that they are willing to try—are admissions officers who know at least one path really well.

In the corporate world, Goldman Sachs, Nike, Procter & Gamble, and McKinsey are often spoken of as organizations with especially astute eyes for management talent. Like Hopkins, they start with big, eager pools of ambitious young people who want to make a name there. And just like Hopkins, they pick out an unusually productive set of prospects each year. They seem to know when to hire the valedictorian, and when to bet on the jagged résumé. Their hiring mistakes are rarer than competitors'; their successful picks race farther ahead.

Where did Goldman Sachs's norms come from? The right starting point is Sidney Weinberg, the Wall Street firm's senior partner during the crucial growth years from 1930 to 1969. He was a high-school dropout from Brooklyn, who started at Goldman as a janitor's assistant, brushing partners' hats and cleaning out spittoons. His scrappy, underdog personality not only propelled him to the top—it became a template for generations of Goldman executives as they sized up applicants in the decades ahead. Other firms looked for well-bred candidates who had grown up in the world of private clubs and high-end restaurants. After all, that's where a lot of Wall Street deal making is done. Goldman looked for strivers who hadn't ever tasted such joys early on, but who wanted entry into the club.

Even after Goldman became prestigious enough to hire mostly from top Ivy League schools, the firm still prized candidates with scrappy, working-class beginnings. In the firm's formal documents or presentations, this was known as "ambition to achieve." Informally, people spoke of "a lusting enthusiasm to jump out of bed every morning to do the deal."

Look at the origins of Goldman's highest achievers, and it's eerie how many emerged from humble backgrounds that rivaled Weinberg's. Lloyd Blankfein, who became Goldman's chief executive in 2006, is the son of a Brooklyn letter carrier. Investment chief John McNulty's father was the groundskeeper at a private golf club. Other partners' fathers ran small businesses making crates or dry-cleaning equipment.

Not only did these recruits work obsessively to advance; they never slowed down even after becoming multimillionaires. Being known as a Goldman partner was the perfect vindication for long-ago snubs. It was a way for life's underdogs to stand in the winner's circle, attracting the admiration and envy of all the rivals they had surpassed. Early retirement and idle wealth paled in comparison.

The full impact of personal judgments hit home for me when I was doing journalistic research about the origins of Amazon.com, the online retailer. There was some mystery about how Amazon founder Jeff Bezos had rustled up the first $1 million that he needed to start his online bookstore. I knew that Seattle go-getter Nick Hanauer had helped Bezos locate his earliest backers. So I figured it would be fascinating to find out what sorts of investors got in—and who passed up this chance.

Over coffee one morning in his Seattle office, Hanauer spun out the story. Back in 1994, Bezos had just quit a hedge fund job in New York and moved west. He knew hardly anyone in Seattle. Hanauer and Bezos had met through a mutual friend, and Hanauer was enchanted. "I had $50,000 that I could commit to Jeff," Hanauer recalled. "That wasn't nearly enough. But I offered to introduce Jeff to everyone I knew who might be able to help."

Hanauer's list was huge. There were various buddies from Alaskan fly-fishing trips, favorite customers from Hanauer's short-lived career as a restaurateur, and all sorts of acquaintances who knew Hanauer's socially prominent relatives. (The Hanauers had become America's down-pillow kings, thanks to their ownership of Pacific Coast Feather Company.)

"I called all of them up and invited them to a series of dinners at my house, where they could meet Jeff," Hanauer recalled. There would be a quick run-through of Amazon's business plan. But there would also be plenty of time to size up Bezos on a more personal basis. If people were curious, he was ready to tell them about his childhood desire to be an astronaut, about his days as a Princeton undergraduate, or about his favorite books. They could take stock of him in any way they wanted.

What happened next startled everyone. The friends that Hanauer had pegged as natural investors—Microsoft executives who knew the most about high tech and the Internet—didn't want anything to do with Amazon. In their eyes, Bezos's operation was too small and too speculative to have much chance of succeeding. Its retailing focus elicited yawns. Microsoft at that time was routinely crushing 100-person or even 500-person software companies that didn't have enough clout to survive. In such a fierce world, what chance did a one-man outfit have? As Hanauer later told me, "They were blinded by their love for their own technology."

By contrast, Hanauer recalled, his friends who ran old-style family businesses—shipyards or timber companies—loved Bezos. They didn't know much about the Internet. They couldn't really tell if Bezos's business idea would work. But they pegged him as a winner.

They liked the fact that he had quit his job in New York and piled his possessions into his Honda, driving west so he could start Amazon in a new location. One way or another, they figured, Bezos would thrive. Some were so enthusiastic that they didn't just write checks themselves; they encouraged their parents or siblings to join in, too.

A few days after chatting with Hanauer, I tracked down one of Bezos's early investors, shipyard operator Nick Eitel. He was a second-generation maritime man; his father had started Everett Shipyard in 1959. As a teenager, Eitel had spent summers scraping barnacles off the sides of boats in dry dock. As a young man, he had sat up nights working through bid sheets, trying to manage the boom-and-bust nature of shipyard work. Not every year at Everett was a good one, but overall, the business prospered.

Nick Eitel remembered that first dinner with Bezos as a warm, bonding moment. "Jeff was a lot of fun," Eitel told me. "He talked a lot about what the opportunity was. He wasn't confused in the least about how to get there." The two men didn't review Amazon's business plan until a second meeting a few days later, but to Eitel, that was a formality. "I had pretty much decided before even seeing the numbers that I would put money into this," Eitel recalled. "He struck me right away as a winner."

Do such moments define newcomers like Hanauer and Eitel as America's best high-tech investors? No, and it's silly to extrapolate their Amazon success too far. At one particular moment, those Seattle investors happened to possess exactly the right framework to make the most of a situation. While Hanauer's happy winners have done well with other high-tech investments, they haven't displaced the titans of Sand Hill Road as America's leading venture capitalists. That's all right. For many of the Amazon pioneers, one great coup was enough. The significance of their success is that it shows how powerful such personal insights can be.

For millions of Americans, such eureka moments are within reach.

Spend long enough in a field, and the winning paths become evident. Anyone who pays close attention over a decade or more will start to see the small clues that presage people's destinies. Sometimes it's common knowledge. Catch the veterans over a cup of coffee or at an airport luggage carousel, and they will know who has "lots of runway ahead," who is "meant for big things," and who is "a disaster waiting to happen." The secrets of judging character are right in front of us. All we have to do is use them.

Yet many people let those potential insights slip away. The reason: most of us dodge the hard work of extracting lasting truths from the zigzags of our own careers. We don't want to know why we stumbled at certain points. We may not even care to pick apart our successes that much. We would rather settle for a soothing narrative—revealing little about the real reasons for success or failure—instead of staring at the raw truths of why some people achieve great things and others don't.

In his book *Vital Lies, Simple Truths*, psychologist Daniel Goleman documents how pervasive such coping mechanisms have become. As he points out, "the mind can protect itself against anxiety by dimming awareness." Evasions shield us in the face of everything from severe physical pain to awkward dealings with friends, colleagues, and societal problems. It takes a special sort of courage to revisit the critical junctures in our lives, and to look at them calmly and with clarity.

Why bother? The answer: because that's where insights are born.

More than a half-century ago, an eleven-year-old boy was admitted to Children's Memorial Hospital with a ruptured appendix. He didn't leave the hospital until three months later. A fierce stomach infection had set in. Antibiotics of that era were barely sufficient to bring it under control. As it finally became clear that the boy would recover, he wanted to know everything about what his doctors and nurses did, and how they helped to heal him.

That unforgettably scary experience became James Weiss's touchstone. It doesn't show up on his résumé. But when we talked at Johns Hopkins, it was clear that a harsh childhood illness still shaped his thinking about what doctors could be—and should be. Without that illness, Dr. Weiss might have become an oboist. Without that illness, "bedside manner" might never have been more than a phrase to him. Without that illness, he might have taken the easy route of guiding Hopkins's admissions committee toward picking strictly the candidates with the best grades and scores, rather than looking for the ones with the most caring souls, too.

One of Dr. Weiss's favorite ways of spotting the nonobvious winners is to see how candidates answer a quartet of essay questions that are aimed at drawing out students' character. Those questions ask students to talk about rewarding experiences, overcoming adversity, areas of pride, and moments of exclusion. Dr. Weiss added those questions shortly after taking command of the admissions effort in 1999. There have been answers, he says, that brought him to the brink of tears.

But, to his surprise, those gentle questions have also provided Hopkins with some of its starkest warning signs. "We've had essays that dripped with breathtaking arrogance," Dr. Weiss says. "And there was one where a candidate said that his proudest moment involved getting his guitar to make a warbling, Pink Floyd sort of sound. I have no idea what he was thinking when he told us that."

5: Auditions That Work

Bob Gibbons and I are sitting side by side in a South Carolina gym, watching a rite of passage in American sports. It's mid-July. About two hundred high-school basketball stars are barnstorming their way across the United States, playing in one giant summer tournament after another. This week everybody is competing in the charmingly named Nike Peach Jam. Other tournaments in Orlando and Las Vegas will follow soon. The big time beckons. College fame and glory feels imminent, with the very best players eventually racing onward to an NBA career.

For now, this is a scout's paradise. Bleachers and courtside chairs are packed with middle-aged men clutching BlackBerrys and taking notes. Most are coaches from big-name colleges, such as Kansas, Texas, Connecticut, North Carolina, and Ohio State. They will watch dozens of games in July, trying to identify whatever extra talent their teams might need.

Sprinkled in the crowd are some longtime independent scouts, like Gibbons. They won't sign any players. But they are conducting the most intense reviews of all. After each tournament, they will publish detailed rankings of the top one hundred or so players in the country. The best scouts blend opinion and facts so skillfully that college sports departments gladly subscribe to the assessors' high-priced newsletters, year after year.

Gibbons is the informal dean of the scouts. He is a friendly, paunchy man from Lenoir, North Carolina, the furniture-making capital of America. He is in his late sixties at the time and has been appraising high-school stars since 1977. Since then, he has watched perhaps 15,000 games in person. We have agreed to observe an early-round game together. So at 10:15 A.M. on a hot Monday, we pull up chairs to see a standout team from the Midwest, All-Ohio Red, square off against a New Jersey team that calls itself Playaz Club.

We've got identical vantage points. But in truth, we aren't seeing the same game at all.

As the game gets rolling, I'm the casual fan, keeping track of which players are scoring a lot of points, who possesses breathtaking speed or agility—and which team is ahead. Such box-score tidbits hardly matter to Gibbons. To him, the game is a forty-minute screening of fine-grained talent. It's a chance to gauge subtle elements of judgment, preparation, intensity, and the like. In the years to come, such factors will separate great players from great disappointments. While I watch the score, he watches for character.

Eventually Gibbons takes pity on me. One of the Ohio team's guards is dribbling the ball on the perimeter, ready to toss up a three-point shot. Gibbons reaches over and pokes me. He gestures toward All-Ohio's six foot eight center, Jared Sullinger. Regardless of what's happening on the perimeter, the big guy is muscling his way toward the basket.

"You will not find a better rebounder than Jared Sullinger," Gibbons tells me. There's an easy confidence to Gibbons's voice; he has seen Sullinger play many times before. It's as if I'm back in childhood, listening to my uncle explain what kind of car to buy. I turn my head just in time to behold proof of Gibbons's point. A sloppy Ohio shot heads toward the rim. Belatedly, the Playaz center tries to challenge Sullinger for good rebounding position. It's hopeless. The 260-pound Sullinger senses the opponent right behind him—and abruptly leans back with all the force of a wrecking ball slamming into a condemned building. The other guy careens away in an awkward stumble.

The missed shot now belongs entirely to Sullinger. He catches the rebound at head height and flicks in an unstoppable layup. If Sullinger had wanted, he could have caught the ball at his ankles and still scored with ease. At that moment, he dominated the court. And if Gibbons hadn't redirected my gaze, I never would have seen the key moment of the play. All I would have perceived was a long, missed jump shot that somehow landed in Sullinger's hands. I would have glimpsed the result, but not the reason.

For the next hour, Gibbons locks into specific players, one by one, starting with an effort to figure out what each one does best. Then he runs through a checklist—memorized long ago—of all the factors that could define a player's destiny. Some of the players that impress him the most aren't doing anything dazzling on the official score sheet. They will finish the game with just six or seven points. But they are strong and fast. They defend well. They make good decisions with or without the ball. And they show extra hustle that can prove decisive in a close game.

"You want guys diving on the floor or crashing into the stands, chasing a loose ball," Gibbons explains. "You look for 'effort' people. It makes a huge difference how dedicated they are. You're always asking: 'Are they willing to do whatever is necessary to get to the next level?'"

As a case in point, Gibbons points to Ohio guard Aaron Craft, who finishes the game with just six points. No matter; he is a tenacious defender who constantly thwarts the New Jersey team's attempts to set up easy shots. Gibbons sees Craft as a player who could make a big contribution at even the very best collegiate programs. By contrast, Ohio point guard Kevin Gray—who leads all scorers with twenty-three points—doesn't impress Gibbons nearly as much. "He shoots too much from the perimeter," Gibbons declares near the end of the first half. "He's not looking to find the open teammate."

As the game nears its finish, Gibbons is ready to pass judgment. He pegs Sullinger as the best high-school player in the nation: a likely superstar in years to come. It doesn't bother Gibbons that other people can outjump Sullinger or make a wider range of shots. As Gibbons sees it, the Ohio big man is brilliant at anticipating the action and getting to the right place on the court. That careful preparation and good judgment will serve Sullinger well his whole career. Meanwhile, Craft earns a more restrained thumbs-up. As for Gray, he is at the back of the pack, rated as someone who could succeed at a mid-major college but probably no more.

Can a scout like Gibbons read the future? I'm fascinated by his efficiency, his calmness, and his confidence. He carries himself like an expert who knows how to get the most out of these summer-tournament auditions. But the only way to tell, of course, is to let time unfold. Then we can see how these athletes fare once they enter college. So in early 2011, about one-and-a-half years after our time together at the Peach Jam tournament, I checked how Gibbons's prospects were faring.

The results were breathtaking.

Jared Sullinger not only made the starting lineup at Ohio State as a college freshman; he helped propel the Buckeyes to a top-five ranking in the country. Sullinger led Ohio State with 10.2 rebounds per game and emerged as a strong scorer. His psychological impact on opponents was even more fearsome. *Sports Illustrated* columnist Luke Winn likened Sullinger to "a battering ram," adding: "He progressively weakens opponents—and eventually breaks them—with a series of blows: from the left block, from the right block, through bodies, through arms, and particularly . . . from the free-throw line."

Before Sullinger's first college season was done, sportswriters predicted he could be one of the NBA's top draft picks.

Aaron Craft wasn't making as big a splash, but he was on his way to stardom, too. He became a key reserve for the same Ohio State team, playing twenty-nine minutes a game and averaging 6.9 points. He led the team in steals, even though he wasn't on the court for as many minutes as the starters. As for Kevin Gray, the transition to college play didn't start well. He won a basketball scholarship to Morehead State, but most of the time, he sat on the bench. As a freshman, he averaged just 3.6 minutes of playing time per game, and 0.8 points. Poor shooting accuracy hurt his chances. He made just 26 percent of his shots from the field.

Millions of auditions take place in America every month. They come in every imaginable form. Some can be as brief as an actor's two-minute reading of a minor movie part. Others involve two weeks of round-the-clock rigors at the FBI's main training facility in Quantico, Virginia. Whatever the format, each audition represents a chance to see what a candidate actually can *do*. At a certain point, it's time to move beyond the indirect insights that can be gleaned from résumés, references, and interviews. It's time to ask the actor to step on stage; the pilot to crawl into the simulator; the educator to teach a class. It's time to see, right there in action, who possesses the right stuff.

The best auditions achieve exactly what Bob Gibbons pulled off that morning in South Carolina. They reveal profound strengths—and flaws—that might not be obvious otherwise. When it's time to make sense of jagged résumés, auditions help identify the Sullingers and Crafts of any field. Just as important, well-run auditions can sound the alarm about candidates who seem spectacular on paper but falter on closer inspection. Every field has its share of high-scoring performers whose shortcomings take a while to perceive. Auditions can uncover those flaws.

Because the most prominent auditions occur in public-performance fields such as sports, music, and acting, it's tempting to regard these sessions as nothing more than a search for individual excellence, in the form of some unique "Wow!" moment. Who can jump the highest? Whose voice has the richest harmonics? Who can clutch a skull while starting a soliloquy, and make us believe that a grieving, wistful Hamlet is right there before us? Those can be powerful moments indeed. But to focus only on the "Wow!" moments shortchanges the full value of a well-run audition.

Ask audition masters what they are hunting for, and the deepest answers involve subjects' character. Regardless of differences in the exact ways that talent is expressed, each domain's underlying quests are strikingly similar: Who tries hard? Who prepares well? Who recovers quickly and calmly from a setback? Who works well with others? Who can size up a turbulent situation and come up with a plan? Or, taken from the other direction, which people cut corners? Who turns brittle under pressure? Who is clueless about group dynamics? Who ultimately doesn't care?

All these queries help illuminate the reasons *why* candidates achieve the results that they do. It's not enough to know that a candidate, for a few brief moments, can deliver what looks like a successful performance. It's far more important to understand the path that particular candidate traveled to achieve that result. Some paths are built upon durable habits that will lead to many more good results. Others involve flawed choices that may work for the moment, but already contain the seeds of future trouble.

Even simple, subject-specific tests turn out to be deeper probes into universal aspects of character. When an Army selector watches soldiers' eyes during long marches . . . or when a Teach For America examiner listens for resilience if a lesson plan goes astray, both are looking for virtues that stretch beyond any particular line of work. Experts in many other fields, too, have developed sly techniques for eliciting larger truths. Examples range from a paper-plate dinner at the FBI to the hidden e-mail addresses of venture capitalists.

Surprisingly, meaningful auditions tend to be taboo in one domain: the hunt for top executive talent at America's biggest corporations. As chapter 10 will show, too many top executives are being picked on the basis of whether they can *talk* a good game with boardroom selectors, rather than whether they can actually *run* the enterprise at hand. That misalignment is so severe that it often seems as if top corporate jobs keep being handed to high-scoring athletes who won't pass the ball to anyone. Even so, some intriguing attempts to improve executive talent searches are under way. Later chapters will explore ways that audition-style simulations, involving on-the-fly problem solving, can help in picking the boss.

To get a sense of talent auditions in their briefest, starkest form, there's no better starting point than Hollywood. Every day, casting specialists quickly round out the lineup for movies or television shows. Dozens of plausible candidates stream into the tiny studios where selections take place. Each actor or actress gets five to ten minutes to learn the part and try out the lines once or twice. Then goodbyes are said; doors swing open, and the next candidate pops in. Decisions aren't announced until days later. Everything is pleasant and vague.

It seems like a superficial guessing game. Or is it? I spent a morning with Los Angeles casting ace Susan Vash, who at that moment was hunting for someone to play "Rainbow," a sarcastic ex-girlfriend appearing briefly in the sitcom *'Til Death*. This was not a deep part. As far as I could tell, Rainbow amounted to a short skirt, big hair, and a pout.

Yet in a morning packed with fifteen auditions, Vash on two or three occasions saw something that intrigued her. She asked an actress to try the lines a few more times, abandoning the original bitchiness of the role in favor of a sweetness or vulnerability that wasn't in the script. The show wouldn't be cast that way. The actress had no chance of landing the part. But Vash knew there would be other roles to audition in a week . . . a month . . . a year. Rainbow's moment provided a way to find talents beyond what one sitcom needed that day.

"I like quirky," Vash explained to me. Over the years, her willingness to go beyond the immediate task of filling a narrow part has paid off repeatedly. One such journey helped Vash waken to the immense potential of Kathy Baker (who became the star of the television show *Picket Fences*.) Another exploration led her to champion Paul Giamatti (who became the star of the film *Sideways*.) "That's what keeps me going," she remarked.

Hollywood's best-known casting experts are famous for their ability to push back against directors' initial stated preferences for a role. If someone intriguing pops up in an audition, why not redefine the role slightly to make room for him or her?

In aviation, by contrast, no one wants to be surprised. Pilots need to land planes on the right runway, every time. Step into a flight simulator, and much of the testing will involve standard, repeatable tasks. Can you hold speed and elevation within tight limits? Do you understand the fine points of each set of controls? Can you keep control in the event of certain equipment failures? Yet even in the highly controlled world of flying aircraft, the savviest assessors look for more than just technical competence at the controls. In a profession where some amount of ego is essential—but too much is dangerous—it's time to learn about the character factors that shape pilots' thinking in a crisis.

A favorite test at many airlines involves the "Bad Weather Reroute." Settled at the controls of a flight simulator, candidates prepare to make the regularly scheduled landing. Soon they are told that harsh weather makes the original destination off limits. That seems tolerable. The original flight plan always includes an alternate landing site. Then the storm (or blizzard) spreads. Now even the alternate destination has fallen below minimum acceptable landing standards.

What to do? Remain airborne too long, and the plane runs out of fuel. Pick one of the impaired landing sites, and there's no guarantee of a safe landing. It's a nail-biting moment, even in a simulator, says Doug Smuin, who spent much of the 1980s and 1990s as a check airman for Evergreen International Airlines, a major cargo hauler. But it's also a great way to learn whether a pilot can stay calm in a crisis.

"There may not be any right answer," Smuin told me. Even so, a good pilot will think through the choices and come up with a plan for managing the risks. He or she will keep processing any new information that comes in. And the pilot will welcome all the help available from a copilot, an engineer, or air-traffic controllers on the ground. Stubborn-minded heroes aren't nearly as effective. "If I can see that the pilot's ego is too big," Smuin remarked, "that's a problem."

When auditions stretch out over days or weeks, then it's possible to probe candidates' character even more deeply. Heidi Roizen, a successful Silicon Valley entrepreneur who went on to become a prominent venture capitalist, told me a few ploys that she found effective. "I'd speak a lot at conferences," she said. "Lots of entrepreneurs would want to get in touch with me afterward, to see if I would fund their businesses. I learned that it actually wasn't a good idea to hand out my business card. I'd just suggest that they find me online and e-mail me." That way, the ones who got through were already telling Roizen something about their perseverance and ingenuity.

After all, great entrepreneurship is all about breaking down walls of apathy or disdain. It means winning over customers who don't want to buy products from an unknown company. It means hiring strong managers by persuading them to abandon good jobs and take a leap into the unknown. Any aspiring entrepreneur can claim all these powers, but venture capitalists need proof before investing millions. That's why it makes sense to create a stumbling-block test, right away. Your venture capitalist isn't in the directory. How can you find her? Entrepreneurs who establish contact anyway are starting to show the moxie needed to succeed.

There's another character test that venture capitalists apply, though it makes former entrepreneurs like Roizen squirm. When entrepreneurs seek funding, they almost always want the money right away. Fresh cash is vital. Yet venture capitalists often dawdle for a few weeks. It's not because paperwork gets lost or bookkeepers go on vacation. It's because during that lull, venture capitalists find out how well entrepreneurs can carry out all the weekly chores of growing a business.

Effective entrepreneurs blast through their to-do lists, day by day. Dreamers keep talking about a glowing future but can't complete the tasks needed to make it happen. So creating drawn-out observation time becomes an audition in its own right. Without knowing it, entrepreneurs are on the spot. Do they keep moving forward after spelling out their growth plans in an investor pitch? Or are they mere talkers instead of doers? A powerful way to find out is to let the funding clock stretch out and see what happens.

In most organizations, it takes a long time for auditions to become fully calibrated to the values that matter. Bosses can't simply snap their fingers and say: "Bring me a good test for resilience—or teamwork." Only people on the front lines can identify the right proving grounds for such abstract virtues. That process can't be rushed.

Army Special Forces, for example, started out in the 1950s with a selection system that largely reenacted the challenges of World War II. That's what its founders knew best. So candidates were assessed for physical strength and the cunning needed to pull off sabotage missions behind enemy lines. Only as the chaotic challenges of Vietnam became clear did the drills change. Now it was time to place greater emphasis on stamina and the ability to regroup after inevitable minor failures.

Teach For America's early auditions looked for charismatic presenting skills, which turned out to be far from essential in inner-city classrooms. It took years for TFA to retool its assessment methods so that its auditions focused on more vital traits, such as resiliency. Hollywood, in turn, became much more willing to cast actors in unexpected ways after the old studio system broke down in the 1960s and 1970s. (That upheaval brought an end to rigid control of career development.) And venture capitalists toughened up their audition norms in the dot-com boom, when many of the cleverest-sounding pitches came from posers who wanted to get rich without doing anything arduous.

For the FBI, one of the great works-in-progress involves the bureau's most elite tactical force, the slightly misnamed Hostage Rescue Team. This is the group of FBI agents who are the best marksmen, the most accomplished helicopter pilots, the savviest explosives experts, and the coolest heads in close-quarters combat. They do get deployed when high-profile kidnappers seize hostages, if federal force is needed. But the Hostage Rescue Team also provides high-level security at events such as the Olympics and political summits. It deals with terrorist threats of all sorts. It is an all-purpose group of master tacticians who often need the patience to hover on the edge for weeks, while negotiators try to bring impasses to a peaceful conclusion.

The impetus to create the Hostage Rescue Team began in 1977, shortly after a Hanafi Muslim group assaulted three buildings in Washington and seized 150 hostages. Existing U.S. police and FBI teams struggled to control the situation, in which one person was killed. Local Muslim diplomats helped negotiate a peaceful surrender, but U.S. policymakers concluded that the country needed something mightier than a standard SWAT team to deal with such delicate, scary situations. A Texas lawyer turned FBI agent, Danny Coulson, was put in charge of creating that new force.

To make the new unit seem like "the best of the best," Coulson could have settled for a superficial definition of excellence by demanding eye-popping physical performance from his new recruits. Instead of hiring marksmen who could hit 90 percent of their targets at fifty feet, why not demand perfect accuracy at even greater distances? Norms for pushups and distance runs could have been jacked up, too. But that wasn't what the FBI required.

Character was crucial, Coulson decided. The new unit needed agents who could knit together well as teams, while enduring the tedium of long waits between assignments without going stir-crazy. It needed agents who cared more about the team than about their own physiques. "I don't want anybody who blows through his cases so he can get in his ten miles (of running) a day," Coulson told subordinates. Eventually he compressed that message to two words: "No assholes."

Quickly, Coulson and his aides built up a two-week selection system where even the harshest physical tests did double duty as a way of gauging whether candidates possessed the humility, self-sacrifice, and empathy to be strong team members. In his memoir, *No Heroes: Inside the FBI's Secret Counter-Terror Force*, Coulson described some ways of doing this. An especially effective method: turning some events into five-person team tests, where the team's score was based largely on how the weakest person fared. There was no reward for high-ego soloists who left their peers in the dust.

Real-world events reinforced Coulson's judgment. In 1987, HRT operators were called into an Atlanta prison to quell a riot. A few years later, agents entered the Grand Canyon to track down an escaped murderer who briefly seized hostages. Those missions worked out brilliantly. Order was restored; bloodbaths were averted. The FBI's agents maneuvered so effectively together that they never needed to fire their weapons.

Even when everything turned out horribly, Coulson's emphasis on selfless teamwork hovered in the air as the lesson to remember. In 1993, dozens of HRT operators participated in the government's two-month standoff against a heavily armed Branch Davidian cult in Waco, Texas. That showdown ended in the firestorm deaths of about eighty cultists. The tragedy generated no end of "what if" questions—most of which focused on the horrendous course of negotiations during the standoff. Vast, disparate parts of government were thrown into the Waco debacle. All these powerful players never figured out how to work together in accord with the Coulson doctrine.

Nowadays, there's a pop-culture view of the HRT selection system that portrays everything as agony for its own sake. In the words of one career guide to the FBI, "to become an operator is to go through a grueling, Darwinian process that only the strongest and fittest can survive." That's an easy stereotype, but in its effort to sound macho, it overlooks a much subtler interplay between toughness and wisdom. The FBI wants both those virtues. And it knows how to get them.

In the course of researching this book, I spent two days at the Bureau's main training site in Quantico, Virginia, where HRT selection and training takes place. It's an eerie experience. The sound of gunfire is constant. Agents with pistols, rifles, and shotguns blast away at targets, constantly refining their aim. Helicopters loop through the air, sometimes unfurling ropes so that FBI operators onboard can practice "fast-roping" their way down to the ground. A simulated small-town street, known as Hogan's Alley, provides a working facsimile of a café, a bank, and an appliance store, so that trainees can practice surveillance and arrests in such settings.

Then there's the Shooting House. At the edge of the FBI complex, there's a giant box of a building, painted drab beige. From the outside, it looks like an industrial warehouse. Inside, though, the facility's central section has been reconfigured to resemble a cheap boarding lodge. There's a common room in the front with a worn-out sofa and some chairs. There's a narrow hallway leading back toward a series of small rooms. Only the rubber walls suggest that no one lives here—or ever will.

This is where Hostage Rescue agents learn how to storm a barricaded house. In a typical day, black-uniformed agents firing live ammunition will seize control of the Shooting House every hour or two. Sometimes they will blast open the front door. Other times they will arrive with police dogs and stake out the house more slowly. On each assault, there's a hostage somewhere in the house who must be protected. And there are multiple villains—in cardboard-cutout form—who must be shot right away. Senior FBI agents peer down from a catwalk above, keeping track of which trainees are making all the right moves and which ones are blundering.

I watched one assault from the catwalk, accompanied by Charles Pierce, a twenty-seven-year veteran of the FBI who was acting deputy commander of the HRT program at the time. It was like watching a tornado. At first the house was calm. Then the front door exploded out of place . . . ten agents swarmed into the front room . . . a blizzard of shots were fired . . . smoke filled the room . . . agents raced down the hallway . . . and the hostage was rescued before I could figure out how it happened.

Pierce looked over and saw my puzzlement. "You'll see more from down below," he said. "They're getting ready to do it again. Come downstairs if you'd like. We'll squeeze you into one of the corners. Stay very close to me—and watch."

When the second assault began, the agents' intricate maneuvers all became clearer. We were in the perfect spot to be observers of a high-speed ballet with bullets. Each step, each shot, each gesture served a purpose. All these delicate insights were overpowered by one stunning image: a black-suited FBI agent thrusting an assault rifle within two feet of my nose—and hesitating a moment before making his next decision. Then his harsh stare softened. Everything was all right. I wasn't a cardboard villain. I would be spared.

The moment lasted less than a second. It seemed like an eternity.

If Pierce had wanted me to spend the rest of my life thinking about good judgment in all its forms he could not have picked a more powerful demonstration. Elite units like the Hostage Rescue Team make headlines when bullets are fired or suspects are caught. Clearly, though, some of their most skillful work involves the shots not taken. As fascinating as it was to see these agents with weapons blazing, the deeper lesson here was that the Hostage Rescue operators' greatest skills involved the ability to use that power judiciously. That couldn't happen unless the FBI was very, very careful about what sorts of people it hired.

During that same visit, one of the Hostage Rescue group's top assessors, John Piser, talked about what the FBI prized most highly in its candidates. As I walked into our meeting, I could hear gunfire outside. I had just withstood a twisting half-hour ride in an FBI helicopter. Two FBI employees and I had swooped amid trees, towers, and berms to see how Hostage Rescue agents can be brought close to crime scenes when regular ground travel isn't fast enough. Now Piser wanted to step back into the world of abstractions to tell me about the nine character traits that mattered most when choosing new agents. In this high-stakes world of cops and copters, I wondered, would any of Piser's remarks make sense to civilians?

The surprising answer: they all did. What the FBI's Hostage Rescue Team wants is remarkably similar to what Johns Hopkins, Facebook, and dozens of other high-talent organizations are seeking, too. The FBI's list is as follows:

- Initiative, perseverance, and compatibility.
- Discipline, trainability, and judgment.
- Loyalty, leadership, and maturity.

It's simple stuff. Almost any organization could embrace a similar or perhaps even identical list. At less successful enterprises, those virtues never become more than slogans on the wall. They remain empty words. Clearly, the Bureau is going to extraordinary trouble to make sure that the HRT program really did pick agents who embodied those values. I wasn't going to leave Quantico until I understood how the agents' shooting, running, and other physical tasks translated into a reliable way of gauging these nine traits.

It didn't take long to find examples. Embedded within each physical activity during the two-week selection cycle was a second, character-assessing component. At the end of one drill, candidates were told to gather sandbags strewn across a field, so they could be used the next day. Some sandbags were tiny and nearby. Others were bigger and farther away. Candidates might think it didn't matter which ones they hauled, but it did. Assessors were standing by, watching to see who took a fair share of the load, who did more, and who shirked work.

On the shooting ranges, candidates were scored closely on their ability to follow directions—exactly—as well as on their target-hitting accuracy. Compliance mattered in ways that went far beyond target practice, Piser indicated. A middling shooter could get much better over time, if there was a willingness to practice hard. An agent who didn't pay attention to directions, even picayune ones, could be a huge liability in the course of a complex operation that required everyone to carry out a precise segment of the plan.

More audition nuggets kept coming. After candidates spend ten hours on a rugged hike with no meals, they are herded into a conference room and told to prepare testimony for a simulated court case. In part, the FBI wants to know how well candidates can focus mentally when they are physically exhausted. But there's a second, hidden test as well. Partway through the exercise, an FBI assessor slips into the room with a plate of fried chicken. It smells great. The tense, hungry candidates long to dig in. Then they realize there are six candidates and only four pieces of chicken. FBI assessors watch what happens. It's just one tiny test, but it's a useful marker of tendencies toward sharing or selfishness.

I asked Pierce why such tests are so pervasive. His answer was blunt: "If you're sharing a muddy tent for three weeks with someone on a mission, you don't want to be with a jerk. You'll be operating with no sleep and lousy food. You don't want personalities that are going to cause friction. We get very strong, type-A personalities here. But at the end of the day, we choose people who can focus those attributes in a way that's constructive."

For anyone wanting to create comprehensive, systematic, well-planned auditions, the HRT selection system is a perfect model. But some auditions take shape much more casually. There isn't a master planner. There isn't a top-down directive about how the system should work. Everything gradually coalesces around an unmet need.

The development of high-school basketball tournaments—and the associated scouting rituals—fits squarely into this second category. Turn the clock back to the 1950s, and most colleges relied on informal word of mouth to know what high-school prospects were worth recruiting. Occasionally a sensational high-school athlete, such as Wilt Chamberlain, attracted national attention. By and large, though, colleges focused mostly on their home states, aided by networks of alumni and friendly high-school coaches. Collegiate coaches didn't look much farther. Great high-school athletes in Los Angeles went to UCLA or USC. Top performers in Eau Claire or Milwaukee ended up at the University of Wisconsin.

Everything began to change as college sports attracted big television audiences. Top programs now had much larger budgets, as well as heightened incentives to track down great players in any locale. That way teams could win championships and more TV revenue. The recruiting maps no longer looked like medieval Europe, with hundreds of small, independent duchies nestled side by side. Coaches at the top programs viewed their rightful recruiting territory as stretching from coast to coast.

The American Athletic Union helped out in 1972 by sponsoring the first national championships for high school basketball players. Sneaker companies began sponsoring additional tournaments in the 1980s, jacking up revenue and publicity. The National Collegiate Athletic Association added to the frenzy by rewriting its recruiting rules in 1989, so that college coaches' access to high school players was greatly restrained during most months, except for July.

The result: high-school basketball acquired a frenzied, blink-and-you'll-miss-it second season. Each day of July became defined by team buses racing from tournament to tournament, or by coaches and scouts dashing in and out of airports. Everyone's efforts reached their crescendos; it was time for the best players in the nation to pair up with the top college teams. High-school coaches grumbled that the process was tantamount to meat markets. For players and college coaches, however, it was the only way to get things done.

Occasionally, a sensational performance at a July tournament will greatly raise a player's standing. I saw that happen once at the 2009 Peach Jam tournament. On a Florida team full of high-school seniors to be, one younger player slipped into the starting lineup. He was Austin Rivers, a wavy-haired guard who had just finished his sophomore year. As the son of a former NBA player (Glenn "Doc" Rivers), the teenager had already attracted scouts' notice, though he ordinarily would have played in a different tourney for younger players. Someone thought Rivers was ready for the big time.

Yes indeed. Rivers took the court against a tough Minnesota team and proceeded to tear his opponents apart. He dunked. He hit multiple three-pointers. He stole the ball repeatedly from players a year older than him. Not only did he thrill the crowd with his eighteen-point performance, he established himself as the most coveted recruit when his graduating class would finally be ready for college. Rivers's decision came a year later, when he opted to enroll at Duke in the fall of 2011.

Such moments are extremely rare. Typically, scouting these tournaments is a group exercise in recalibration rather than a solo journey of discovery. Nobody scouts in isolation. Everyone has some sense of which players already are regarded as possible stars and which can't stir any interest. Most of the time, scouts are fine-tuning earlier assessments, looking for situations where they might see extra strengths or flaws in a player's game that others have missed.

Because basketball is such a physical game, scouts devote part of their attention to players' obvious speed and stature. Tall, skinny players that haven't filled out yet are credited with "room to grow." As longtime scout Tom Konchalski puts it, "the guards excel early, but eventually the big men get their revenge." Players with well-chiseled physiques are actually at a disadvantage in scouts' eyes: they may already have reached the upper limits of their physical potential.

The art of scouting, however, tends to involve more delicate assessments of players' character. I sat for a while with Rob Judson, a savvy Midwesterner in his early fifties who has been a head coach or assistant coach at five different colleges over the years. He was fascinated by what happens during time-outs. "You'll see some players run into the huddle, paying attention to the coach, eager to do everything right on the next play," he told me. Others drift on the court, ignoring their teammates. For Judson, that brief moment informs him about which players are likeliest to respond well to coaching over the next few years. Those are the ones who keep improving. The others are far more likely to clash with authority; they may never live up to their potential.

Judson's checklist included more such tidbits. "Watch what happens when a ref makes a call that a player doesn't like," he remarked. "Then watch that player more closely on the next play, especially if he accidentally dribbles the ball off his shoe. The best players will regroup and shrug it off. Other players can't do that. Their temper will get hold of them. You have to take them out of the game for a few minutes."

Dozens of coaches and scouts are looking for similar, telltale clues. As Bob Gibbons explained to me, most of the colleges with solid, "mid-major" basketball programs don't stand much of a chance of landing the sensational high-school talents. Those players are likely to end up at Kentucky, Duke, Kansas, or other schools that compete each year for the national championship. Yet mid-majors such as Gonzaga, Davidson, and Butler can put together strong winning seasons by pursuing athletes with slightly less raw talent but extraordinary discipline and character.

There's a big pool of impressive high-school players who aren't quite amazing enough to be in the top ten, Gibbons adds. Somewhere in that pool are relentless hard workers who will raise their level of play, year after year, by sheer grit. Those are the players the mid-major coaches are seeking. That's why so many scouts and coaches watch time-outs. That's why the best scouting insights tend to happen at moments that will never appear on ESPN's *SportsCenter* highlights show.

"I remember the first time I saw Michael Jordan play," Gibbons adds. It was a high-school tournament in North Carolina in 1981. Jordan excelled on the court. But what stuck forever in Gibbons's mind is what happened after the game. "Michael came up to me," Gibbons recalls, "and said: 'Hello, Mr. Gibbons. What did you think about my game, and what can I do to improve?' It's so rare to see that. Most players want to brag about their dunks. He didn't. He wanted to get better."

That season, Gibbons says, he rated Jordan a 98 on his 1-to-100 rating scale for high-school talent, marking him as the best high-school player in the country. Most other rating services gave top honors to other players with higher scoring averages. But Gibbons thought he saw an extra character edge in Jordan. Time proved the scout right.

I asked Gibbons, toward the end of our shared game-watching time, what he sees that the average fan doesn't. "Being a total team player is so underrated," he said. "So is the knowledge to make the right decision. What is overrated is points scored." There is an old-school simplicity to Gibbons's view. He won't be beguiled by a flashy player puffing up his own statistics at the expense of his team.

Just at that moment, Gibbons was finishing up his evaluation of a shot-happy guard on the court. Most of this player's game irked Gibbons. At one point, when the guard drove toward the basket without a clear path to a layup and ended up being stripped of the ball, Gibbons penciled in a dour 90 as his evaluation. That would be the rating of a player with uncertain prospects even at the collegiate mid-major level.

Now the guard had the ball once more. He fired a three-point shot under pressure—and this one whizzed through the center of the basket, snapping the net as crisply as a drumbeat. Gibbons blinked. Then he grinned. "Having said all that," Gibbons remarked, "I'm going to move him up to a 91."

6: Talent That Whispers

In late 2006, Facebook Inc. confronted a serious problem. New users were signing up faster than anyone expected. The social networking service was rocketing into prominence as one of the world's most popular Web sites, and Facebook wasn't ready to handle that growth. Understaffed and flat-footed, the company required more software engineers in a hurry. Otherwise its computers would freeze up; its services would stop functioning properly, and its hopes of an orderly expansion would disintegrate in an out-of-control sprawl.

At the time, Facebook's brainpower consisted of about twenty scruffy young engineers, working in a graffiti-covered office in downtown Palo Alto, California. They saw themselves as top-gun programmers, capable of building a company that could someday rival Google and Microsoft. But they desperately needed first-rate reinforcements. Within Facebook, there was a dread that if bosses started hiring any available engineer just to fill some empty seats, everything good about the company's fast-moving, highly innovative culture would become polluted. Mediocre engineers were seen as silent saboteurs, spewing out flawed computer code that could take years to fix.

To succeed, Facebook needed to beat the big guys at the hiring game. In some cases, Facebook could poach individual Google and Microsoft stars by offering big stock-options packages and exciting

121

jobs. Raiding alone couldn't solve Facebook's needs, though. University recruiting had great potential over time, but Facebook hadn't yet built ties to more than a few schools. Becoming well known at top campuses across North America would take many months and lots of engineers' travel. Facebook couldn't wait. It needed a faster way to become known as a haven for really smart programmers.

"We should come up with programming puzzles," declared Facebook's chief technology officer, Adam D'Angelo, a recent Caltech graduate. If the puzzles were clever enough, they could be posted on Facebook's Web site as a form of "brain candy," inspiring gung-ho solvers to think about working at Facebook. So Facebook engineer Yishan Wong cobbled together some jaunty stories with sneaky-hard puzzles imbedded in them. Most of his creations were so gnarly that he couldn't solve them. D'Angelo liked that.

As Facebook's puzzle inventory grew, so did the company's understanding of the national talent pool. "We developed this theory that occasionally there were these brilliant people out there who hadn't found their way to Silicon Valley," Wong recalled. "They might be languishing in ordinary tech jobs. We needed a way to surface them." Goofy puzzles looked the perfect bait. So Facebook began looking for ways to get its brainteasers in front of whatever desk-bound slackers might have hidden aptitudes for top-flight programming.

Meanwhile, something intriguing was happening on the southeast coast of Maine.

In downtown Portland, just a few blocks from the harbor, there is a curving, cobblestoned road known as Milk Street. A century ago, this was a warehouse and factory district. Today, these massive brick buildings have been converted into lofts and office suites. Inside are the classic denizens of any small-city business district: five-partner law firms and tiny consulting shops that tend to local customers. Everything is cozy and off the beaten path. Big-company recruiters don't come here except on summer vacation.

Inside one of those Milk Street offices, Evan Priestley chafed for something better. A large, round-faced fellow in his early twenties, he was marking time as a back-office computer coder at Portland Webworks. His bosses drummed up business building corporate Web sites; he executed the details. Sometimes Priestley fiddled with shades of blue until clients were happy. Other times he moved logos from the top, to the side, and then back to the top again. He found clients' ignorance both amusing and pitiful. "They were always saying: 'Can you build us some Internets?'" Priestley later told me.

No big-league software recruiter was likely to rescue Priestley. "I had a pretty terrible résumé," he later observed. He had quit high school a few weeks before graduation because classes became unbearably slow-moving and dull. He switched majors three times in college, at the University of Southern Maine, for similar reasons. Eventually he left college a semester or two short of graduation as well.

In a world where fascinating job candidates come in three varieties—"jagged résumés," "talent that whispers," and "talent that shouts"—Priestley epitomized the middle group. In early 2007, none of the standard success markers suggested he was gifted at *anything*. His choice of college didn't dazzle. His transcript was a mess. His work history wasn't much better. There was no sign of enduring dedication toward any type of project. Unlike a flighty but clearly brilliant graphics wizard like Alan Kay, Priestley hadn't shown any of the high points of a jagged résumé.

Most people pegged Priestley as just another slacker. He did little to fight that perception. On the afternoon in question, he had finished all his assigned tasks ahead of schedule, so he started reading online sites for engineers, including reddit.com and xkcd.com. (xkcd is weird but hilarious—take a look.) One posting alluded to a programming puzzle page that Facebook had just introduced.

Priestley hadn't heard of Facebook. Still, any fresh mental challenge was welcome. A few minutes later, he began wrestling with the ways that a group of friends can be seated in a movie theater, given that best friends want to be side by side and rivals need to be far apart. The puzzle looked hard and shapeless at first. After forty-five minutes, Priestley cracked it. He double-checked his programming solution, decided it worked, and e-mailed it 2,500 miles west, to Facebook headquarters.

Facebook liked Priestley's approach so much that it flew him out to Palo Alto for a job interview. There, Facebook engineer Marc Kwiatkowski tested the newcomer, face-to-face, on a trickier problem. As Priestley later recalled, "I told Marc what answer he probably wanted—and I explained why it was a badly constructed problem. You were supposed to speed up one piece of the code. But it didn't address the fact that 98 percent of the time was being wasted on network requests."

Kwiatkowski blinked, and decided Priestley was right. A week later, Facebook offered Priestley a job. His patchy background didn't matter; his analytic and programming skills seemed outstanding. Perhaps there was a new way to beat Google and Microsoft in the hiring derby.

Priestley's first few months at Facebook became the stuff of legend. He started on a team of programmers figuring out ways to speed up Facebook's underlying computer infrastructure. Then he helped develop a framework that made it easier for users to add games, maps, and other applications to their Facebook experience. He was a computing polyglot, switching from PHP to Ajax to other programming languages as needed. He worked days; he worked evenings; he worked nights.

Whatever Priestley didn't know, he learned, in gung-ho tutorials that he ran himself. One time, Facebook's site stopped working for a small group of users. It turned out their computers were burdened with an obscure, out-of-date security program. No one at Facebook knew how to untangle this snarl. At 11 P.M. that night, Priestley rustled up the Internet's only publicly available information about this security program—which happened to be written in Dutch. Annoying? Yes. Impossible to decipher? No way! By daybreak, Priestley and a partner had gained a working familiarity with Dutch terms such as *foutmelding* and *beveiliging*. They rejiggered Facebook's internal code and voilà: the problem was fixed.

Even Priestley's goofs added to his mystique. In his third week at Facebook, the entire site abruptly crashed one morning. Engineers on the day shift examined records of computer-code alterations in the previous six hours, only to learn that Priestley had been tinkering in the middle of the night. "I had changed something at 3 A.M., and the change was a little bigger than I had intended," Priestley ruefully told me. Colleagues fixed the blunder within minutes and quickly forgave the rookie's mistake. "I berated myself about it more than anyone else did," Priestley added.

Priestley wasn't the only "genius from nowhere" who showed up on Facebook's doorstep. Facebook's puzzles began attracting a cult following among programmers worldwide. Utter strangers spent as much as forty hours trying to devise solutions. Most of their efforts didn't work. About 10 percent of submissions, however, amounted to accurate, runnable programs. Within that pool, a much smaller number amounted to genuinely elegant work. Those standout candidates earned job interviews at Facebook. Contestants who passed all the regular tests for new hires were invited to come on board.

Among these new hires was Jonathan Hsu, a graduate of Harvey Mudd College in southern California. He joined Facebook's engineering team in July 2007 and began working with online ad software. Soon a much more beguiling side job opened up. The company's original puzzle creator, Yishan Wong, was taking paternity leave. Facebook needed someone new to oversee its growing collection of software quizzes. At the very least, that meant sizing up the candidates' attempted solutions. Beyond that, Facebook needed someone to whip up excitement, silliness, and buzz around the puzzle-solving program.

It was time to create Facebook's Puzzle Master.

Hsu was perfect for the job. Not only was he technically savvy enough to size up candidates' work, he also understood the geeky fascinations of young engineers who could spend days in front of their computer screens. After all, he was one himself. He drank Red Bull to stay energized at night. He dashed around the Facebook office on a RipStik scooter to unwind; he devoured science fiction and fantasy novels in his spare time. He knew his audience. He became Facebook's equivalent of the party-happy characters that surface at summer beach resorts, inviting everyone to join the fun.

Each time Hsu posted a new puzzle, he adorned it with mischievous details that offered a peek into Facebook's jaunty culture. A mainstream problem involving garbled-text analysis, for example, was repackaged as "Breathalyzer." Contestants were asked to help Facebook identify intoxicated users who couldn't type properly anymore. To deal with this imaginary scenario, contestants' programs needed to catch flurries of typos in unfamiliar text samples, while absolving those with rarer errors. It proved to be an intricate challenge, because some garbles could represent ~~avariousty~~ a variety of different words. Solving it required shrewd use of a sophisticated look-up function. Hsu's version made this task seem like a late-night dorm game.

Even the Puzzle Master's own identity became a puzzle in its own right. The puzzle site's opening picture never showed Hsu or any other individual. Instead, visitors saw an odd version of a lowercase f, consisting of many brightly colored rectangular slivers, all pressed together. Most viewers thought it was abstract art. The cleverest ones realized that the f was a puzzle in its own right, written in Piet. What, you might ask, is Piet? It is a computer language (mastered by Facebook engineer James Leszczenski and very few other people) in which all terms are represented as rectangles in the style of the abstract artist Piet Mondrian. Thousands of people looked at the f each week. During a two-and-a-half-year span, just forty-two figured it out. The program yielded a secret e-mail address at Facebook, so that solvers could alert the social networking company to their prowess.

The purpose of the Puzzle Master's merriment, of course, was to generate as much interest as possible in Facebook's unorthodox tests, particularly among avid programmers. When I first met Hsu in late 2008, Facebook's puzzle page had about two thousand fans. Within a year, that total had soared to ten thousand. By early 2011, the puzzle page had forty thousand members. It didn't matter if each new wave brought only a few people who would ever work at Facebook. It was so easy, fast, and cheap to evaluate entries automatically—and then have Hsu take a closer look at the best submissions—that puzzle solving became Facebook's most efficient way of recruiting new engineers.

More than two hundred submissions arrive each day, from all corners of the world. Some contestants hold advanced degrees; others may be college dropouts. Many are short on corporate charm. They won't make good salespeople or public speakers. But they all believe they possess a gift for programming. All they need is this gossamer-thin link, allowing them at least a slim chance of connecting with Facebook's central hiring system. As of early 2011, the Puzzle Master had helped find 118 engineers—nearly 20 percent of Facebook's programming cadre.

"This is how we capture the long tail," Hsu told me. "This is how we find the great engineers that would never show up through our regular recruiting systems."

When Hsu sums up his work that way, he is speaking a universal language. In almost any field, most prime candidates come from a narrow, time-tested set of backgrounds. If you want concert violinists, check out the graduates of Juilliard and other top conservatories. If you want future U.S. senators, do your scouting among congressional representatives, state governors, and top business leaders. If you are looking for comics with hit-movie potential, pluck someone from the cast of *Saturday Night Live*. Those patterns of talent concentration are so well established that they keep working to some degree, decade after decade.

Hunting strictly in those familiar zones doesn't find everybody, however. When selectors apply such rules too tightly, lots of fascinating candidates on the fringe get overlooked. There's no mechanism for considering the 100-to-1 long shot, let alone the 1,000-to-1 candidate. On a one-at-a-time basis, it's easy to say that such candidates aren't worth the time it would take to assess them. Yet in aggregate, ignoring all of these outsiders can mean squandering access to a vast amount of talent.

Statisticians coined the term "the long tail" generations ago, as a way of describing increasingly uncommon events that stretch on, seemingly forever, on a graph of probabilities. The term took on new life in 2004, when *Wired* magazine editor Chris Anderson wrote about the ways that the Internet makes it much easier to find and sell uncommon goods. In his book *The Long Tail*, Anderson observed that companies such as Amazon.com and Netflix have established very powerful businesses by offering customers a near-endless collection of rarities, along with the big hits.

Is there a long tail of talent? Absolutely. For a showcase illustration, consider Major League Baseball's draft of amateur players, which takes place every spring. Generally, about 60 percent of the players chosen in the first round go on to achieve at least some level of success in the big leagues. That percentage drops to about 50 percent for second-round picks and tails off steadily, to the point that by the tenth round, barely 10 percent of those picks will make it to the top.

By the end of ten rounds, the amount of unclaimed big-league talent is limited—*but not zero*. Longtime baseball executives are smart enough to know this. So each team keeps picking. Entire rounds may go by without identifying any athlete that will ever play more than a few innings of major league ball. Yet the teams keep picking. Why? The answer is simple: somewhere in this collection of slim-chance leftovers are future All-Stars such as Keith Hernandez, Mark Buehrle, Jeff Conine, Junior Spivey, and Raúl Ibañez. Each was picked in the thirtieth round or later.

Could teams stop after thirty rounds? Yes they can, and each year, some do. By that stage of the annual baseball draft, nine hundred players have been chosen. Top college teams' rosters have been picked clean. All the high-school pitching sensations with 95 mph fastballs have been claimed. It takes a lot of diligence—or optimism—to keep pressing onward. In 1988, the baseball draft stretched past the sixtieth round. By that point, only seven of the league's thirty teams were still choosing, including the Los Angeles Dodgers. As a favor to a family friend, Dodgers manager Tommy Lasorda urged the team to pick a slow-footed first baseman playing college ball in Florida. As a result, the Dodgers won a place in baseball fame (and in statistical lore) by landing a future big-league All-Star, Mike Piazza, in the 62nd round.

"Nobody wanted me," Piazza later told an interviewer. "Coaches said: 'You know what? You're never going to make it.'" Piazza couldn't crack the starting lineup at the University of Miami's elite team in 1987. Although he got more playing time after transferring to a nearby junior college, coaches dismissed him as just another slow-moving power hitter. The doubters, of course, were spectacularly wrong. Recast as a catcher, Piazza played for sixteen seasons in the major leagues. He made the All-Star team twelve times and hit 396 home runs as a catcher, more than anyone else who ever played the position. He is regarded as a shoo-in for the Hall of Fame when he becomes eligible for voting in 2012. As for those early snubs, Piazza said, they became "fuel for motivation."

How can anyone find the next round of Priestleys and Piazzas? Luck might help, but a sound strategy is even better. Alert organizations find clever ways to widen their net without wrecking the careful checks and balances involved in a conventional hiring system. Often the pioneering work can be done by a few explorers who approach the hunt for talent in a radically different manner. The winning methods are so ingenious—and so powerful—that the next three chapters will explore in detail how the most successful innovators have succeeded against the odds.

The key techniques are as follows:

Break down barriers that restrict where you look. As the Puzzle Master example shows, the talent universe is full of overlooked people, shunned for reasons of geography, status, or background. This chapter will show how the best talent scouts break from the pack, spending time in places where no one else visits. Sometimes all that's required is a willingness to consider Kansas when everyone is fussing over the same limited pool of candidates on the Eastern Seaboard. Other times, looking in new places involves the courage to start hiring women on Wall Street when other firms aren't. It may feel safer to stick with the pack. But scouting the same way everyone else does amounts to paying a huge "conformity tax."

When you're exploring, ask: "What can go right?" Most conventional assessment is all about finding candidates' flaws. That's appropriate in the final stages of selection, when top-tier candidates have already established their allure. But as the Puzzle Master example showed, the outer fringes of talent work differently. Great discoveries happen only if assessors are willing to suspend their skepticism at first, so that the underdogs get a chance to show a spark of promise. Chapter 7 will explore the ways that a new ethos—defined by open-mindedness, optimism, and curiosity—can lead to epic talent discoveries in unexpected places.

Figure out how to take tiny chances—so you can take more of them. When it's expensive to consider candidates who might not work out, the long tail of talent becomes off-limits. Organizations can't stomach the costs, distractions, and emotional fatigue associated with frequent mismatches. The Puzzle Master approach is a high-tech way of making that problem vanish: evaluations are automatic and misfires hardly cost anything. In many other fields, success is still so mysterious that everyone relies on hunches and patience. But the most successful talent spotters steal an edge anyway. Chapter 8 will show how these leaders take their boldest risks with their smallest dollars, spreading bets around so that long-tail prospecting can pay off even when yields seem meager.

The search for "geniuses from nowhere" is especially intense in fields such as music, acting, comedy, and the rest of the performing arts. But similar hunts can be found in investing, advertising, book publishing, politics, and other creative fields. In all these areas, it's well known that some of today's biggest stars won hardly any notice at first. Figuring out how to catch those early stirrings of promise is a marvelous, maddening obsession for any organization that wants to win in the talent hunt. After all, no one wants to walk past the next Priestley or Piazza without realizing it.

Some of the most intriguing experiments in this direction are taking place in downtown San Francisco, at the advertising agency of Goodby, Silverstein & Partners. It's an ambitious, high-swagger shop that likes to tout its campaigns for world-renowned brands such as Chevrolet, Comcast, Hewlett-Packard, Sprint, Netflix, and the Nintendo Wii. About five hundred people a month apply for jobs at Goodby. Many have strong enough credentials to earn a job in advertising somewhere. At Goodby, there's room to hire only a very small number of them.

Yet Goodby's director of talent, Zach Canfield, spends barely half his time reviewing mainstream applications from mainstream candidates. When he does, he grumbles about it. "I would put a gun to my mouth if I just looked at résumés all day long," he told me. "I would be miserable. I would go completely crazy. We need to refresh the pond. The more interesting people I can find outside this industry, the better." So the core of his job involves hunting for smart, high-intensity people who never knew they wanted to work in advertising until Canfield contacted them.

For a while, Canfield scouted the world of stand-up comics. As he later explained, they are marvelous storytellers. They hone their material relentlessly, so that it connects with an audience. (If they don't, they become sit-down comics.) And they are keenly aware of audiences' short attention span, in ways that other narrators often overlook. Canfield came back from that quest with several standout hires, including one ex-comedian, Andrew Bancroft, who became of one of Goodby's top creative talents on the "Got Milk," Häagen-Dazs, and Chevrolet accounts.

Emboldened by that success, Canfield started talking to lawyers, police detectives, private investigators, and college debate champions. Nobody else regards those professions as feeder systems for ad agencies. But Canfield saw these unlikely specialties as hotbeds of superb researchers with a deep curiosity about what other people think and believe. Turn such people loose in a top ad agency with big research budgets, and there's a greater chance for them to "change culture and change the way that we operate as humans." As Canfield observes, "Really smart, passionate people tend to be drawn to that sort of thing."

Three of Canfield's four targeted professions turned out to be dead ends. Lawyers, detectives, and private eyes had already settled on steady careers. Backtracking to make a fresh start in advertising didn't fit their plans. But with the college debaters, Canfield hit the jackpot. They liked Canfield's pitch. For at least some of them, advertising sounded a lot more exciting than their standard career option: heading off to three years of law school, followed by the highly constrained life of a corporate litigator. If Goodby needed research aces who could analyze the seventeen reasons why people buy the cars that they do—why, that was fine stuff!

Thanks to debate-focused chat boards such as cross-x.com and planetdebate.com, Canfield learned a lot about his quarry without leaving the comforts of Goodby's offices. Some top debaters turned out to be unspeakably arrogant or rude. Canfield crossed those off his list. Others came across as smart, well organized, and likable in their own quirky ways. Those became his chief prospects.

At the top of Canfield's list was a shaggy-haired Harvard student with oversized glasses: Ralph Paone. Nobody would mistake Paone for a teen idol. But there was something sweetly disarming about Paone's delivery. On Web videos, Paone showed a knack for slipping bits of his vast knowledge into everyday conversation in ways that made him seem helpful, rather than bossy. Even when picking apart the views of German philosopher Friedrich Nietzsche, Paone came across as a gentle explainer.

Goodby could use someone like that, Canfield believed. There was room inside the firm for a vast range of skills, going beyond the classic stereotypes of brilliant but fussy "creatives" and smooth, assertive account managers. There was a natural role for Paone on Goodby's research team. Not only was he packed with more facts than an overprepared *Jeopardy!* contestant; he also delivered them as if he were a younger, nerdier version of beloved essayist Bill Bryson.

After a short phone chat to see if Paone was interested in a career in advertising, Canfield flew him out to Goodby for an interview. Paone wore a suit, while everyone at Goodby was in jeans. Partners decided they liked the new guy anyway. Two weeks into his new job, Paone cranked out research for a JetBlue business pitch. He analyzed the American public's flying habits with clarity and verve. Goodby's executive creative director, Rick Condos, declared Paone to be a genius.

Within a year, Paone had a full-time job at Goodby as a junior brand strategist—and a mischievous informal title, too. He was now "an amateur detective of culture."

Bringing in outsiders like Bancroft and Paone brings big spillover benefits, Canfield argues. "Our whole mission as an ad agency is to connect with people," he observes. That's best done if the firm includes people with the full spectrum of skills, attitudes, and perspectives. Overload Goodby with too many people who came into advertising through the same paths, and blind spots start to occur. The best way to fix that, Canfield believes, is to add a few people "who know nothing about advertising but have a great perspective on the world."

His conclusion: "You have to dig in unknown places. You have to spend 50 percent of your time trying to find those wild cards."

For smaller organizations—especially those with limited spending power—sheer economics may force them to concentrate on the long tail of talent. Realistically, they can't win the costly bidding wars to hire the obvious superstars. They need to adopt more of a guerrilla strategy, picking up nonobvious talent that larger rivals can't be bothered to pursue. And sometimes, that can work out quite well.

In big-time sports, Bill Polian is seen as one of the savviest general managers around. He runs the Indianapolis Colts, a football team that has twice been to the Super Bowl in the past decade, and that hasn't had a losing season since 2002. Long ago, he learned his trade in a much humbler setting: working for the Montreal Alouettes in the Canadian Football League. There, his budgets were less than one quarter of what U.S. pro teams in the National Football League could muster. Polian could draw up as many lists of top college prospects as he wanted, but it was futile. Nearly all the great players would sign for bigger money with U.S. teams. They had no interest in seeing what skimpy offer a Canadian team could muster.

So Polian and his head coach, Marv Levy, decided to stop scouting the top U.S. college teams. Instead, he told me, they redirected their resources toward hanging out on the edges of NFL training camps. Week by week, the U.S. teams would trim their rosters as the season approached. Ninety players might come to camp; only forty would make the team. The first few rounds of discards didn't offer much. But when the forty-third best player, or the forty-second best player, was let go, Polian pounced.

"Those guys were good," Polian told me. "They were nearly as good as the ones that made the team. And when they got cut, man, they were motivated. They wanted to play pro ball. They felt they deserved a shot. We could come in, sign them to contracts, and let them live out their dream. Even if all they wanted to do was get back to the NFL, we could get a couple extraordinary seasons out of them."

On Wall Street, investment expert Jack Rivkin developed a similar, equally successful strategy. Working for Lehman Brothers in the 1980s as head of investment research, Rivkin wanted to build up a top-flight team of stock-picking experts. His firm could try to poach top analysts from the likes of Merrill Lynch, Goldman Sachs, and Salomon Brothers, but the odds were that any job offers he made would simply be used as bargaining chips by those analysts to get even richer pay from their existing employers. Unless Rivkin wanted to overpay wildly for proven talent, poaching wasn't going to work.

So instead, Rivkin and his chief operating officer, Fred Fraenkel, decided to hire young unknowns, full of promise, and see if they could be groomed into high-profile analysts, too. Most Wall Street firms in those days did their recruiting at elite business schools such as Harvard, Wharton, Columbia, and the University of Chicago. There was a big pool of male and female candidates to choose from, but recruiters tended to pigeonhole prospects. Women were interviewed for sales jobs. Men were tapped for everything else, including research.

Rivkin defied the norms. He met with the female candidates no one else wanted, pitching them on the notion of a career in investment research. Before long, 30 percent of his analysts were female, compared with industry norms of 10 percent. Each year, when *Institutional Investor* magazine released its rankings of top investment analysts, Rivkin-era hires such as investment strategist Elaine Garzarelli or textiles analyst Josie Esquivel achieved number one status. Overall, 60 percent of Lehman's female analysts earned *Institutional Investor*'s acclaim, compared with just 40 percent of their male peers.

Facebook, of course, started out in the underdog camp. Tight budgets, urgent hiring needs, and the burdens of being small combined to nudge the company into adopting its imaginative ways of seeking out talent that whispered. What's striking, though, is that as Facebook got bigger, richer, and better known, it didn't send the Puzzle Master into retirement. The exact opposite occurred. Puzzle solving became a more prominent part of Facebook's hiring strategy, with even mainstream candidates being encouraged to take a shot at some puzzles if they wanted to improve their chances.

I asked Hsu and other Facebook engineers why this was so. They pointed me toward two quite distinct ways that programmers become really good. Most top-flight programmers learn their craft in centers of excellence. They may start at high-powered high schools or at tech camps for teens. They refine their abilities at leading engineering programs such as MIT, Caltech, Stanford, Harvard, Waterloo, Carnegie Mellon, the state universities of Illinois, Washington, Michigan, and so on. At each step, these nascent programmers are surrounded by smart, motivated students, while being inspired by prominent professors and other instructors.

Yet some other top programmers rely much less on formal education, and end up being largely self-taught. They may not have considered applying to a high-prestige university. They may have latched on to the excitement and discipline of cutting-edge programming only after their college days were done. Or their personalities may include so many mordant, sassy elements that their traditional bosses and professors would mistakenly write them off as lifelong underachievers. Whatever the reasons for choosing unconventional paths, these programming wizards aren't likely to catch anyone's eye via the usual recruiting methods.

No matter how big Facebook got, it still wanted some of these scrappy characters on its payroll. They were good. The best ones worked enormously hard. And their seat-of-the-pants programming style strengthened the company's overall programming culture, creating a hybrid of careful, by-the-book methods and timely improvisation. The Puzzle Master's realm was the best way to keep finding such candidates.

One of Hsu's favorite finds was David Alves, a 2001 high school graduate who still hadn't finished college in 2009. His degree came from San Jose State, not generally thought of as an elite school for computer programming. But once Alves solved a puzzle and caught the eye of Facebook's recruiters, the sidelights of his résumé commanded attention. He had been regularly entering computer-programming contests with as many as six hundred contestants. He was regularly finishing in the top ten. He was president of San Jose State's computer science club. Alves might be stuck at an obscure school. But he was eager to make a name for himself.

Other top puzzle solvers carried themselves in such blithe, jaunty ways that they couldn't master the social graces of traditional campus job interviews. But if they were given a computer, an Internet connection, and a chair, they could accomplish great things on their own. Typical was James Leszczenski, a Carnegie Mellon graduate who had worked at three major software companies by age twenty-five. On his LinkedIn page, he identified his job at Facebook as "saxophonist." His entire job description: "I do stuff." Hsu regarded him as one of Facebook's most persistent and cunning programmers.

In 2010, Facebook engineers decided that they would stop asking classic brainteaser problems entirely during interviews. Traditional riddles such as "Can you estimate the number of piano tuners in Chicago?" turned out to have only hazy correlation with genuine programming skills. The best way to see who could write good computer code was—surprise—to ask candidates to write good code. In fact, Hsu said, puzzle submissions revealed even more than he expected about candidates' strengths and weaknesses.

"Look at this," Hsu said one afternoon, as he pulled up a contestant's successful entry. At the top of the submission, before the dense mix of numbers and symbols that constituted the actual programming code, was a neatly blocked off rectangle of type, with asterisks all around it.

"That's his annotation," Hsu said. "He's explaining how his program works. Look at how clearly he defines all his parameters. Someone who goes to the trouble of doing that is making life a lot easier for anyone else on the team who needs to get into that same program someday. Do that annotation, and it's clear how the program works. Without it, you can spend hours trying to make sense of another person's work."

"I've never met him," Hsu continued. "I've never seen his résumé. But I know a lot about him already that I might not have learned from his résumé or an interview."

7: What Can Go Right?

In the winter of 1960, Austrian cardinal Franz König got caught in the worst journey of his life. Vatican leaders wanted him to represent the church at the funeral of Cardinal Alojzije Stepinac of Yugoslavia. Traveling for hours along icy roads, König never reached his goal. About an hour north of the burial site, his Mercedes sedan skidded off course and smashed into an oncoming truck. The crash killed Konig's driver and left the Austrian cardinal badly injured. Carried away unconscious, König awoke in an unfamiliar hospital, with his face heavily bandaged and his jaw wired shut. He couldn't move his head.

Everything about the trip at that point was a total failure. Efforts to send Catholic dignitaries to the graveside were for naught. Cardinal Stepinac ended up being buried in obscurity. As König later told interviewers, he lay for days in his hospital bed, staring at a Communist portrait in his room, trying to find some rallying thought. At first nothing clicked.

Then König found his plan. Even if he hadn't succeeded this time as the Vatican's envoy of hope, König could try again. Somebody needed to connect believers throughout Europe, no matter how harsh conditions might be behind the Iron Curtain. He could become

139

one of those connectors. In his memoirs, König described that hospital stay as "a crucial watershed in my life."

Over the next eighteen years, König explored Eastern Europe with the zeal of a new priest getting to know his first parish. He celebrated mass in Warsaw. He consoled the elderly in Budapest. He kicked soccer balls at seminaries; he went for hikes with Polish bishops; he even toured a museum of atheism in Leningrad so he could better understand the Communist mind-set toward religion.

In this new mission, König gained deep insights into Eastern Europe's leaders, including a charismatic younger cardinal in Poland, Karol Wojtyła. By the late 1970s, König was talking about Wojtyła as a possible future pope. Most other cardinals didn't see that possibility. König persisted anyway. In October 1978, König prevailed. Thanks to the Austrian cardinal's influence, the church picked its first non-Italian pontiff since 1522, gaining a leader who came to be seen as one of the strongest popes of all time.

The selection of Pope John Paul II is more than just an astonishing zigzag of fate. It's a reminder that in a time of crisis, even an institution as deeply steeped in history as the Roman Catholic Church can be inspired to break with its past. In such situations, it's possible for a few high-energy optimists to get everyone else thinking about new paths—and what can go right—rather than being governed by apprehensions about what could go wrong.

This is a chapter about the Franz Königs of the world: a rare breed of explorers whose lives are defined by the chance to roam beyond familiar territory. They enter the talent-hunting narrative only rarely: when an organization is so young, so carefree, or so caught up in crisis that it doesn't intend to follow the careful, predictable methods that have been documented so far in this book. In such situations, these pioneers earn renown by discovering or championing talent that no one else sees.

These explorers don't just find popes. They also succeed at

humbler and more worldly missions. They size up the frontiers of talent in highly unpredictable fields such as acting, music, and literature. They play a big role in ferreting out corporate inventors. In an especially intriguing role, they help pinpoint the twenty-five or so "geniuses" that win MacArthur Fellowships each year. Regardless of their official titles or authority, they all come at the world with a wide-eyed vigor that resonates with Isaac Newton's famous quote: "I seem to have been only like a boy playing on the seashore . . . whilst the great ocean of truth lay all undiscovered before me."

Consider Catharine Stimpson, who ran the MacArthur Fellows program from 1993 to 1997. She grew up in Bellingham, Washington, in the 1940s, surrounded by academic achievers in all disciplines. Her father was a doctor. Her aunt was a chemist. Her mother ran a small insurance company. She taught herself to read at age three and later whiled away the afternoons flipping through encyclopedias. "The Second World War was under way when I was little," she told me. "Every man of military age in my family was away. There was an edge of anxiety. Reading was a way of trying to get some control over a world that was out of control. I liked doing it. It's your source of power."

As a young academic, Stimpson built her reputation as an English professor at Barnard College, specializing in women's studies. But the explorer's spirit never left her. She had been one of three girls in her high school class to study physics at a time when few women did, and she kept reading about physics on her own as an adult. She taught a course on African American studies at one point, partly as a way of educating herself. Breaking down the walls that separate academic disciplines, she counseled other scholars writing books on everything from Islam to the blues.

When the MacArthur Foundation approached her, Stimpson hoped she might be in line for a "genius" award herself. No such luck. She was targeted instead to oversee the MacArthur Fellows program, which awards substantial five-year grants (currently $100,000 per year) to about two dozen highly creative people each year.

The program was just twelve years old at the time, but it already had attracted worldwide renown. It was born in mystery, created by a handful of foundation trustees after eccentric billionaire John D. MacArthur died in 1978 without leaving clear directions about what to do with his money.* Each year the prizes were scattered among a kaleidoscopic assortment of people, as the foundation refused to be pinned down about where great creativity might surface. Early recipients included poets, geologists, civil-rights lawyers, historians, and a scientist who studied baboons. The money could be spent in whatever way the winners wanted.

Adding to the intrigue, ambitious achievers couldn't apply for the prizes or rally support behind their candidacy. The MacArthur program scanned the nation's talent pool by itself, as invisibly as possible, using a vast, informal network of tipsters, evaluators, and judges. Then the foundation announced the winners each summer. The result, said one early recipient, composer Charles Wuorinen, was "the most civilized award ever invented."

Stimpson received the MacArthur offer at an awkward time; she was serving as graduate school dean at Rutgers University. But she couldn't resist. "I felt we were in one of those decisive cultural moments where older stereotypes of creativity were being exploded," she recalled. "My job was to bring in people who were familiar with what was going on at the cutting edge."

During Stimpson's time at the helm, prizes went to a handful of people in her longtime areas of academic interest, as well as many others in

---

* According to biographer Nancy Kriplen, MacArthur's main concern was keeping his insurance and real-estate fortune away from the tax man. That led him to create a giant, hazily defined foundation. The chief advocate for the "genius" awards was MacArthur's estranged son, Rod MacArthur, who believed the world was full of potential Einsteins who never got the funding and unfettered time to pursue their dreams. By some accounts, Rod MacArthur saw himself as such a person.

wildly different fields. Feminist poet Adrienne Rich got a fellowship one year. So did literary scholar Susan Stewart and theater director Elizabeth LeCompte. Meanwhile, the fellowship program continued its famous explorations of creativity in all its forms. Other winners include jazz musician Ornette Coleman, mathematician Andrew Wiles (who proved the three-hundred-year-old stumper known as Fermat's Last Theorem), and astronomer J. Roger Angel.

The way the MacArthur program is set up, anyone sitting in the director's chair can't pack the annual awards list with personal favorites. The final roster of prize winners is assembled each year by a rotating committee of outsiders, known as "selectors." But the director still enjoys considerable power in shaping the early stages of the hunt. With the program's wide-roaming definition of creativity, there is always discussion about where else to turn. Should the program consider sculptors? What about radically new approaches to farming? Or metalworking?

"I felt we should run an avant-garde program," Stimpson told me. "We should recognize things that haven't been done before." When I spoke with Stimpson in 2009, she warmly recapped popular and controversial choices during her tenure. Her main regrets were the areas she hadn't reached. "I wish we had looked more at the military," she said.

When Stimpson moved on, MacArthur Foundation leaders in 1997 put an even more eclectic spirit in charge of the Fellows program. Their choice was Daniel Socolow, who cloaked his kaleidoscopic résumé behind the safe euphemism of "educator." True, Socolow had spent several years as president of the American University in Paris. But in prior jobs, he had bought animal glands from Argentine slaughterhouses; he had been the Ford Foundation's man in Uruguay; he had set up a Canadian studies department at an upstate New York university, and he had been one of the few white administrators at historically black Spelman College.

"I didn't want to do anything for very long," Socolow told me during a long coffee-shop chat in Chicago. "I was always restless. Whenever I started to get comfortable, I wanted the next challenge, where I would have to start from scratch." At Spelman, he worried that he had stretched too far, to the point that he would never fit in. When he left that school, though, Socolow recalled, "they made me an honorary black woman. It's something I felt very good about."

Coming to the MacArthur Fellows program, Socolow sensed that at last he had found a place where novelty-seekers would never grow tired. "For God's sakes, I was going to try to help pick people in the sciences and other areas," he said. "It seemed wonderfully challenging."

During Socolow's time in charge, the MacArthur program has shown more interest in going beyond the university, looking for people with big ideas that defy characterization. Slightly fewer prizes are being awarded to people in the humanities and social sciences. But the clearest trend is that the program keeps redefining its focus, at least slightly, each year. New categories of recipients emerge in fields ranging from computer security to bridge safety and hand-letter carving. As Socolow drolly remarked, "The pattern is that there is no pattern."

For the MacArthur Foundation's leadership, that's as it should be. "As long as Dan keeps bringing us these marvelous bouquets, filled with fascinating people, there's no reason for us to intrude at all in the way he does his job," says John Seely Brown, a MacArthur Foundation trustee. Unlike most philanthropic entities, the MacArthur program doesn't ask (or even encourage) its prize winners to provide an accounting of what they accomplished with their awards. The program's mere existence is seen as success enough.

Step back a bit in American history, and this eagerness to corral talent in any area—without much more than an optimist's desire to see it all work out well—helped build some of the nation's leading universities. At Cornell University, for example, benefactor Ezra Cornell famously declared in the 1860s: "I would found a university where anybody can study anything." Once the school was open, administrators took him at his word. They stretched the definition of university far beyond the era's usual norms of classics, theology, and sciences—making room for experts in agriculture, engineering, and a host of other fields.

Harvard's great ascent in the late nineteenth century was guided by Charles William Eliot, a chemistry scholar from a family of prominent Boston merchants. His forty-year tenure as Harvard's president was marked by a never-ending hiring spree, as Eliot roamed beyond the familiar pools of talent to find people who he thought might help the school. As one earlier biographer noted, Eliot "has appointed professors from outside without the advice or consent of the departments, much to the good of the departments in question."

The University of Chicago's first president, William Rainey Harper, built his institution with similar gusto. So did David Starr Jordan, the first president of Stanford University. They had no other choice. Their patrons (oilman John D. Rockefeller and railroad tycoon Leland Stanford, respectively) had put up millions of dollars in hopes of creating world-class universities from scratch. Greatness in a hurry was desired. Mistakes might be tolerated, but dawdling or hesitation would be inexcusable.

As organizations grow older, a lot of that exuberance fades. Familiar paths for adding talent get established. Leaders become more certain about which types of people they want (and which they don't). Cultures turn more conservative. Unfamiliar ideas of any sort, particularly ones involving what might seem like oddball hires for important jobs, are more likely to be viewed with suspicion or disdain.

But in Silicon Valley, where even well-established companies try to retain the friskiness and childlike curiosity of their early days, the willingness to ask "What can go right?" never dwindles. The model in many executives' minds is Bill Hewlett, cofounder of Hewlett-Packard. During his heyday in the 1950s and 1960s, he developed a famous three-step approach for dealing with engineers who were excited about what they hoped was an amazing breakthrough.

At the start of the process, one chronicler recalled, "Bill immediately put on a hat called 'enthusiasm.' He would listen, express excitement where appropriate and appreciation in general, while asking a few rather gentle and not too pointed questions." Later, Hewlett would revisit the issue, in effect wearing new hats called "inquisition" and "decision." In those later stages, Hewlett could turn fiercely critical. Shortcomings in either the idea or its champion would be bluntly aired. But the critiques wouldn't happen until Hewlett had first enjoyed a chance to see what could go right.

As a result, the best ideas (and the most talented engineers) prospered within HP. The duds were culled. Thanks to Hewlett's willingness to begin with an open-minded look, morale stayed strong, no matter what the outcome. The boss's overriding message: new ideas and new talent were welcome at HP.

At Apple, founder Steve Jobs is famous for pursuing a similar strategy. Many commentators tend to focus on his fierceness during the middle stage of inquisition. In *The Perfect Thing*, a book recounting Apple's development of the iPod music player, author Steven Levy wrote about "Jobs's maniacal attention to detail and harsh way of communicating." In Levy's words, such barrages "proved incredibly effective in producing products that were many cuts above the clunky efforts of his competition."

Apple insiders say the harangues are only half the story. Daniel Walker, Apple's former chief talent officer, said what struck him about Jobs was the Apple founder's willingness to see the best in any idea at the beginning. Jobs's supposed brilliance in finding the next technological wave ahead of everyone else may actually reflect an unfiltered enthusiasm for everything at first. If only the best ideas and people survived Apple's internal beat-downs, then only Jobs's successes would be visible.

There is a powerful benefit to this strategy of opening the doors wide at first, and then getting picky as newcomers reveal their full strengths and limits. It becomes much easier to hire someone intriguing without a fully formed view of what she or he might accomplish in the years ahead. All that matters at the beginning is a willingness to get started.

Take a look at the principals' lineup of Gensler, one of the world's biggest architectural firms. One of the company's top achievers has been Jun Xia, design director of Gensler's Shanghai office. He is best known for leading the design effort on the 2,073-foot Shanghai Tower, which is due to be the tallest building in China when completed. But when Xia joined Gensler in 1991, the firm didn't have a Shanghai office. In fact, Gensler didn't do any meaningful business in China. And there wasn't an active plan to expand into that market.

No matter. The director of Gensler's Denver office, Phil McCurdy, was looking to hire bright young architects in the early 1990s. It didn't bother him that Xia, a recent Chinese immigrant, was still perfecting his English language skills. McCurdy was blown away by the quality of Xia's drawings and admired the younger man's passion for architecture. There were lots of ways that Xia could succeed at Gensler.

At first, Xia worked in the background, helping to design airport terminals and office parks in Colorado while McCurdy handled the client relationships. Then McCurdy nudged Xia to start making presentations. They weren't Dale Carnegie–perfect, but clients loved the younger architect's intensity. "I told him: 'I'm not one hundred percent sure what you're doing, but keep doing it,'" McCurdy later told me. By the time Gensler did decide in 1999 to size up the Chinese market, it was clear that Xia would be a vital part of the team.

"We didn't have any idea at the beginning how well it would all work out," McCurdy said. "But we saw enough to get rolling."

In the case of Franz König, the Austrian cardinal who "found" Pope John Paul II, there wasn't a master plan of discovery, either. Instead, König possessed the courage to tiptoe into an intriguing new world, even after the catastrophe that marked his first trip to Eastern Europe. After that, good things started to happen. That was how his life worked. From childhood onward, he was driven by the explorer's unshakable quest for new experiences.

Languages were König's first fascination. As a little boy, he recalled in his memoirs, "foreign words on tins or cardboard boxes immediately attracted my attention." His school days included lessons in Latin and French, but that wasn't enough. He cajoled rural priests into teaching him English and Spanish, too. Russian and Italian followed soon afterward. Later, he developed a reading knowledge of Hebrew, ancient Persian, and Syriac, so he could do deeper theological research.

Foreign travel and advanced degrees came next. At various stages in his life, König studied philosophy in England, taught theology in Austria, and spent months in Rome, helping to refine Catholic thinking on the nature of the church at the Second Vatican Council, known as Vatican II. While Catholicism was his life, König's writings suggested that he found every religion fascinating. At one point, he spent years studying Zoroastrianism. He set up a publishing company in Austria that promoted study of Eastern faiths. When he came back from conferences in Beirut, Iran, or India, he bubbled with enthusiasm about new acquaintances and new insights into Islam or Hinduism. Genial curiosity propelled him forward.

So when a badly injured König ended up in a Croatian hospital in 1960, it wasn't in his character to pray for an ambulance ride home, hoping never to see the back roads of Eastern Europe again. He regrouped. The Vatican set the agenda at first, sending König to sort out church issues in Budapest and other Eastern European cities. Over time, without any master plan, König gravitated to Poland.

There, faith was deepest, the opportunities to help were greatest, and the local church leadership was most inspiring.

Papal historians have documented a long series of casual contacts between cardinals König and Wojtyła over about a fifteen-year period before Wojtyła became John Paul II. No individual encounter towers over the others. What emerges instead is a sense of a strong professional friendship that formed gradually, with deep roots. The two men worked together at Vatican II, where König praised the younger man's astute research. They got to know each other socially over meals and walks in Poland. Most important, König got to see Wojtyła's charismatic presence among lay Catholics while saying Mass, talking to church-goers, and so on.

All the while, Wojtyła was becoming one of the best-known senior churchmen in the world and a rising star in the eyes of Vatican leadership, too. In 1976, Pope Paul VI invited Wojtyła to give the Vatican's entire Lenten retreat, a rare honor for a visiting cardinal. Also in 1976, Wojtyła visited the United States and Canada, meeting with church leaders there. Philadelphia's Cardinal John Krol, of Polish origin himself, said later that he was particularly impressed by the visitor's energy, warmth, and wisdom.

At the cardinals' conclave in October 1978 that elevated Wojtyła to the papacy, König's greatest impact was in reassuring the approximately 120 other electors that the church would be in good hands if Wojtyła was chosen. As papal historian George Weigel noted in his book *Witness to Hope,* many of the voting cardinals were "in a state of spiritual shock." They had wrapped up an earlier conclave that summer, believing that God had directed them to pick the short-lived pope known as John Paul I. That pontiff's death within weeks of being chosen led anguished cardinals to wonder: *Is God angry at us? Did we make a mistake? Is there something different that He wants from us?* Tensions increased during the first day of voting, when it became clear that there wasn't a majority in support of any of the leading Italian candidates. To pick a new pope, the church needed to look elsewhere.

König argued that Wojtyła could be part of a bright future for the church. The fifty-eight-year-old Polish cardinal was in the prime of life, healthy, and charismatic, which hadn't exactly been true of his predecessors. Wojtyła's East European heritage might provide special insights in the church's long struggle with atheistic communism. And in a world where 95 percent of Catholics were non-Italian, maybe it was time for a non-Italian pope. It was König's nature to think about what could go right. This was a rare moment when conditions were right for the entire conclave of cardinals to become swept up in that optimism, too.

In hindsight, the papacy itself was ready for a fundamental transformation. By the late 1970s, two big societal changes—jet travel and the global ubiquity of television—were redefining what it meant to be a religious leader. It wasn't enough anymore to operate mostly inside the Vatican. Now it was possible, maybe even essential, for popes to bring their energy and convictions to the people wherever possible. No one foresaw how much John Paul II would redefine what it meant to lead the Catholic Church. But forward thinkers like König had glimpsed enough of this future to point the conclave in the right direction.

It's hard, in the normal give-and-take of life, to step away from our usual concerns about loss aversion and to think instead about what can go right. But when bad news is so persistent that the status quo seems intolerable, an entire nation can make the leap. Think of the presidential elections of 1932 and 1980—the two most transformative ballots in twentieth-century U.S. history. In 1932, the country's plunge into the Great Depression made President Herbert Hoover a hated man. It wasn't entirely clear what Franklin Roosevelt meant by "a new deal," but voters overwhelmingly were willing to give him a try. Much the same dynamic happened in 1980, when inflation, runaway gasoline prices, a recession, and the Iran hostage crisis made the United States seem like an enfeebled nation. When Ronald Reagan promised to "make America great again," he connected with voters. Instead of granting Jimmy Carter another four-year term, Americans overwhelmingly opted for a newcomer, hoping he could solve the country's problems.

Big corporations go through the same dynamic, too. The classic example came in 1993, when International Business Machines needed a new chief executive officer. At the time, IBM's stock was in freefall; its financial results were horrid; its costs were out of control; and its market share in many key computer markets was being gobbled up by smaller, nimbler competitors. Directors had lost faith in John Akers, a career IBM executive who had been running the company for the past five years. Akers had been squeezed out and directors were looking for a replacement. Most analysts expected IBM to limit its search to computer-industry experts. But IBM director James Burke, the former head of Johnson & Johnson, led a push to recruit Lou Gerstner, a former McKinsey management consultant whose main operating experience had been at American Express and the RJR Nabisco food-and-tobacco conglomerate. Other people saw Gerstner's lack of computer experience as an immediate disqualifier. Burke believed Gerstner's ability to give IBM a fresh look was actually an advantage, coupled with Gerstner's leadership skills and ability to make change happen.

When other directors agreed, and picked Gerstner to run the company, they made a giant bet on what could go right. Events played out better than they dared hope; Gerstner enjoyed a very successful eight years as IBM's boss, retiring in 2001 with the company's finances, reputation, stock price, and competitive strength in far better shape.

Everything seems so clear in hindsight. But at the moments when assessors must decide on someone's potential, listening for clues about what could go right can be as delicate as trying to pick up a baby's heartbeat through the muffled layers of heavy winter clothing. It's so easy to hear nothing. It's so easy to walk away. Even the scouts who get it right sometimes wonder how they did it.

There's another problem with swooping in after the fact, trying to gauge the power of asking: "What can go right?" The best success stories become immortalized. They are held up as examples of courage and its rewards. The failures tend to disappear from sight. At some point, it's only natural that explorers' healthy optimism can shade into naïveté or outright gullibility. Any thorough look at these experts' impact needs to distinguish between journeys of hope that work out and those that are doomed.

In the world of theater, the directing career of Bill Rauch is a poignant illustration of relentless optimism's allure and pitfalls. Over the past thirty years, Rauch's explorations have taken him from the comforts of Harvard to the austerity of an old railroad bunkhouse in North Dakota, and many other strange places as well. These days he is living well again, as artistic director of the Oregon Shakespeare Festival in Ashland, Oregon. He says he is proud of his choices and wouldn't change anything if given a second chance. Yet for people who knew him at the incandescent start of his career, there will always be a question of what he could have accomplished if he hadn't embarked on some of his oddest detours.

As a Harvard undergraduate in the early 1980s, Rauch whipped up enough plays to become a one-man theater festival. He directed a staggering twenty-six productions during his four years in college. They ranged from Shakespearean classics to a wild outdoor interpretation of Vladimir Mayakovsky's Communist satire *Mystery-Bouffe*. Some of his most imaginative works were staged in an abandoned room in a dorm basement—a setting that Rauch imbued with excitement by declaring it to be the artistic home of "The

Kronauer Group." (Kronauer was the surname of a Harvard instructor who slipped Rauch the chamber's keys.)

"Bill embraced what was beautiful and good in each person," recalled Ted Osius, a Harvard classmate. "His stable of actors continually expanded, because people saw his talent and were amazed by what he could evoke from them." Sometimes Rauch made "peculiar casting decisions," Osius added, particularly bypassing a polished performer in favor of a rawer talent that Rauch thought could expose a character's essence. Still, Rauch liked those gambles. Even his failures were fascinating.

After graduation, Rauch took a temporary position as an assistant director at Washington's Kennedy Center. His boss, Peter Sellars, was an earlier Harvard graduate who had just been proclaimed a MacArthur "genius" at age twenty-five. When that association came to an end, Rauch was eager to try something quite different from another mainstream directing job in a big city.

Instead, Rauch and Harvard colleague Alison Carey set out to bring Chekhov, Molière, and Shakespeare to small-town America. They created the Cornerstone Theater Company, a traveling ensemble of eleven Harvard buddies. Rauch bought a big blue van and mapped out a series of madcap routes across the United States, visiting an Indian reservation in Nevada, a Nebraska farm town, and so on. The more obscure the better. Cornerstone might be in town for just a few weeks, but with luck it would change people's lives forever, creating a theater-minded culture where one never existed before.

Who would act in these plays? Cornerstone provided several trained actors, who could help keep everything coherent. But the energy of each production was meant to come from inviting local farmers, welders, or grandmothers into the cast, too. It didn't matter if residents' acting skills were ragged at first. "Given a chance to relax and take artistic chances, their potential becomes obvious," Cornerstone declared in one of its manuals.

In October 1986, the Cornerstone players attempted their first big expedition, to Marmarth,* a worn-out railroad town in North Dakota. Their goal: to produce *Hamlet* on the Great Plains. Thanks to a briefing from the state tourism board, the Easterners knew that Marmarth was tiny, near the Montana border, and contained a small, working theater that hosted a cowboy poetry festival every September. Free lodging was available at the old railroad bunkhouse.

What Marmarth lacked was any deep desire to stage Shakespeare's most intricate play. There was a vaudeville tradition in town, but it didn't involve an anguished Danish prince wondering whether it was time "to sleep, perchance to dream." On the few occasions when Marmarth's ranchers, farmers, or bartenders took the stage, it was to goof around with cap guns and fake vomit. Undaunted, Rauch's crew started chatting up strangers in bars and handing out fliers with pizza deliveries, hoping to interest somebody—anybody—in becoming part of the cast. Hardly anyone responded at first. Rancher Merle Clark took a look at Cornerstone's copies of the famous play, singled out a few especially obscure turns of phrase and declared: "This will go over like a turd in a punchbowl."

So the Cornerstone players regrouped. They cut one thousand lines of Shakespeare. They changed "proud contumely" to "the crap we take from assholes." They bought cowboy boots and hats. They hung out at barbecues, tasted buffalo for the first time, and even learned to milk goats. Eventually townspeople relented and joined the project. "We didn't want them to feel bad," explained Dan Flor, a Marmarth rancher.

---

* The town was founded in 1905 by the Chicago and Milwaukee railroad, whose tracks stretched from the upper Midwest to Seattle. The town's name was an amalgam of Mary and Martha, two daughters of a prominent railroad executive. At its peak in the 1920s, Marmarth had about 1,500 residents and a small opera house. By the time Cornerstone arrived, the population had shrunk to 139. The opera house had been shuttered for decades; its interior was covered with inch-thick layers of dust. There was a small, seldom-used movie theater available for use.

To find acting talent, Rauch and his crew developed the "newspaper audition." Anyone wanting to be in the play was given a copy of the local county weekly, *The Slope Messenger*, and told to read routine stories as if they were insults . . . love letters . . . denials of something embarrassing . . . and so on. It was an easy, lighthearted test that let newcomers show what kinds of emotions they could convey. Before long, Rauch had his Laertes, his Rosencrantz, and his gravediggers. A few weeks later, the makeshift cast put on seven sold-out performances in the town's 150-seat theater.

Rauch's impact was charming but fleeting. After Cornerstone left, there wasn't any theatrical awakening in that corner of North Dakota. The vaudeville players went back to magic tricks, juggling, and cap guns. One of the most energetic local actors got in trouble with the law over alcohol issues that a minor brush with the stage didn't change. As for everyone else, in the words of town maintenance chief Jim Carroll, "Bill tried to make us into better actors, which was impossible." When Cornerstone left, so did any prospect of staging more Shakespeare.

Rauch stayed on the road for five years. In some towns, Rauch and company created an enduring awakening of theatrical ambition. Local residents kept staging plays after the visitors left, savoring the ways drama could bring a community together. For all their good intentions, however, Rauch and his colleagues weren't magicians. Cornerstone couldn't turn farmers or laid-off steelworkers into Broadway-bound actors. When the glow of a well-staged play faded, people went back to their regular lives, which weren't always happy. Judged by its own yardstick, Cornerstone's long road trip was a remarkable success. To the wider world, it was a brave, poignant tribute to hope and its limits.

In 1991 Rauch moved Cornerstone to Los Angeles and stayed as the troupe's artistic director for another fifteen years. His passion for community theater helped make Cornerstone a durable and beloved California institution. By the end, though, Rauch was taking frequent breaks to be a guest director at Yale, at the Guthrie Theater in Minneapolis, and especially at the Oregon Shakespeare Festival (OSF). He was ready to rejoin the world of full-time actors whose polish and technique could support a whole new range of theatrical ideas.

I first met Rauch in June 2009, two years after he left Cornerstone to become artistic director at OSF. Now he was running a seventy-four-year-old institution that sold nearly 400,000 tickets a year. He employed nearly one hundred members of Actors' Equity for a nine-month season on three stages. Money and talent were at his disposal again. A cautious newcomer would have altered very little. Rauch's appetite for experimentation, however, couldn't be contained.

At first, Rauch poked at the edges. He and Carey (who made the migration from Cornerstone as well) retooled OSF's lineup of non-Shakespearean plays, which usually accounted for about half the schedule. The Cornerstone alums were ready to stretch audiences' horizons, introducing them to plays about Mexican immigrants, Navajo issues, and the upheaval associated with a modern-day assassination. It took a while for Rauch to figure out what to do about Shakespeare. By the time I arrived, he had declared he would direct *Hamlet* for the 2010 season.

What would Rauch do with Shakespeare's best-known play? Over the years, OSF had staged at least a dozen versions of *Hamlet*. "Every version is slightly different," Rauch said enigmatically. Then he added: "We're still settling on the casting and the set design. It's very early. But if you want, come watch rehearsal in January." So I did.

On a bare stage, actors worked from noon to 10:30 P.M., sorting out three of the play's final scenes. I had expected to see Rauch methodically tugging the actors into delivering each line his way. But that wasn't his style at all. He had mapped out an overarching interpretation of the play, in which the Danish court had become a carnival of wickedness, full of schemes and suspicions that were bizarre beyond words. Now he wanted the actors to become his partners in a nonstop exploration of how to make that vision come true.

In Rauch's *Hamlet*, the minor courtiers Rosencrantz and Guildenstern would be even more miserably out of step with everyone else; they would be played by a lesbian couple. Hamlet's murdered father, seen mostly as a ghost, would struggle even more than usual to convey the facts of his death to his son. On Rauch's stage, the ghost literally could not speak; he would be played by deaf actor Howie Seago, who would use sign language in a crucial scene.

How should Hamlet treat other people? Rauch invited each scene to become a laboratory of emotional choices. "This is a minefield— as it should be!" Rauch declared at one point. The company's choices weren't always consistent. But the net result was for the actors themselves to find deeper meaning and more complexity in each of their scenes.

During the rehearsals that I watched, it wasn't just OSF veteran Dan Donohue, playing Hamlet, whose energy level kept ramping higher with each new challenge. Other actors, playing Laertes, Claudius, Gertrude, and Osric, were swept up in the excitement, too. They came to view each exchange as a pivotal moment in the entire play—whether it involved grief, petulance, slapstick wit, or disdain. As the intensity ratcheted up, Rauch could pull back and simply voice astonishment at what an amazing play it was. In his words: "It's sick. Really wild."

During OSF's 2010 season, Rauch's *Hamlet* was performed 110 times, more than any other play. Most performances were sellouts. On average, 99 percent of all available seats were filled. West Coast reviewers raved about the performance, though they generally have kind words for OSF. The play's capstone review came from *Wall Street Journal* critic Terry Teachout, who applauded Rauch's audacity.

"Mr. Rauch's 'Hamlet' may sound like a cornucopia of postmodern clichés," Teachout wrote, "but no sooner does it get moving than you find yourself swept up in the momentum of a show that makes compulsive sense. Every scene is shaped with easy authority. Every line, even 'To be or not to be,' is read with a freshness and snap that makes it new."

8: Lottery Tickets

When Scott Borchetta founded his own music label in Nashville, at age forty-three, he was trying to rebound from a run of bad luck. He had been squeezed out of MCA Music years earlier because of a personality clash with a boss. He lost another job in the summer of 2005, when DreamWorks Nashville shut down. After those setbacks, it wasn't clear who might hire him. The chatter in town was that Borchetta knew how to do one thing supremely well—drum up radio station airplay for top artists—without realizing his limitations.

Borchetta yearned to be in charge of picking talent. He had spent twenty years in Nashville, taking orders from a long series of music label chiefs. They decided who should be a star. Borchetta's job was to get on the phone with radio station music directors and programmers around the nation, trying to make someone else's business plan come true. By the end of his DreamWorks days, he later estimated, he had made at least twenty thousand calls on behalf of big-name singers such as George Strait, Reba McEntire, Toby Keith, and Jimmy Buffett. As these artists' hits kept piling up, Borchetta came to see himself as more than a marketing guy. He couldn't help but think he could spot tomorrow's stars, too.

Right after leaving DreamWorks, Borchetta moved his work gear into an aging bungalow on Nashville's Music Row—and declared himself CEO of Big Machine Records. ("We were anything but big," he wryly acknowledged later.) He printed up business cards. He designed a splashy logo. His bohemian new premises couldn't match the corporate offices where he once worked. No matter; the little building could serve as world headquarters of his new label.

To succeed, Borchetta needed to sign the singers America wanted to hear. This posed a problem. Country music's big names were under contract with other labels. Hardly anyone was eager to switch. Even if a few top performers might be tempted, Borchetta lacked the money and credibility to launch much of a raid on anyone else's talent stable. He couldn't pay the hefty up-front sums that a Nashville superstar would demand for switching labels. Borchetta's shot at success involved a much trickier path: he had to *discover* talent that the rest of the industry didn't see.

Most of the time, such prospecting is a never-ending stumble through the fog. Nashville—like any hub city for creative performers—is packed with baristas, cab drivers, students, and nail salon workers hoping for their big break. Few of them make it. Even when a remarkable new performer shows up, it's hard for the old guard to realize what they are hearing.

In 1988, for example, Garth Brooks rattled around Nashville for months, unable to get any music-label executive interested in him. Perhaps they didn't like his sound. Or they didn't care for his hat. Whatever the excuse, the skeptics were horribly wrong. It wasn't until Brooks began performing at the Bluebird Café that one scout was willing to take a chance on him. A decade later, after Brooks had sold more than 68 million albums, the notion of "catching Garth at the Bluebird" had become a rueful Nashville expression. It was music executives' way of reminding themselves how befuddled even the pros can be when talent is in its earliest stages.

In fields like music, where so much depends on the mysteries of how a mass audience relates to something new, the champions do three things right. They take a lot of small risks. They make the most of their fortunate hunches. And they let go of mistakes before these become ruinously costly. That's all anyone can do. Everyone is forced to guess about what might work. No one gets it right every time. The dividing line between success and failure comes down to how well executives can manage their portfolio of guesses.

Borchetta's wild ride with Big Machine illustrates all those points. During his final year at DreamWorks, he had been prospecting for talent without knowing for sure what label he would call home as the next stage of his career played out. He sampled a lot of demo CDs and MP3 files. He hung out at the cafés and bars where musicians congregate, including the Bluebird Café. As his hunches took shape, he started the label with five largely unknown artists.

Three of Borchetta's artists were gritty male soloists who had cut a few songs for other labels. None had hit the big time yet. Another addition was an astonishingly good-looking woman whom Borchetta had met at a sushi restaurant. The fifth arrival in Big Machine's lineup was a tall, blond high-school girl, just fifteen years old at the time. She didn't fit into any familiar category, but Borchetta really liked her lyrics.

In essence, Borchetta had bought five lottery tickets.

Ultimately, Borchetta's venture paid off in ways he hadn't dared hope. During Big Machine's first five years, his artists sold more than 20 million albums and won four Grammy Awards. One of his performers made the cover of *Rolling Stone*. Big Machine became country music's top-selling label in 2009, which changed the way Borchetta was seen in Nashville. He became a powerful man. Journalists sought his opinion on music industry trends; leadership conferences wooed him as a featured speaker. Within the music industry, people who might have snubbed him at the low points of his career now wanted to hang out with him, flatter him, and perhaps catch a bit of his magic.

What's striking about Big Machine's surge is that success didn't flow the way Borchetta had planned. Practically all of Big Machine's success came from the teen artist nobody noticed at first: Taylor Swift. When Borchetta first met her, she was working with a seasoned Nashville songwriter to make her lyrics even crisper. Then she found a producer who crafted the right sound for her music. When her debut album hit the stores, she won fans in small towns and big cities with her candor, poise, and warmth. Eventually Taylor Swift ended up with more than 19 million fans on Facebook. That put her ahead of Barack Obama and the Beatles. She turned out to be the unlikely superstar that made Big Machine the hottest ticket in Nashville.

That slow unfolding is what makes Scott Borchetta's success so instructive. He signed Taylor Swift without glimpsing more than a tenth of what she might become. In Big Machine's first few months, she consistently got number three billing on the label's Web site. Borchetta started with an understandably modest view of what his youngest singer might achieve. No matter; he saw enough.

In early 2009, I visited Borchetta in Nashville and asked him to flip through his old appointment calendars, curious to see exactly how his discovery of Taylor Swift took shape. Borchetta began that part of the conversation by telling me: "I knew right away that Taylor was going to be a star. I wrote it down. Give me a minute or two, and we'll find it."

Borchetta started looking through the calendar pages for November 2004, when he first heard Swift sing. No sign of the magic phrase. He moved to his 2005 calendar. We flipped through the earliest dates together. Still no sign. Finally, after much page turning, we found the exclamation: "Taylor is a star!" Borchetta was slightly flustered that his euphoria took longer to build than he had remembered.

He shouldn't have been embarrassed at all.

In areas of artistic creation, such as music, our first encounters with greatness very seldom amount to "Wow!" moments. All we notice at the beginning is a slight flutter. We see, hear, or read someone who stands out. How much? We're not sure. We need to know more. But our curiosity has been engaged. We certainly will take stock of this new presence some more. Those follow-up sessions—the second, third, fourth, and fifth encounters—are where we gradually gain the conviction to say: "That really is someone extraordinary."

When we fiddle with the narrative afterward, trying to create a sense of awe at the first encounter, we do so because it feels as if events *should* have unfolded that way. But when such retouching of the story takes place, we shortchange the most impressive part of the talent spotter's art. If bells went off every time someone amazing walked into sight, it wouldn't be hard at all to recognize the first stirrings of greatness. The great art lies in being open-minded enough to see faint possibilities at first, and then being methodical enough to keep coming back for more impressions, until the full picture is clear.

In the filing cabinet that holds this book's research files, there is a thin folder labeled "BASEBALL—RIVERA." Inside is a one-page scouting report filed from Panama on February 17, 1990. Looking at it is a bit like visiting the captain's deck on an ocean liner, and being directed to look at the tiniest dot possible on the horizon, with the assurance: "That's land."

I got the report from Herb Raybourn, the former head of Latin American scouting for the New York Yankees. He had heard good things about a tall, skinny shortstop who had switched positions and was trying his luck as a shortstop. Raybourn and another scout scheduled a private workout in a field near the player's home. Compared against a legitimate major-league hurler, this twenty-year-old prospect at that exact moment was "below average," Raybourn wrote. The Panamanian's fastball wasn't that fast. (It clocked in at 84 to 87 mph.) The mechanics of his windup weren't quite right yet.

All the same, Raybourn packed his write-up with a dozen hints that Mariano Rivera might get better. Rivera pitched with a loose, easy motion that was a joy to watch. He had a good pitcher's body: "tall, lean, broad shoulders, long arms, big hands." Even his scrawniness might be a hidden asset. The old scout had spent much of his thirties playing outfield for Panama's Los Novatos team. He knew what patchy diets most young Panamanian men subsisted on. If Rivera filled out and got stronger, good things could happen.

Raybourn promptly signed Rivera to a $2,500 contract with the Yankees. It was a pitifully small sum, but it was sufficient. No other major-league clubs had noticed Rivera yet. Overall, Raybourn rated Rivera's major league potential as somewhere between average and above average. That won Rivera an invitation to spring training with the Yankees, and a spot on a Rookie League team in the Florida Gulf Coast League.

From there, Rivera's career took off. By 1995, Rivera was pitching in the major leagues. Two years later, an All-Star. Two years after that: two saves and a win in the World Series, earning him a "most valuable player" award. By the end of the 2010 season Rivera was earning $15 million a year. His career achievements ranked him among the best relief pitchers of all time.

When I chatted with Raybourn, he didn't claim to be a prophet. Instead, he reminded me how much guesswork there is in scouting a player so early. As Raybourn put it, "A lot of things had to go right for Mariano to become as great as he did." During Rivera's Rookie League days, former baseball pitcher Hoyt Wilhelm helped Rivera greatly with both his mechanics and his on-the-mound judgment. Later on, some accidental tosses in a game of catch led Rivera to develop the spinning "cut fastball" that became his most effective pitch. Without it Rivera might never have advanced as far. And in a line of work where injuries shorten many pitchers' careers, Rivera stayed healthy.

Each year, baseball scouts render thousands of early, even premature, judgments about young players in the United States and Latin America. That is what the scouts have to do. There's a constant scramble among thirty big-league clubs to commandeer the next generation of talent. Teams that wait too long—until all the evidence is in—will find their best prospects are already playing for someone else. So guessing early and living with the consequences is unavoidable.

Inevitably, even the best scouts' ledgers end up riddled with far more failures than successes. Of the prospects getting contracts from big-league teams, less than 10 percent make it to the majors. Yet because most signing bonuses are small, and because scouts typically accept long hours and low pay, those mistakes aren't lethal. Teams know they can experiment a bit with their early guesses. Over time, player development systems will finish the job, sifting rare winners from the many near-misses.

As the Rivera example shows, the rewards for being right are so huge in baseball—or any hits-driven field—that strategists don't burn up much energy trying to reduce the number of bad guesses. Small mistakes fade quickly from memory. These fields aren't governed by the same anxieties as, say, aviation. (There, a single unduly optimistic assessment of someone's talent can be catastrophic.) The inherent optimism of a hits-driven field washes away any compulsion to ward off errors via the classic maxims of quality control, Six Sigma, reducing variation, and the like.

Mistakes don't matter, as long as they are small. The nightmare scenario for any chief of a hits-driven business isn't the isolated goof. It's getting trapped in an environment where talent hunting becomes so chronically costly and inefficient that even periodic hits can't save the day. Instead of spending $100,000 in signing bonuses and scouting fees to procure $1 million of talent, the ratios invert. Spend $1 million to find $100,000 of talent, and trouble arises. It's time either to find a new talent-picking chief or to call a bankruptcy attorney.

So as organizations get bigger, the outer edges of their scouting systems need to be as lean, comprehensive, and efficient as possible. In other words, it's time to create a hands-on, low-tech version of the Puzzle Master schema that was featured so prominently in chapter 6. In such systems, the very first assessments are simple and cheap. They aren't meant to be the last word on someone's potential. They function as a first-round gating system: finding unexpected candidates who at the very least deserve a closer look. The more frugal and streamlined such a system can be, the more candidates it can consider.

Something as basic as keeping track of ten thousand prospects is an art form in itself. The high-school basketball scouts of chapter 5 make their living by monitoring sixteen-team weekend tournaments, full of fast-moving athletes visible only by jersey number. Each starter needs to be evaluated in some form. Heaven forbid that Woodside's No. 12 gets logged in as Woodlawn's No. 21. In this clipboard clutter, only the apostles of efficiency and order survive. To my surprise, none of the middle-aged scouts doing the initial assessing on behalf of college clients is a former player or coach. All of them are number-crunchers by trade. Bob Gibbons, the savvy assessor in chapter 5, started out as a data-systems analyst for the state of North Carolina. Another top scout, Tom Konchalski, was a high school math teacher. A third, Van Coleman, began as a purchasing manager for Rockwell International.

How did the data jockeys seize control of basketball scouting? It turns out their spreadsheet wizardry is what coaches cherish most. Any coach who subscribes to these services gets a rough but orderly roadmap of where the better prospects are likely to be. Later, coaches and their staffs can fill in the details via their own recruiting trips. The basketball experts can show up later. When the data mavens' reports land on the desks of top coaches at Duke, Kansas, Connecticut, and North Carolina, basketball's elite gains a quick scan of hundreds of prospects. The cost: as little as 50 cents a name. Round one of scouting belongs to the quants.

Ordinarily, looking for cheap solutions invites shoddy work. But on the outer edges of scouting, ordinary economics doesn't apply. While full-time scouts need enough income to pay their bills, part-timers are a different species. For some—including highly skilled and successful people—scouting every now and then is a delightful hobby that doesn't need to be justified on an earnings-per-hour basis. Think of all the college alumni who interview freshman applicants, free of charge. Or consider all the high-tech executives who volunteer their time to judge the Intel Science Talent Search each year. Pay is irrelevant. The thrill of seeing a future Nobel laureate's earliest work is what inspires experts to work pro bono.

Dan Socolow, the director of the MacArthur Foundation's Fellows program, told me a charming story that bears out people's willing-ness to scout for free. In its earliest years, the foundation invited about a hundred experts in various disciplines to nominate nonobvi-ous people for the foundation's "genius awards." It paid nominators $1,000 apiece for their trouble. When Socolow took charge, he de-cided that he needed more nominators, but didn't want to raise his overall budget. So he signed up a fresh batch of two hundred people and cut the stipend in half. "The results got better," he recalled.

Socolow kept pressing ahead. A few years later, he eliminated the stipend entirely and recruited a new, even wider pool of nominators. "There's no end to where creativity might be, and now we aren't constrained in looking for it," he explained. "We've been able to reach out into areas such as farming and blacksmithing." What's more, some of the foundation's most detailed and thoughtful nomi-nations of all time came from the volunteers. Offering token pay made people stingy with their time. Offering nothing but the fun of helping a worthy project unleashed much greater generosity.

Of all the industries where the lottery-ticket analogy seems apt, book publishing deserves special mention. Editors spend their careers trying to gauge in advance how well a book will sell, only to be surprised constantly in either direction. As *New York Times* writer Shira Boss declared in 2007, "Most in the industry seem to see consumer taste as a mystery that is inevitable and even appealing, akin to the uncontrollable highs and lows of falling in love or gambling."

"It's guesswork," editor Bill Thomas at Doubleday Broadway told Boss. "The whole thing is educated guesswork, but guesswork nonetheless. You just try to make sure your upside mistakes make up for your downside mistakes . . . Nobody in publishing is smart enough to know which of the big books will be fiascos, which of the little books will be successes, and which in the middle might go up or down."

Editors have been guessing wrong since at least 1797, when London publisher Thomas Cadell turned down the chance to publish an early draft of Jane Austen's *Pride and Prejudice*. Her book is still in print. His publishing house went bust in the 1830s.

Even the distinguished house of Alfred A. Knopf, which is generally regarded as one of the most discerning U.S. publishers, has gone astray at times. Knopf's internal memos for much of the twentieth century are now publicly accessible at the University of Texas's Harry Ransom Humanities Research Center. A cavalcade of scholars and frustrated authors has unearthed a wide range of rejections that the publishing house surely wishes it could revisit. Sylvia Plath's *The Bell Jar*—"ill-conceived and poorly written." John Barth's *Giles Goat-Boy*—"labored and heavy-handed." Anne Frank's *Diary of a Young Girl*—"very dull . . . a dreary record of typical family bickering."

There's no way to avoid at least a few such missteps, contends Speer Morgan, a scholar at the University of Missouri who has studied the Knopf files in detail. "Any publisher that endures more than a few years misses plenty of good work," he observes. Even the most popular books are bought by less than 3 percent of all readers. By implication, 97 percent or more of readers decide that such a book isn't to their tastes. Whether editors trust their own judgment or rely on market research, they won't be able to spot every winning manuscript that crosses their desk.

As author John Thompson pointed out in his book *Merchants of Culture,* many successful books win their audiences for reasons that defy prediction. War in Afghanistan can turn an academic treatise on the Taliban into a bestseller. An unexpected movie deal has the same effect. So does a kind word from television personality Oprah Winfrey. Trying to predict such strokes of good fortune is a bit like trying to evaluate Mariano Rivera as a pitcher *while he is still playing shortstop*.

In an industry where 70 percent of books don't sell enough copies to justify the advances paid to authors, the best way for publishing houses to stay solvent is to make the intermittent winners count for a lot. A single book that vastly exceeds expectations can cover the costs of many medium-sized disappointments.

J. K. Rowling's first Harry Potter novel, for example, attracted barely a flicker of interest in the summer of 1995, when the manuscript was first shown to several British publishers. Editors may have thought it was too long for casual readers, too fanciful to be a "realistic" book, or simply too much bother to read when vacation resorts beckoned. For whatever reason, the book attracted only one bid, of £1,500 (equivalent to about $2,500), from Barry Cunningham, who ran Bloomsbury's children's books division. When it became clear a few years later that the Harry Potter franchise would be worth many hundreds of millions of dollars to Bloomsbury, the company's share price more than doubled.

Why did Cunningham buy a lottery ticket when no one else did? The children's division at Bloomsbury was quite new. Cunningham was still trying to fill out his catalog. He had been in publishing long enough to know that in an annual list of a dozen or so new books, each new title didn't have to be a success. But all of them needed to have a prospect of succeeding. Sometimes, if each title aimed for a different home in the marketplace, the odds would be better that something in the overall portfolio would succeed.

So while other editors were looking for ways to say no, Cunningham was looking for ways to say yes. That opened the way for him to do what's often the wisest, rarest, and least dramatic thing in such a situation: to take a small step forward amid massive uncertainty. As Cunningham recounted to one interviewer, "I read it (the first Harry Potter manuscript), and really the sky didn't part and the lightning didn't come down, but I just really liked it."

Often, the most fruitful chances are taken by little-known editors at little-known publishing houses. They have less to lose and more time to explore. Lacking access to the pipeline of proven bestselling authors, they are compelled to experiment more. And they may be less inclined to turn up their noses at something different. The lessons of the previous chapter hold true here, too. Being snide can be a huge mistake. Being able to ask "What can go right?" is the crucial first step toward opening new pathways to success.

In 2004, Ian Malcolm was in his sixth year as philosophy editor at Princeton University Press. He had acquired about a hundred titles for PUP, chiefly scholarly works such as *Kierkegaard's Concept of Despair*, and *Wittgenstein on the Arbitrariness of Grammar*. Such books sold . . . about as one might expect. They were pillars of thought in a good university library; they didn't find much readership elsewhere. Meanwhile, in his browsing time, Malcolm had come across an odd essay by Princeton philosophy professor Harry Frankfurt. It was called *On Bullshit*.

The essay enchanted Malcolm. It was enjoying weird, underground distribution among academics, almost like Russian dissidents' samizdat literature in the 1970s. Frankfurt, at age seventy-five, had a lot to say about why people fake their way through situations, why society tolerates such nonsense, and why that is harmful. What's more, Frankfurt employed a vexed, bombastic tone that was screamingly funny at times. Many of Malcolm's contacts knew the essay and loved it. No one had ever proposed turning the screed into a full-fledged book.

Malcolm decided to become *Bullshit*'s champion. So what if the title was profane? So what if Princeton hadn't ever published anything remotely similar as a standalone book? So what if the essay was so brief that even the fluffiest approach to typesetting couldn't stretch the book beyond eighty pages? Malcolm guessed that the tract could become a quirky but appealing addition to the university press's catalogue anyway. He began marshaling academic support. Some leading philosophers warmed to the idea of publishing *On Bullshit*. So did Bill Jordan, the former chair of PUP. Malcolm coaxed them all into writing formal reports. He brought their testimonials to a board meeting of Princeton's press and won formal approval for his idea. Frankfurt would get a modest, $3,000 advance, reflecting a 5,000-copy first printing. Malcolm hoped it might eventually sell 20,000 copies.

The book promptly spent more than five months on *The New York Times*' bestseller list. It sold 390,000 copies in hardback in its first year. *On Bullshit* became one of the Princeton press's most popular books of all time. And Malcolm—who until that point had been regarded as one of the most obscure editors in all of publishing—started getting phone calls from outfits such as *The Washington Post*, which wanted to chronicle his role in launching one of the year's blockbusters.

Six years later, Malcolm was still puzzling over what lessons (if any) could be drawn from the project's runaway success. Within Princeton's press, publishing an eighty-page book stopped being seen as absurd. While academics might regard books as infinitely expandable suitcases that can hold every scrap of imaginable knowledge on a subject, their editors didn't always need to agree. Sometimes it takes courage to write (and publish) an extremely short book. Princeton stepped up its experiments with miniature books, often with good results.

Beyond that, *On Bullshit* came to be seen as a one-of-a-kind triumph. Frankfurt tried to follow up with a more somber book called *On Truth,* which didn't sell nearly as well, despite being well regarded by reviewers. A handful of authors tried to talk Princeton's editors into publishing more books with foul-mouthed titles, only to be shooed away. Future editors at Princeton might champion projects with a different sort of offbeat appeal, in an informal salute to Malcolm's daring. No one was hunting for an obvious follow-on.

"It's tough to duplicate any freakish success that relies in part on novelty," Malcolm explained to me. "You can't do something for the first time twice."

In entertainment and the performing arts, the struggle to find lasting successes amid constantly changing public taste is especially intense. There's proof every year in the "stiff ratio," the percentage of new music releases that fail to sell enough copies to warrant labels' advance payments to artists. Estimates are that 80 percent of albums and 85 percent of singles come up short. That makes book publishing's failure rate of 70 percent seem outright soothing.

"All hits are flukes," the sociologists William and Denise Bielby famously declared in 1994. They were writing about the troubles that network television executives faced in coming up with popular prime-time series. They could just as easily have been writing about pop music, Broadway theater, or stand-up comedy. Sticking to familiar genres sometimes reduces the risks; banking on stars or writers with strong reputations can help, too. But no one then or now has found a formula that worked every time.

When music executives try to fight the public's fickle tastes, disaster often ensues. In 1999, MCA Music began a doomed, heroic effort to get people excited about an Irish singer, Carly Hennessy. The label ultimately spent $2.2 million on her debut album, hiring two producers, a series of musicians, and spending $100,000 on "imaging" for her, such as clothes, photos, and makeup sessions. The result: an album that sold just 378 copies in stores in its first few months, according to reporter Jennifer Ordoñez, who chronicled the snafu for *The Wall Street Journal*.

I spent some time chatting with John Hart, the head of Bullseye Marketing Research in Nashville, about what country music audiences want. His data sheds light on some aspects of public taste. Female listeners often like low, throbbing bass tones. Ballads do best in the autumn. Up-tempo songs thrive in the spring but lose their appeal quickly. Male tastes are hard to peg. "Mostly," he says, "guys don't like anything."

"If radio stations really wanted to be safe," Hart told me, "they should stop playing any new songs. It's too hard to guess what will be a hit." That's a cynical perspective, he concedes. His approach couldn't really work if everyone tried it. The avenues for new music to be introduced would vanish. But his basic point is serious: anyone who tries to define the next round of music tastes is stepping into a world that is both exciting and very risky.

From childhood onward, Scott Borchetta saw only the excitement. In the 1960s his father, Mike, was a record promotion executive for Capitol Records, Mercury Records, and RCA on the West Coast. As a toddler, Scott jumped up and down on the backseat of his mother's 1964 Volkswagen Beetle, singing along to the Rolling Stones' "Satisfaction." As a teenager, he saved up his money to see Kiss and Led Zeppelin. He collected autographs from the Monkees and Bobby Womack. There wasn't the least bit of discrimination to his tastes. He liked everything.

His parents divorced and father Mike moved to Nashville in 1979. The younger Borchetta came to visit in the summer of 1981 and quickly made Nashville his new home. After a brief stint working in the mailroom of his father's promotion company, Scott Borchetta got a job handling promotion for MTM Music, a label set up by Mary Tyler Moore. Photos from the day show him as a hipster with intense brown eyes and ringlets of curly black hair coming down to his shoulders. He played bass and guitar in local bands and had dreams of making it himself as a musician, a hope that slowly faded.

Borchetta was impatient then, sometimes too much so. He barely said hello to the part-time receptionist at MTM Music, a quiet college student named Trisha Yearwood. A decade later, she became one of country music's biggest stars. Borchetta had worked alongside her for months and never even knew she liked to sing. From that awkward gaffe, Borchetta told me, he took away a lifelong lesson: "Talent can be anywhere."

During the 1990s, working on radio promotion for Nashville's largest labels, Borchetta embraced what he believed was a second essential truth about the music business. Most of the recording companies were run by executives who had started as music producers. They cared most about how an artist sounded in the studio. Not Borchetta. As he saw it, Nashville was full of artists who could cut a good record. What differentiated the stars from the hangers-on, he believed, was whether performers thrived on the road—or fell apart.

Some artists lost their way once fame swept into their lives. They made the wrong friends; they didn't know who to trust; they came to hate touring because it was too lonely and too draining. Once they got stuck in one of those downward spirals, they couldn't connect with fans anymore. Their music stopped selling. For others, it was just the opposite. They loved getting out, meeting existing fans—and making new ones. Even if they weren't well known at the start of a road trip, they won people over with ebullient personalities. Radiostation programmers liked to see them. Hotel clerks did, too. They created an aura of success around themselves that was self-fulfilling. Those were the people Borchetta wanted to sign.

So in the course of getting to know each of his new artists, Borchetta pressed for answers to two deceptively simple questions: "Who are you?" and "What do you stand for?" Almost any answer, delivered with enough conviction, was fine. Borchetta knew how to promote jokers, prophets, mourners, temptresses, wise uncles, and wayward nephews. As long as a performer knew his or her central message, Borchetta could convince the folks at scores of major-market country stations to grant that artist enough airplay to have a decent chance of ringing up a big hit.

Trying to pick winners in music might be a perilous business, but at least Borchetta felt he was buying the right sorts of lottery tickets.

Borchetta started with especially high hopes for Jack Ingram, a Brad Pitt lookalike from The Woodlands, a Houston suburb. Ingram had been rattling around the Texas club scene since the late 1980s, singing about stuck-up women and the pleasurable side of arson. (In "Mustang Burn," a male quarrel ends up with one guy's car ablaze.) Over the years, Ingram had built up a cult following among angry young men. Big-time success kept eluding him.

"I was tired of having hits that weren't really hits," Ingram told me. He wanted to be at the top of *Billboard*'s charts. He was ready to do whatever it took to get there.

Borchetta had a plan. Ingram could be repositioned as a gentle ballad singer, targeted toward the melancholy moms who were country songs' most dependable buyers. Ingram's flair for writing or cowriting his own edgy lyrics would be put on the shelf. Instead, romance-minded songwriters would supply him with suitable creations. Jack Ingram would be relaunched with "Wherever You Are," a tender song in which an errant man pleads for "one more last chance." With luck, Borchetta believed, the song could go top ten—or maybe even number one.

Ingram was game to try. He released the song in late 2005, and then hit the road in early 2006 to promote it, mixing concert stops and radio interviews around the clock. "I'd come back to the hotel at two A.M.," Ingram told me. "Then we'd get up at four A.M. to go make calls to any radio station in the country that would let us do an interview during drive time. We'd work the phones for hours and then drive to the next town and do it again." In late April 2006, it all paid off. Ingram got word that his song was at the very top of *Billboard*'s Hot Country list for the next week. He was driving, alone, on a Texas highway and nearly had to pull over to collect himself, his emotions were so intense. A year later, Ingram was named Top New Male Artist by the Academy of Country Music.

Unfortunately, Borchetta and Ingram couldn't figure out how to build on that success. Ingram's next album, *Big Dreams and High Hopes*, aimed for the same audience, but reviewers thought it sounded forced. One critic called it "a commercial disappointment and not quite an artistic triumph—the work of an intriguing artist caught betwixt and between." A ballad called "Seeing Stars" only made it to number fifty-four on the *Billboard* country charts. Overall the album peaked at number twenty-one.

Danielle Peck, an alluring brunette from rural Ohio, was supposed to be Big Machine's top female prospect. When Borchetta's talent hunt began, she was dabbling at songwriting and paying the bills by waitressing at Virago, an upscale sushi restaurant. Borchetta was one of her customers. On a lark, he asked her to sing a big hit from a few years earlier: "Heads Carolina, Tails California." She belted it out, right there at the table. He liked it enough to invite her to a proper audition. When that went well, she came away with her first recording contract.

Borchetta guided Peck to what they both hoped would be a spectacular debut. In December 2005, she launched "I Don't," a wistful single about romance gone cold, followed up two months later with "Findin' a Good Man," a sassy denunciation of cheating boyfriends. Big Machine helped her assemble very smooth music videos for both, showing off her glamorous features. Her voice was strong; her lyrics were catchy. Somehow, though, her sound just wasn't quite what America wanted to hear. Her first album made it only to number twenty-three on *Billboard*'s charts, and a second one, released in digital-only format at the end of 2008, never made the charts at all.

The winning ticket turned out to be the unknown teen, Taylor Swift. When Borchetta first met her she had a songwriting contract with Sony/ATV, which turned into a thriving partnership with experienced lyricist Liz Rose. Swift also had an "artist development" contract with RCA, which wasn't nearly as satisfying. RCA at the time was paying her $15,000 a year. She had completed one year under the contract and was being offered a renewal on the same terms. It wasn't clear to the Swift family that much "development" was actually happening. RCA seemed content to let her accumulate some more birthdays before trying to launch her on tour or in the studio. "They weren't going to say yes to anything until she was nineteen or twenty," her father, Scott Swift, told me.

Borchetta was ready to move faster. During his first meeting with Taylor Swift, she played a song she and Rose had written about a teenage couple breaking up. The opening lines painted a picture of a romance gone sour and a boyfriend ready to disparage his former sweetheart. A moment later, Swift lashed back with all the taunts she was ready to hurl at him: mocking his manhood and poking fun of his truck.

Borchetta chuckled with delight. He hadn't seen that one coming. The song was brave, scared, petulant, and funny—all at the same time. It was everything that made high school so intense and unforgettable for teenagers. Adult songwriters couldn't convey that anymore. For them, the moment had passed. This girl was capturing it all. Even though conventional wisdom in Nashville was that labels almost always regretted signing a teenage singer, Borchetta was ready to break the rule. He wasn't sure yet what Taylor Swift would amount to, but he was willing to find out.

Once Big Machine got started, Borchetta began calling up Tennessee radio stations to see if their programmers wanted to meet Swift. She didn't have an album yet. There wasn't any reason to expect they would put her on the air. Still, Borchetta thought it would be a useful, low-key way to build relationships. So one Monday afternoon, Borchetta and Swift arrived in Knoxville, Tennessee, at the offices of WIVK. The program director politely escorted the two inside the station, and they settled in his office for what was supposed to be a quick visit. She played one of her songs.

"That's very nice," the program director said, ready to escort out his visitors.

"Thank you!" Swift replied. "Can I go on the air and play it right now for your listeners, too?"

The manager was powerless to resist. And Borchetta—who now tells the story with great glee—was grinning at the scene. Here was an artist with a pitch-perfect sense of how to win friends on the road. She was going to do just fine.

In February 2009, when I visited Borchetta in Nashville, we spent part of an afternoon in a cavernous recording studio on the outskirts of Nashville, where Taylor Swift and another teen star, Miley Cyrus, were rehearsing a duet that they would perform at the Grammy Awards a few days later. Between takes, Cyrus provided earthy, hilarious commentary on whatever topic crossed her mind. Her monologues touched on what to do about creepy boys on the Internet . . . whether it's wise to shave your arms . . . and what the Houston rodeo smells like. Most of us giggled like schoolboys at each new digression.

Swift smiled a time or two. But what Swift really wanted to know, during the breaks, was how to put on the best possible concert at the Houston rodeo. She would be performing there in the spring for the first time. Some 75,000 people would be in attendance. Cyrus had played there before. So during the breaks, Swift wanted to know the answers to questions like: *When can you set up your band? Does the stage rotate? How long are the sets?* For Taylor Swift, fame meant an obligation to get even better.

Talking with Borchetta at the end of the day, it became clear he could thrive for years by focusing strictly on Taylor Swift's career. Yet his horizons stretched much further. Over the next year or so, he planned to build up a second label that he had created, Valory Music, which was already the new home of country legend Reba McEntire. A third label (Republic Nashville) might follow later. There was room to add more artists for Big Machine, and perhaps a need to wrap up some contracts that weren't working out, so that more slots could be opened for new acts.

Around dinnertime, a music scouting specialist, Allison Jones, came into Borchetta's office with a dozen or so MP3 files of artists that might want to join Big Machine's stable. For the next hour, the two of them listened to track after track. If the new songs were the least bit appealing, Borchetta pushed back his leather armchair, pressed his fingers together, and closed his eyes. Then he began to smile. There would be time, later, to worry about whether that particular artist belonged at Big Machine. For the moment, Borchetta wanted only to discover the best in each performer.

He was in the mood to buy some more lottery tickets.

9: Talent That Shouts

Decades after they scrubbed together, surgeons across the country still hear John Cameron's voice in the operating room. Dr. Cameron is in his seventies now, yet the mentor's impact lingers. At some of America's finest hospitals—including the Mayo Clinic in Rochester, Minnesota, and Brigham and Women's in Boston—when surgeons get to work, it's as if they were back in Baltimore, finishing their training while their former chief stands beside them. Nothing the younger surgeons are doing is good enough. The testy, silver-haired boss is demanding perfection.

His voice begins gently. It is the cadence of a patient teacher, sharing maxims and anecdotes. Everything is delivered at a smooth pace that is just right for full, first-time comprehension. Dr. Cameron wants you to learn. Yet every few minutes, there's something odd that he wants to single out. Now the pitch rises. The frequency of words slows down. Dr. Cameron lingers on a single word with incredulity. A puzzled, mocking tone takes hold. The great teacher has come across something that makes utterly no sense. Now he wants you to realize how wrong-headed this is. Even before you can absorb the reasons he will share, he wants you to shudder at this bad practice.

Should you forget for a moment to clamp off a blood vessel, Dr. Cameron's high-pitched whine will assault your ears. *"Jeez, Mike, every surgeon in North America . . . knows . . . better . . . than to do that."* Start working around the incision and the voice keeps reminding you to handle the patient's tissues as delicately as possible. Make a single awkward move, and the voice will snap: *"Wooden hands!"* Teeter on the edge of a difficult decision, and the voice arrives for a third time, more combative than ever. *"If you were going to do that, why didn't you just throw the patient down the elevator shaft?"*

Yet when the operation is over, Dr. Cameron's voice is gentle again. *"You did a good job,"* the voice says. *"I hope you don't mind me yelling. Yelling makes me feel better."*

For twenty years, Dr. Cameron ran what amounted to an extraordinary boot camp for America's most ambitious surgeons. Starting in 1984, his general surgery department accepted about thirty young doctors a year as Hopkins trainees. All of them had been winning competitions their entire lives. They were academic standouts in high school, college, and medical school. Many had worked part-time in top research labs; some had been standout athletes, too. Each beat out fifteen or more rivals to win a place at Hopkins. They represented talent that shouts.

Those aren't easy people to manage—and they can be even harder to assess. What seems like bountiful, overflowing talent can turn into a minefield of petulance, frustration, and selfishness. Many organizations suffer their worst setbacks when dealing with "can't miss" talent. The best strategies involve a tough-love approach, as epitomized by Dr. Cameron's marathon training programs. He bombarded young doctors with fierce challenges and lofty goals. As each round of apprenticeships played out, Dr. Cameron could see who the true winners were. The result: an extraordinary crop of future medical leaders, and a talent-grooming system that ought to be an archetype.

If there was a better surgery department in the world than Hopkins, Dr. Cameron didn't believe it. Once, when a prospective patient broached the idea of going elsewhere for a second opinion,

Dr. Cameron shot back: "Here's your second opinion! If you want a second-rate operation done by a second-rate surgeon at a second-rate institution, you are out of your mind! If you want it done right, you come here to Hopkins." The patient stayed.

Protégés were expected to pick up that swagger, but also to see themselves as part of an unbroken line of pioneers that dated back more than a century. So in the midst of operations, Dr. Cameron told stories to his disciples. They learned about long-dead doctors and about pioneering operations of the 1930s. They learned a great deal about Dr. Cameron's hero, William S. Halsted, who founded Hopkins's surgery department in 1889.* As young doctors absorbed Dr. Cameron's version of the past, they became conscripted to his view of their destiny. Great surgeons put in long hours and didn't complain. They became their own toughest critics. Their highest goals shouldn't involve big paychecks and fast sports cars. Their calling was to stretch the frontiers of surgery in ways that could benefit patients worldwide.

One of Dr. Cameron's most important protégés was an intense, black-haired young doctor from New York named Rob Udelsman. He arrived at Hopkins in the early 1980s, at age twenty-six, bearing a résumé that radiated success. Udelsman had been the top student in his class at George Washington Medical School, out of 150 students. He had been publishing his lab results in medical journals since his junior year of college. Udelsman was proud but polite. He epitomized talent that shouts.

Dr. Cameron toughened up the newcomer right away. One evening, a patient wasn't doing well after surgery. Most doctors had

---

* Halsted's name still pops up in medical textbooks as the father of Halsted's law, Halsted's sign, and Halsted's suture. He pioneered the use of sterile gloves in the operating room. He also won acclaim for developing radical mastectomies as a way of fighting breast cancer. There was another side to Halsted: his long-running struggles to shake a morphine and cocaine habit acquired through some ill-advised experiments in his youth. Modern biographers have documented the surgeon's private turmoil in fascinating detail. Dr. Cameron was less inclined to share those stories.

gone home, including interns such as Udelsman, who were supposed to coordinate nighttime care as needed. When a nurse phoned Udelsman at home, seeking advice, the trainee wanted his boss's counsel on what to do. Reaching Dr. Cameron at home, too, Udelsman started to describe the problem, when the older doctor interrupted.

"Where are you?" Dr. Cameron demanded.

"At home," Udelsman replied.

"You're not at the bedside," Dr. Cameron shot back. "If you aren't in the hospital, I'd rather talk to the nurse than you." The next thing Udelsman heard was a dial tone. Dr. Cameron had hung up on him. Udelsman was angry and embarrassed. In the fiercely hierarchical world of teaching hospitals, it was as if Dr. Cameron had just yanked off the short white coat identifying Udelsman as one of the hospital's newest and least experienced doctors. If Udelsman couldn't muster the energy for a bedside update, no matter how weary he was, he didn't deserve to talk to the boss.

Some interns quit after a few such humiliations. Udelsman didn't. He drove back to the hospital, helped stabilize the patient, and vowed never again to be compromised like that, no matter how tired he might be. Before long, Udelsman became a full-fledged resident at Hopkins, entitled to wear the long white coat that signified "real" doctors. Then he rose to be chief resident, telling younger trainees how to survive in Dr. Cameron's surgery department. "There are three things that Dr. Cameron can't stand," Dr. Udelsman later summarized for me. "They are laziness, stupidity, and dishonesty." Of the three, laziness was the worst.

Dr. Cameron liked this disciple's progress. Dr. Udelsman's surgical judgment was excellent; his dedication flawless. His emerging interest in thyroid tumors suggested great promise. So in the spring of 1988, Dr. Cameron tabbed Dr. Udelsman to be the hospital's next Halsted Resident. That one-year job was akin to becoming a Supreme Court clerk or a White House fellow. It paid just $40,000 a year, but it meant being groomed for greatness. At age thirty-two or so, Halsted Residents were like junior faculty members. They led clinics; they ran meetings; they made hundreds of life-and-death decisions on emergency cases. Halsted Residents typically became star professors at Hopkins; later they often were recruited to take charge of some other university's entire surgery department.

When Dr. Cameron summoned Dr. Udelsman to hear the good news, a rude shock awaited. Dr. Udelsman didn't want to be the Halsted Resident. It was a fine honor, he told his boss. But he had other plans. The National Institutes of Health in Bethesda, Maryland, was offering him a senior investigator's position. He had already expressed interest in it. In a few months, Dr. Udelsman indicated, he planned to pack up his belongings and leave Hopkins behind.

Dr. Cameron was stunned. "You belong at Hopkins," he told Dr. Udelsman. The younger doctor didn't budge.

Unwilling to lose the argument, Dr. Cameron asked his protégé to walk through the hospital with him. They paused in front of a musty chamber near Dr. Cameron's own office. It was an informal museum of Halsted's life. As they stepped inside, they could see a bronze bust on the left, showing the nineteenth-century pioneer at his sternest. On the right, the great man's roll-top desk, medical books, and pipe were preserved as if he had stepped away a few hours ago. Even an ancient surgical glove had been turned into a relic, preserved inside a Lucite block.

"Dr. Cameron kept saying: 'This is where Halsted worked,'" Dr. Udelsman told me. "'This is where other great doctors worked. Rob, it's the only place for you.' Dr. Cameron kept talking about the way that we all build off our predecessors, and how there was this one-hundred-year heritage at Hopkins."

Hammering home his message, Dr. Cameron brought over Halsted's cane for Udelsman to hold. After that, Dr. Cameron handed him Halsted's top hat. The emotional impact of the Hopkins legacy was overwhelming. "I lasted for half an hour," Dr. Udelsman later confided. "Finally I gave in. I had every intention of going to NIH. But John can be very persuasive. I got up and made a very difficult call to the man who would have been my boss at the NIH."

Dr. Udelsman ended up staying another thirteen years at Hopkins. He became an expert on thyroid surgery, and one of the school's best-known professors. In 2001, Dr. Udelsman left for Yale, where he became surgeon in chief of the Yale–New Haven Hospital. Soon afterward, he was elected president of the American Association of Endocrine Surgeons and subsequently president of the International Association of Endocrine Surgeons. When Dr. Cameron retired as chair of Hopkins's surgery department in 2003, he cited the successes of younger doctors such as Dr. Udelsman as some of his proudest achievements.

For bosses like John Cameron, it's not enough to discover talent that shouts. That much is easy. The great challenges come later, once such people are on the payroll. That is when everything hinges on an ability to make the most of such people's wide-ranging ambitions and restless spirits. If top performers don't feel tied into the organization that hires them, all their marvelous potential may be useless. Their careers may be marked by quarrels, betrayals, squandered opportunities, and repeated job-hopping in moments of anger.

In extreme cases, organizations decide it isn't worth accommodating such high-intensity turmoil. No matter how brightly a star might shine before a hiring decision is made, everything can blow up once a contract is signed. If events don't play out as planned, talent that shouts can turn impatient, selfish, or frustrated. After too many such failures, some leaders retreat. They would rather surround themselves with amiable plodders than tangle again with the unruly side of talent.

Fortunately, there's a way around this agony. Top teaching hospitals like Hopkins are a fine place to look for clues. So are elite military units. These organizations don't flinch at filling their ranks with ambitious personalities. That's because they know how to get everyone pulling together toward shared goals, rather than ending up with a quarrelsome bunch of prima donnas. Step into the corporate world, and similar triumphs exist as well. None of these organizations equates talent and treachery. Instead, they are the world's best snake charmers, if you will, figuring out how to get the most out of high achievers without being led astray.

What's the key insight? These benchmark organizations hardly ever coddle their stars. Instead, they set huge goals and run the hardest auditions. They hurl their best candidates through drawn-out tests of valor that may last for years. They have the audacity to portray hardship and possible failure as selling points for their jobs, rather than as liabilities. Run-of-the-mill candidates don't want any part of this. For exceptionally talented souls, however, such long-running gauntlets are thrilling and addictive. Such people are defined by what dancer Martha Graham once called "divine dissatisfaction: a blessed unrest that keeps us marching and makes us more alive than others."

One of the mysteries that this book set out to explore involves the reasons why some organizations fare so well with talent that shouts, while others lurch from calamity to calamity. This time, the answers go beyond the fine-grain details of how to find talent that other people miss. The next three chapters will show how to reconcile an organization's needs and a star's ambitions, when to realize that it's not going to work, and how to make wise choices in some of the hardest hunts of all: looking for chief executives.

The central ideas of these three chapters are as follows:

Talent wants to be challenged, not coddled. Even the nicest perks and bonuses don't buy lasting loyalty if they aren't accompanied by a chance to do great work. High achievers' desire to make a mark in the world is so intense that it usually trumps every other motivator. Talent-rich organizations know this. They cater to people who are always looking for harder challenges, bigger arenas, and greater mastery. Often this takes the form of endless tests of valor, almost like a medieval quest. This chapter will show how organizations such as Pixar and General Electric harness this competitive dynamic to their advantage. (Army Special Forces, Facebook, and Teach For America will make brief return visits, too.) A crucial part of these winners' edge comes from doing exactly what John Cameron did with the Halsted cult: instilling a belief in his best prospects that they aren't just in it for themselves; they are part of an enduring and ennobling movement.

Great talent is no substitute for the right talent. Glistening résumés have been caught up in some of the bitterest leadership failures. A brilliant Cabinet secretary stumbles as a university president. An All-American college quarterback can't make it in the pros. A famous entrepreneur plunges his second start-up into bankruptcy. Chapter 10 will explain what goes wrong in such situations, and how to avoid similar hiring catastrophes. The key insight: the more prominent a talent hunt may be, the easier it is for selectors to lose track of what they really need. Candidates' prestige, social affinity, and other factors become huge distractions. Assessors focus on what's easy or gratifying to evaluate, not what is important. Only afterward is it clear how much got overlooked in the stampede to make a decision that looked good.

Sometimes, even CEOs' résumés need to be read upside down. The moment-by-moment virtues of resilience, efficiency, and consistency that opened this book don't just matter for soldiers and teachers. Such time-honored traits can be crucial at the top of an organization, too. Ironically, of all the talent hunts going on in America at any given time, the searches for CEOs are most likely to become caught up the mismatches of chapter 10. Directors and their advisers are trying so hard to come up with someone heroic that they lose sight of the many small capabilities that add up to greatness. The best ways of avoiding this trap involve radical new ways of taking stock of candidates, looking for patterns of conduct that often are hidden in plain sight.

Ask anyone in the movie industry about "talent that shouts," and the name Brad Bird will enter the conversation within seconds. His enormous abilities as an animator and director—coupled with his exasperating personality—left a long string of bosses seething for decades until Bird finally found his rightful home. Growing up in Oregon, Bird began sending work samples to Disney at age fourteen. Older animators were awed. Milt Kahl, one of Walt Disney's pioneering animators known as the "nine old men," befriended Bird in high school. Bird went to college on a Disney scholarship. He started working for the big studio in 1979. Bird lasted less than two years. His strident insistence on doing things his way, or not at all, made it impossible for Disney to keep him.

After that, Bird animated some of *The Simpsons* television episodes. People loved his work, but they didn't love Bird. He rattled through a series of other employers. In the late 1990s, he directed *The Iron Giant*, a full-length, computer-animated movie about a boy's friendship with a doomed robot. Warner Brothers, which produced the movie, implored him to add some pets and sidekicks that could generate merchandise tie-ins. Bird refused. Financially, *The Iron Giant* proved to be a flop. It cost $48 million to make and took in just $23 million in box office revenue.

Bird didn't flinch. If the public wasn't rushing to see his film, maybe it meant he was ahead of his time. As he told salon.com in 2000, "I was, and am, willing to look foolish in an attempt to get you to feel something."

In late 2000, Bird was out of work, again. Executives at Pixar Inc. invited him to pitch his next idea. This time, in a departure from everything Bird had heard from movie studios before, the Pixar executives encouraged him to be daring. They already knew how to make cute movies with animated toys and animals. They didn't want to confine themselves to endless knockoffs of *Toy Story* and *A Bug's Life*. When Bird sketched out a story about aging superheroes in a witness-protection program, Pixar gave him a green light to make *The Incredibles*, with immense artistic control and a bigger budget than he had ever enjoyed before.

Pixar executives knew how to handle talented, edgy people. The company's president, Ed Catmull, was part of the amazing cluster of free-spirited computer graphics pioneers who trained at the University of Utah under David Evans. The company's chief creative officer, John Lasseter, had worked briefly at Disney early in his career and had been fired, too. "Our philosophy is: You get great creative people, you bet big on them, you give them enormous leeway and support, and you provide them with an environment in which they can get honest feedback from everyone," Catmull explained in a 2008 *Harvard Business Review* article.

Bird fit the bill. "He has no patience for people willing to compromise," Lasseter told a newspaper reporter. "He used to work at studios where executives didn't understand him. They felt they couldn't 'control' him. It was like having the most amazing racehorse strapped to a plow. We unhooked him from the plow and gave him this huge meadow to run in."

Simultaneously, though, Pixar asked a lot from Bird. *The Incredibles* would be animated with a degree of three-dimensional reality that computer-generated movies hadn't tried before. Bird didn't know that technology well. He would have to learn it. Instead of getting angry all the time about other people's failings, Bird would need to stretch his own skills to make the movie succeed. During the movie's four-year development, Bird would enjoy all the "divine dissatisfaction" that he could stand.

The gamble paid off. *The Incredibles* grossed $624 million

worldwide at the box office, making it one of the top fifty movies of all time. It won two Oscars. Its success led Pixar to sign up Bird to direct *Ratatouille* and *Toy Story 3*, both of which proved to be huge successes as well. Lots of interviewers flattered Bird after his movies' success, and he deflected their praise in ways that were sometimes graceful, sometimes awkward.

Bird's keenest memories involved the moments he stared down failure—and won. On *Ratatouille* especially, he wrestled with a disjointed script, an absurdly tight set of deadlines, and the challenges of making an animated Paris look old. There was a brilliant premise at the center of *Ratatouille*, and he wasn't sure he could draw it out. Pixar's projects were pushing him harder than anything he had ever done before. That was what he craved. "It was like driving down the freeway the wrong way, just trying to live," Bird told one interviewer. "My heart is still racing from it."

In elite military units like Army Special Forces, similar challenges never stop. Soldiers who make it through the three-week selection course are rewarded with . . . a new gauntlet that runs at least a year. Once trainees are chosen, they return to the North Carolina pinelands for advanced training in foreign languages and cultures as well as lessons in how to fire machine guns, set land mines, perform ambushes, and negotiate with tribal leaders. Failure is never far away.

Soldiers who get sloppy with firearms safety are pulled aside and quietly counseled. If they make the same mistake again, there won't be any more training. Such soldiers are shunted back to the regular army without a word to the rest of the trainees. They know what happened. Attrition during the full training program can be as high as 50 percent. In Special Forces, the stresses of selection never end. For the soldiers who prevail, there's undeniable pride in withstanding tests that others couldn't handle.

Author Dick Couch, who followed a full cycle of training, wrote about one sergeant who told trainees after a hellish week of rainy nighttime exercises: "On deployment, you will get less sleep, be colder, carry more, do more—and you know what? You'll have a hell of a lot of fun doing it. . . . This is the best organization in the Army—in the world. So when it gets cold and you're hurting, drive on."

One of the most intriguing soldiers I met at Camp Mackall was Dazerell Fleming, a ten-year veteran of Special Forces. He was a tall, skinny African American man with pianist's fingers. He looked too flimsy to last long. But appearances deceived. He had endless stamina on marches, as well as startling, wiry strength. He had mastered radio signaling and the Thai language. He was an extremely effective member of Special Forces teams that helped Thai drug-enforcement teams patrol their northern borders. I asked him how he came to join Special Forces.

"I was in the Army Rangers for a while," he said. "All these other guys in my unit kept trying to get into Special Forces. None of them made it. Seven or eight of them came back from selection, having failed. So I went to my commander and said: 'I'm going to give Special Forces a try, too.' They didn't expect me to do it. But I said, 'I want to see what it's like to quit.'"

I stared at him. There was just the faintest trace of a smile. We both nodded. He wasn't a quitter. He knew it back then, too. When he came to Camp Mackall the first time, it was because he believed he could absorb everything this elite Army outfit could throw at him, including a thirty-hour solo march at the end. If others couldn't handle it, too bad. He could.

Even in supposedly cushy Silicon Valley, there's nothing like a round-the-clock battle against the demons of failure. At companies such as Facebook, LinkedIn, Lonely Planet, and Atlassian, dozens of engineers set aside their ordinary duties for a day. Instead, they form tiny teams and race to complete a new software project, from start to finish, before the next sunrise. When they do so, they are taking part in a computer-hacking marathon, or "hackathon."

For the best engineers, hackathons are addictive. When I ask why, engineers say it's partly for the camaraderie, but mostly because the challenge is so intense. The allotted time is absurdly short. There's no guidance; no supervision. All the careful and sometimes burdensome routines of corporate projects are stripped away. Each project's destiny is on its own. All that matters is how nimbly team members can fit everything together. Brainstorming at 10:30 P.M. may need to be followed by radical overhauls at 1 A.M., a frenzy of programming, a few minutes of debugging—and then either triumph or failure at daybreak.

"Hell yeah, I want to hack," one Facebook engineer, Bob Trahan, declared on a company bulletin board, hours before a hackathon began. Colleagues chimed in with jaunty comments about "sniffing packets." Within Facebook, it was common knowledge that some of the social network's catchiest features (such as chat and friend finder) came to life this way. The engineers who created those programs walked through the hallways a little differently; among their peers, they became seen as unusually gifted coders. Everyone accepted that many projects would fail, and that no one got paid extra for all this late-night work. Being part of an all-night hackathon was worth it anyway. It was a chance to prove one's mettle.

Can big, mainstream companies harness this spirit of "extreme auditions"—which proves so valuable for maverick outfits like Army Special Forces and Facebook? Often, the answer is no. In corporate settings, most leadership development programs stretch participants a bit, but not too much. Dropout rates are low, by design. Companies run such programs with the goal of creating many dozens of promotable executives, rather than staging all-out tests of valor that elicit extraordinary efforts from everyone left standing at the end.

There's one prominent exception, though.

At General Electric, 140 of the company's rising stars are drawn into an elite auditing/consulting program each year. They are dispatched on four-month projects across the globe, switching from one focus to another. One job might involve equipment leasing in Brazil; the next, insurance accounting in Hong Kong; the third, trade finance in Utah. It's not enough to get the numbers right; participants need to figure out local cultures and make business allies in a hurry so that their recommendations won't be ignored. Work often starts at 7 A.M. It may not finish until 11 P.M. Weekend work is required.

The program starts with a two-year stint as a roving auditor. For many participants, that is enough. Upon graduation they head back to a GE operating business and a solid career. For an elite cadre, though, the fast track beckons. They spend another one to three years as top guns on what is known as the Corporate Audit Staff (CAS). Throughout this time, they do not have a permanent home address. Working for GE this way means living in a series of hotels or extended-stay apartments. "You commit to travel one hundred percent of the time," says Peter Mondani, a GE senior executive who oversees the human resources side of CAS.

People who prevail through the entire five-year CAS program are likely to rise to the highest levels of GE's hierarchy. That's partly because they are bright, hardworking people getting superb training. But it's also because the program's whirlwind pace and constant travel amounts to a multiyear immersion into the GE way of life. Participants find that other CAS members have become their best friends. The road-warrior life stops seeming odd. Survivors of the CAS program may decide there isn't anywhere else except GE they want to work.

Does a showcase program like GE's amount to a well-crafted way of identifying underlying talent? Or is it primarily a leadership program, focusing on specific skills? Or is it an exercise in inspiring people (or indoctrinating them), until their psyches are most attuned to the company's needs?

The GE program is all three at once. The payoff for GE may come years later, when the corporate culture calls for rocketing some of the company's brightest hopes through a series of quick-stop promotions that will provide broad exposure to different industries. Executives who can withstand the geographic relocations associated with that career phase will emerge as GE's highest leaders. Not many people care for such upheaval. It's hard to sell the spouse and kids on relocating to, say, Erie, Pennsylvania, so that the next GE legend can spend a couple years helping to run the locomotive business, before she or he moves on to the next promotion. After putting people through the rigors of the corporate-audit program, however, GE's leaders know where to turn. The hard-nosed leadership program pinpoints candidates with the talent, skill—and adaptability—to make the jump.

It's noteworthy, too, that GE does not pay especially lavish salaries to its rising executives. For a time, GE's steadily climbing stock price sweetened the value of overall compensation packages (including stock options). By and large, though, GE counts on its most ambitious performers to feel a tie to the company that goes beyond dollars. They may like GE's global reach, its stability, its straightforward, results-oriented culture, or the fact that most of their friends work there. Whatever the reason, GE keeps standout talent close by tapping into ambitions that go beyond collecting the next paycheck.

In the nonprofit world, being part of a cause is even more crucial. Talent flocks to organizations that can sustain a strong sense of purpose. Meanwhile, highly capable people abandon places where the mission feels flawed or contrived. If the organization's message is especially inspiring, remarkable people will clamor for the chance to do even the hardest, most poorly supported tasks.

A half-century ago, Peace Corps slogan writers tried to harness this magic in a hurry. Stresses such as odd locations, hard work, and poor preparation weren't failings of the program; they became advantages. In 1961 Peace Corps fliers told participants: "You will stand in the eyes of the world as examples of the moral purpose that established the United States." Some 15,000 people, including many college graduates, raced to join. The bare-bones pay of $75 a month only made the job seem even nobler.

Today, socially minded enterprises such as Teach For America woo prospects with similar exhortations. A case in point: TFA's efforts to send thousands of new teachers to the Mississippi Delta. Recruits balk at first, seeing New York City and Los Angeles as more appealing destinations. When I was at TFA's Berkeley recruiting session, recruiters didn't deny that Delta jobs might involve dilapidated schools, poorly prepared students, and isolation from the comforts of big-city life. All those shortcomings were turned inside out—and portrayed as reasons why brave new teachers could take this region by storm. No sports programs? Be the pioneering coach who starts something. Hardly any other college-educated adults? Become the role model who opens a whole town's eyes to the value of higher education. Most Berkeley students listened impassively. A few were clearly being drawn into this dream.

Rallying other people to become part of a movement is as delicate as can be. Push too hard on save-the-world imagery, without enough substance to back it up, and everything collapses into self-parody. The Peace Corps overreached badly at first, making it hard to recover. Early brochures claimed that corps members' efforts "contributed directly to world peace." Yet many recruits ended up in faraway villages doing little more than manual labor, often with so little training that they weren't even doing it very well. In the words of one jaded corps executive, the Peace Corps relied on "pure ideals and pure publicity."

When big, shared goals take hold, it's because they are seen to be working. People who join the team feel that they and their peers are accomplishing great things. It helps to have totemic symbols of this shared identity, such as the cult of Halsted at Johns Hopkins. What's most important is that these cultures function like coral reefs, constantly renewing themselves. As old ties and legends fade, new ones take their place.

The strongest cultures don't mind opening their doors to people who haven't fully mastered this "greater good" mentality, as long as the prospects of instilling all-out loyalty are strong. Early months of selection, initiation, and training include much exposure to the group's values. Exposure, in fact, may be too gentle a word. Often it borders on outright indoctrination. Candidates who accept these values thrive. Those who don't are likely to walk away at some point, deciding such settings aren't for them.

In surgery, the hard-driving values of John Cameron's operating room began taking shape many decades earlier. Growing up in Detroit, Dr. Cameron told me, he began making hospital rounds at age eight, tagging along with his surgeon father on weekends. "We'd go from bedside to bedside," he remembered. "It was a big influence." In 1958, Cameron arrived at Hopkins for medical school. People who knew him then describe him as brilliant but overbearing. He remembers worrying that he wasn't as smart as the other students. "All I knew was that I could work harder than anyone else," he recalled. So he did.

Dr. Cameron built his reputation by treating pancreatic cancer, a rare, deadly disease that many doctors regarded as hopeless. Dr. Cameron disagreed. From the 1970s onward, he pinned his hopes on a heroic operation known as the Whipple procedure that involved taking out parts of four organs. When Dr. Cameron got started, a quarter of all patients who underwent Whipples died from the surgery itself—making the operation too dangerous to be of much use. Over time, Dr. Cameron drove that surgery death rate down to just 1 percent at Hopkins. There wasn't one giant breakthrough. He made all his progress inch by inch, with dozens of small improvements. Stubbornness and hard work paid off.

As surgery department chair, Dr. Cameron looked for high-achieving residents who could be molded to the Hopkins way of doing things. They needed fierce internal drive. They needed enough self-confidence to withstand the stresses of a surgeon's life. And they needed a strong desire to belong. Dexterity didn't matter; he could teach that. He could tolerate some emotional rough edges, too. If surgeons were eager enough to make it, he knew, they could subdue their tempers, or at least bring them within the bounds of what is acceptable at a hospital.

Initiation into his values started with "Sunday school." This was the Hopkins nickname for a series of informal hospital chats each Sunday at 8 A.M., where Dr. Cameron shared stories about the surgeon's art with the rawest interns. Attendance was optional. Anyone who wanted to sleep in on Sunday could do so. But the trainees who wanted Dr. Cameron's respect showed up every time. As they did so, they bought into his values that surgery was a seven-day-a-week calling. Surgeons who weren't comfortable with that level of intensity probably would drift away from Hopkins before long.

More indoctrination and selection followed in the operating room. One trainee, Kenneth Kern, years later recalled a time Dr. Cameron used intense heat to close off blood flow in a surgical zone right next to the senior surgeon's finger. Bubbles of fat were popping; smoke was pluming up. "At that moment," Dr. Kern recalled, "I thought Dr. Cameron has got to be the toughest surgeon I have ever met. I had never seen anyone take pain like that. I turned that vision into an epiphany: for the sake of the patient, surgeons have got to get the job done, whatever the personal cost."

When we spoke, Dr. Cameron acknowledged: "I had the reputation, in the OR, of beating on people, being very critical of their technique. Mostly I'm tough because I'm trying to make them think and do the right damned thing every time. Not ninety-five percent of the time, but one hundred percent. I'd say: If you could do it all perfectly, you'd have MY JOB! So don't worry. You don't have my job. But you're going to get it."

In 2009, Dr. Cameron counted thirteen of his former protégés who had become general-surgery department chairs at major academic medical centers. His disciples were at the universities of Minnesota and Pennsylvania and the University of California, San Diego. They were running surgery departments at the main teaching hospitals of Harvard and Yale. Many were pancreatic cancer specialists, performing their versions of the Whipple procedure that they had learned at Hopkins. Others, such as Yale's Dr. Udelsman, were stretching beyond their mentor's horizons, developing new surgeries for other conditions. That's what the old boss wanted. "If they're not better than me," Dr. Cameron remarked, "I haven't done my job."

10: When to Say No

It's time to talk about serious talent-picking mistakes—and how to dodge them.

Much of this book has celebrated the adventurous spirit of people willing to make daring hires, based on considerations like "What can go right?" That approach is tailor-made for situations where potential gains are big and risks are small. It's the right way to find the inventors, authors, engineers, scholars, designers, and entrepreneurs who will help define America's future in exciting ways. Even the occasional stumble isn't really a mistake; it's a low-cost lesson in how to pick better next time. But when an organization's destiny hinges on a single hire, everything changes. The financial risks of a blunder are alarming; the reputational risks even worse. Knowing when to say no becomes crucial.

Guess wrong on a $30 million quarterback, and a pro football team's entire budget is shot. There won't be enough money left over to rebuild the squad into a winner. What's more, for the hapless executives who sign off on a disastrous hire, there won't be a "next time" to apply this hard-won knowledge. Owners of sports teams, music labels, and similar ventures aren't willing to squander millions on high-profile blunders. Smaller risks are tolerable. Executives who

199

fail to get the big calls right can expect to be treated as scapegoats. They will be fired without so much as a "Thanks for trying."

Step into America's boardrooms, and the same nail-biting goes on, too. Picking a new CEO touches a company's fate in countless ways. Even though directors hope to find a hero, the odds aren't in their favor. Many corporate bosses last only a few years in office, before job-hopping or being forced out. Pick the wrong person, and the penalties include a skidding stock price, vanishing customers, tattered brand reputations, and intense employee cynicism.

So when big money is at stake, big anxieties enter the picture. Ordinary assessment methods are ramped up to triple-strength dosages or discarded altogether. Decision makers get swept up in an emotional maelstrom. They are full of excitement about perhaps making the best choice of their lives; full of anxiety about perhaps making their biggest blunder. At such moments, they lose the ability to take stock of themselves—and to recognize the new pressures and distortions weighing on their own judgment.

The central issue: When picking talent at the highest levels, it's easy to get star-struck. All the top candidates exude success. They each seem so gifted in their own way that it feels churlish to spend much time wondering whether these stars will thrive in a new setting. So such questions aren't deeply explored. Instead, euphoria takes hold. Giddy yeses are blurted out when the situation calls for a measured no. Organizations foolishly talk themselves into hiring people with great talent, but *not the right talent*.

Rakesh Khurana, a Harvard Business School professor, flagged part of this problem in *Searching for a Corporate Savior: The Irrational Quest for Charismatic CEOs*. In his view, corporate boards in a crisis seek out charismatic new bosses, regardless of whether these people know much about the industry or company that they are supposed to run. Such appointments often work out badly, he found. They bring a momentary boost to a company's stock price, as investors for a day or two applaud the arrival of a new CEO with "star power." Then, as the new boss's tenure plays out, lack of industry knowledge and an inability to connect with the company's existing management team proves fatal. Directors end up in the awkward position of having bet the company's future on what turned out to be a talent mirage.

Khurana could just as well have evoked biblical and ancient Greek tales of tragic temptation. The fundamental problem hasn't changed in three thousand years. When exquisitely alluring people enter the picture—for whatever reason—it's easy to become so enchanted by their strengths that good judgment collapses. In the talent hunts described earlier in this book, that wasn't a problem. Anyone prospecting for jagged résumés and talent that whispers needs courage to press ahead in the face of public indifference or disdain. When talent that shouts is in play, however, runaway optimism is more likely to translate into recklessness than a rare discovery.

The related question of "What price, talent?" becomes much more crucial, too. Economists since the 1960s have been studying the awkward miseries of what's known as "the winner's curse." This macabre condition reflects the fact that when people outbid everyone else for a coveted prize, they may not have done themselves a favor after all. Examples of overpaying range from oil-lease auctions to the salaries of free-agent baseball pitchers. Even people who believe they are very careful in their budgeting keep making the mistake of showering too much money on prospects that may be pretty good—but *not that good*.

Each of these predicaments deserves a closer look.

An excellent place to start is in Boise, Idaho, in the winter of 2001. At that time, the Albertsons Inc. grocery chain—one of the twenty-five biggest companies in the United States—needed new leadership. The Idaho company's longtime CEO, Gary Michael, was about to retire. Company directors thought about promoting an internal candidate. But they decided they could do better by looking outside. After all, America was full of hard-charging executives, making names for themselves at other companies. Albertson's was ready to do some poaching.

"It's the right time to have a change agent at this company," Albertsons director Paul Corddry told *Wall Street Journal* reporter Joann Lublin in early 2001. So the executive search firm of Spencer Stuart identified twenty-nine outside prospects for Albertsons to consider. Recruiters cast a wide net, while warning that the odds of a successful hire would be greatest if everyone stuck to candidates with extensive grocery experience. Board members felt more daring. The candidate who intrigued them the most was Larry Johnston, the head of General Electric's appliance business in Louisville, Kentucky.

Johnston was a good-looking, six foot seven bear of a man. He was a lifelong GE manager, well versed in the rough-and-tumble world of big-time manufacturing. He could land $100 million contracts from key customers. He could keep a factory running. He could draw a hard line on union demands and endure a strike, if necessary, to keep labor costs down. Within GE's world, Johnston was a star. In a company where finance specialists held many of the top jobs, he had proven that a onetime salesman like himself could race ahead, too. Still, he hadn't ever worked in retailing, let alone the grocery business. By his own account, Johnston hadn't even heard of Albertsons when the first recruiter called.

Albertsons directors waved those gaps aside. "GE has very bright people, and our business isn't that difficult," Albertsons director Teresa Beck told me in 2003. "We're not building the space shuttle."

In those days, GE was seen as the world's best breeding ground for management talent. GE's longtime boss, Jack Welch, not only delivered world-class financial performance; he was a bestselling business author, sharing management tips that seemed universally applicable. "Be No. 1 or No. 2 in your markets," he wrote. "Create a vision and then get out of the way." Rank employees by performance and get rid of the weakest ones. The more Welch's precepts circulated, the easier it was to believe that a big dose of GE-style thinking could help any company. Executive recruiters in that era were snatching GE managers to run the likes of Boeing, Intuit, Pfizer, Home Depot, and Fannie Mae.

Caught up in this excitement, Albertsons directors decided they wanted a GE-trained chief executive, too. Thanks to a giant acquisition, Albertsons in 2001 was vastly bigger than it had been a few years earlier. Directors weren't sure the company's in-house management capabilities had kept pace. Albertsons' next CEO would need to run a company with $40 billion a year in sales and 235,000 employees. This was uncharted territory. If Albertsons' own people didn't know how to operate at such scale, perhaps some newcomer did. As Corddry later explained, Johnston "was the guy we thought embodied the best strategic planning skills."

Two years into Johnston's tenure, I spent time at Albertsons' headquarters to see how the new boss was doing. It was a poignant visit. Johnston had packed his office with trophies and mementos of his GE days, as if to remind himself what it once felt like to be a winner. At Albertsons he was adrift. Trying to recreate the tools that had made him so effective at GE, Johnston brought in a new finance chief, who could give him more detailed data on how the business was doing. To gauge employees' performance more analytically, the way GE did, he brought in a new head of human relations.

But Albertsons wasn't meant to be a GE clone. Success in the grocery business is all about making millions of casual shoppers feel good about walking into your stores. That's best done by upbeat store managers who feel they have the freedom to win customers' loyalty with the right blend of prices, promotions, and good cheer. Johnston's GE playbook took him in the wrong direction. The harder he tried to set up the sorts of rigid quality measures that worked so well in GE factories, the more lifeless and rule-bound his stores became.

Even Johnston's gung-ho personality wasn't an asset anymore. Great retailers need to be extraordinary listeners. They succeed by picking up the mood of the customer more skillfully than anyone. That wasn't Larry Johnston. He liked to take command of a conversation, steering other people around to his way of thinking. That paid off at GE, where he was sensationally good at wrapping up big sales contracts with Home Depot (for appliances) and leading health systems (for medical imaging equipment). Still, even at GE, Johnston had been told to talk less and listen more. At Albertsons, Johnston couldn't transform into a different person.

When we went on brief store visits together in Boise, Johnston would park his canary yellow Hummer in front of each store, and then deluge local managers with suggestions about how to rearrange their shelves. They nodded token approval. Everything about their body language said: "It's more complicated than you think. We could change that, but it won't help."

Two years into the job, Johnston was an embattled boss. Albertsons' stock price was weak; some of its stores looked tawdry, and the company was having a hard time holding market share against tough competitors. Directors insisted they still felt good about their prize CEO, but investors and analysts weren't so sure. By early 2006, the final verdict on Johnston's tenure had come in, and it wasn't good. The company's financial performance had faltered to the point that Albertsons was put up for sale. Three buyers each took chunks, and the Albertsons name largely disappeared. Johnston was out of a job, though he received a sizable severance package.

Other GE alumni ran into trouble, too, in their efforts to lead unfamiliar companies. Robert Nardelli, a go-getter at GE who had done a fine job of running GE Power Systems, stumbled as CEO of Home Depot and ultimately was asked to leave. Former GE finance chief Gary Wendt was unable to turn around Conseco, an ailing Indiana insurer. In general, companies looking for new leadership "got overenthusiastic about the GE glow," declared University of Chicago business school professor James Schrager in 2007. "They forgot that there's a big divide between selling appliances and light bulbs to stores and running the stores that sell them to consumers."

How did the Albertsons board feel about this final chapter in the company's history? Directors generally stayed mum. But I caught a tantalizing clue in 2007, when former Albertsons CEO Gary Michael showed up at a high-powered directors' conference in San Francisco. One of the speakers had just wrapped up a presentation about the perils of bringing in charismatic outsiders to run companies. Michael stood up as the presentation was adjourning and said to no one in particular: "We learned a lot about that." He refused to say anything more.

On the East Coast, a similarly tortured story was playing out at Harvard University. In the summer of 2000, America's oldest university began what turned out to be a nine-month search for a new president. Search committee leaders announced they were looking for four key traits in Harvard's next leader. At the top of the list was "high intellectual distinction." Leadership came next, followed by devotion to excellence. In fourth place was the "capacity to guide a complex institution."

Harvard's priorities were oddly shaped. Modern-day university presidents channel most of their energies into fund-raising and being the public face of the university in dealing with alumni, politicians, and other outsiders. Presidents also are expected to be the school's great conciliators in the event of sit-ins, scandals, faculty spats, and natural disasters. Newly appointed university chiefs need some level of scholarly achievement to earn the faculty's respect. But in the ego-rich world of major universities, the big names of the faculty senate don't need or want a president who claims to dwarf the rest in intellectual horsepower. The most effective presidents win acclaim over time for their diplomatic skills, rather than their erudition.

Harvard, for whatever reason, wanted brainpower in its next president—and lots of it. When the search committee came up with its list of three finalists, two were well-regarded academic administrators with decades of experience: Lee Bollinger, the fifty-four-year-old president of the University of Michigan, and Harvey Fineberg, the fifty-five-year-old provost at Harvard. The third was a younger economist whose university experience didn't include so much as a department chairmanship. But, man, could he think!

Lawrence Summers started college at age sixteen and became a tenured professor at Harvard at the stunningly young age of twenty-eight. While most economists pick a single narrow specialty and stick to it for their whole careers, Summers became the Bo Jackson of economics, mastering any subdiscipline he wanted. In 1986, he established himself as one of the top thinkers on European unemployment. A few years later: hostile takeovers. After that: economic growth and central bank policy. A *Boston Globe* profile in the 1980s portrayed Summers as someone who could work on six projects at once. In 1993, his admiring and exhausted colleagues awarded him the Clark Medal, given to America's top economist under age forty.

In the 1990s, Summers brought his audacious ways to Washington. He became chief economist at the World Bank in 1991, and U.S. treasury secretary in 1997. People who tried to match wits with him came away bruised. Strobe Talbott, who later became president of the Brookings Institution, quipped that getting into an argument with Summers was "like being run over by a tank with a Lotus engine." In the early 1990s, Summers signed off on a staffer's World Bank memo that suggested using desolate parts of Africa as dumping grounds for the world's toxic waste, because there was so little productive economic activity there. When environmentalists howled, spokespersons for Summers said the memo was meant to be sarcastic. In point of fact, such "thought grenades" are well accepted among economists, who like to test out belief systems with extreme hypotheticals. To the rest of society, the idea of trashing Africa is horrifying.

Harvard's presidential search committee found Summers's intellectual strengths so dazzling that they carried the day. There was something thrilling about landing a new president who had already been on the cover of *Time* magazine, whose signature appeared on the dollar bill, who might someday be a contender for the Nobel Prize. Any concerns about Summers's edgier ways were smoothed away by Washington insiders, who asserted that the brilliant economist was maturing and becoming more tactful. Search committee leader Robert Stone hailed Summers as "one of the most respected scholars and one of the most influential public servants of his generation." There was talk Harvard could be gaining one of its finest presidents since Charles Eliot vaulted the university to greatness in the late 1800s.

"It's good to be home," Summers told reporters on the day of his selection. Then—unable to be anyone except himself—Summers began doing the academic equivalent of ripping up the lawn, repainting the house, and getting rid of all the furniture that he didn't like. Harvard might be his home, but he was bursting with ideas about how to fix it.

First Summers tried to overhaul the undergraduate curriculum to make it more rigorous. Then he upbraided a leading African American Studies professor, Cornel West, for what Summers believed was a lax approach to research and student grades. When Princeton offered West a better job, he was glad to go. Some Harvard professors chafed at what they regarded as Summers's domineering style, but he brushed their worries aside. He was the boss, and they would be well advised to go along or get out of the way. As Summers later told Britain's *The Guardian* newspaper in 2004, "You know, sometimes fear does the work of reason."

In January 2005, Summers tossed out another thought grenade—and this one cost him his job. Vowing "to provoke you," he told an academic conference in Boston that he was wondering why women were so scarce in math and science scholarship. Summers said the reasons weren't clear. Possible explanations included "what I would call different availability of aptitude at the high end." Women in the audience felt his remarks were tantamount to saying: You're not smart enough. Biologist Nancy Hopkins said she walked out of the talk, aghast, because if she had stayed any longer, "I would've either blacked out or thrown up."

Within days, a full-fledged faculty rebellion was under way. Petitions were drafted, denouncing Summers's leadership. Various scholars called for his resignation. Some believed his gender remarks were abhorrent; others found his style too domineering and dismissive for their tastes. That spring, Harvard's faculty senate passed a vote of no confidence on Summers's tenure. Friends rallied to his defense, portraying Summers as a truth-seeking scholar who supported women's opportunities. But Harvard's recent promotion record didn't help Summers's cause. In the previous academic year, Harvard had offered tenure to thirty-two professors in arts and sciences. Just four were women. In February 2006, Summers resigned as Harvard president after five years in office, citing faculty "rancor." Harvard, he conceded, would be better off without him at the helm.

As a lone economist, Summers could offer up any ideas he wanted. As a university president, overseeing tenure decisions, he occupied a more precarious perch. The truth is CEOs don't enjoy freedom of speech. They are stewards of their enterprises, as federal judge Richard Posner has observed, with a duty to "speak publicly only in ways that are helpful to the organization." Trying to shoehorn a born provocateur like Summers into such strict rules was doing an injustice not just to Harvard, but to Summers himself. As it happens, he rebounded from his Harvard travails to achieve new prominence in 2009 as director of the White House National Economic Council. In Washington, Summers could be himself again: a brilliant "idea man" whose headstrong ways wouldn't destroy his effectiveness.

After Summers's resignation, Harvard's overseers regrouped and went looking for another president. Officially, their job specifications remained the same: intellect first, diplomacy fourth. As a practical matter, Harvard hewed a new path. It picked Civil War historian Drew Gilpin Faust, who had already shown a sure hand as an administrator by running the Radcliffe Institute for Advanced Study at Harvard. People who saw her in action assessed her in measured tones: reasonable, earnest, thoughtful. As author Nicholas Lemann argued, that might be what university presidencies are all about. "Being verbally provocative isn't the job of Harvard's president," Lemann wrote in 2006. "The job is to make a successful but fragmented university cohere intellectually and educationally. A publicly bland president who did that would be a hero."

It took Harvard two tries and six years to straighten out its thinking about what talent it needed for the presidency. That's a maddeningly slow timetable, yet it is probably typical. The reason why is best understood by a classic engineers' parable: the car door that won't open.

What do we do when our car key doesn't work? In his book *The Design of Everyday Things*, engineering design specialist Donald A. Norman describes the logical yet absurd routines we follow. First we try again, holding the key at a different angle. Then we try the key upside down. Then we consider switching keys. "Then the door is wiggled, shaken, hit. Finally the person decides that the lock has broken, and walks around the car to try the other door . . . at which point it is suddenly clear that this is the wrong car."

Oops! When talented people like Larry Johnston or Larry Summers don't work out in big jobs, much the same haphazard thinking takes place. Outside commentators and actual decision makers rebuke the candidate—hesitantly at first and then with increasing ferocity as problems get worse. *(Blame the key.)* It takes a lot of humility and self-awareness to ask if the search itself was wrongly constructed. People in charge would much rather mask their own gaffes and denounce their former favorites instead.

Some of the harshest name-calling arises when gifted performers turn lackadaisical on the job. The denunciations that ensue are as heated as if a con man had come to town and swindled a whole community of trusting people. Beating up on such perceived slackers has become such good sport that bookstores now offer titles such as *Talent Is Never Enough, Talent Is Overrated,* and my favorite: *You're Not the Person I Hired!* What's missing in all this indignation is a candid perspective on whether the dawdler ever showed much inclination to work through the hard stuff—and whether the decision makers who were so eager to hire this new legend ever cared.

In pro football, one of the most vilified prospects of all time is Ryan Leaf, a star college quarterback at Washington State who stumbled through a short, unhappy career in the pros. He was the second player drafted in 1998, which earned him a multiyear contract worth $31 million. Unfortunately, his confidence and composure fell apart quickly and never recovered. He screamed at reporters. He missed NFL games and practices because of injuries, yet was seen playing other sports during his recovery time. He drew a four-week suspension at one point for yelling at his coach. In his brief pro career, Leaf played in twenty-five games, winning just four of them, while throwing a total of thirty-six interceptions.

In the run-up to the 1998 draft, Leaf's future looked so bright that the Indianapolis Colts seriously considered making him the league's number one draft pick, ahead of eventual superstar Peyton Manning. I spent an afternoon with Bill Polian, the Colts' vice chairman, who called the shots back then in terms of which player to pick. For Polian, that was a make-or-break moment in his career. "If I had got that wrong," he said, "you wouldn't be talking to me now. There would be someone else in this office. I'd probably be across the street, parking cars."

As we reconstructed the Colts' decision-making process, what came across was that Polian and his aides couldn't reach a clear decision simply by studying game films and running various tests on the two players. Everything the young quarterbacks had done on the football field to date was essentially a tie. Both were Heisman Trophy finalists in college. Both were six foot five and in sound health. Manning was slightly more polished; Leaf might have more potential. Dithering over details wasn't getting the Colts any closer to a decision.

"Did we overanalyze?" Polian asked rhetorically, conceding that they did. He and his aides watched video footage of all 880 of Leaf's college passes. They watched video of all 1,381 of Manning's passes. Then they hit rewind and watched each player's final-season passes three more times. They checked both quarterbacks' scores on a modified IQ test, known as the Wonderlic exam. Leaf scored a very respectable 27. Manning scored an essentially identical 28.

More tests of valor followed. In the weirdest one, the Colts paid for each quarterback to fly to Indianapolis, stand immobile at one end of the football field, and hurl a football as far as he could. It was supposed to be a measure of raw arm strength. No human quarterback throws like that in a game. Even a poorly designed robot wouldn't throw that way. Footwork is such a crucial part of a quarterback's performance that asking anyone to throw a football without moving his feet is like asking a singer to perform without moving her lips. For their trouble, the Colts learned that Leaf could throw a football sixty yards that way. Manning was good for fifty-eight. "Some of the coaches saw a ceiling in Peyton's arm strength," Polian conceded. It was hard to say whether Leaf's edge amounted to anything.

Eventually, Polian and his aides realized, the Colts' decision wasn't going to hinge on microscopic differences in technical skills. The Colts needed to take a stab at big, murky issues of temperament. Who was more likely to survive a tough rookie season with his confidence intact? Who could gradually turn a losing team into a winner? Who wholeheartedly wanted to play NFL football, no matter how grim things got? "We were likely to lose a lot of games no matter who was the quarterback," Polian told me. "The question was: 'Did whoever we chose have the ability to withstand that?'"

Once that issue was on the table, clues were everywhere. When Leaf and Manning came to the NFL's big predraft workout in February, Manning arrived at his usual playing weight of 230 pounds. Leaf tipped the scales at 261 pounds, nearly twenty pounds above his playing weight, and blamed it on too many off-season banquets. When Colts coach Jim Mora scheduled one-on-one meetings with both players, Manning showed up on time. Leaf got sidetracked by a medical exam and didn't let Mora know of the delay.

In isolation, any single lapse was forgivable. But in the Colts' eyes, a pattern was forming. Manning, the son of an NFL quarterback who had endured many losing seasons, wanted to play pro ball more than anything in the world. Leaf's motivation was shakier. He was a great athlete who looked forward to the cheers and money of an NFL career. But he had other goals, too. When both players were asked what they would do the moment after being drafted, Manning said he would study his new team's playbook. Leaf said he would fly to Las Vegas.

Polian's lesson from the Manning-Leaf conundrum is so blindingly simple that most decision makers never stop to think about it: you can't take motivation for granted, even when the job pays $30 million. The most glamorous jobs can get ugly at times, with nonstop commitments, relentless travel, public setbacks, and media scrutiny of a person's weakest moments. Anyone who wants to pick winners in high-prestige, high-stress fields needs to know as much as possible about people's true stamina. Looking into candidates' psyches and figuring out: "Do you really want to do this?" may be one of the most important ways of deciding whether someone truly has the right talent.

From a distance, Leaf and Manning seemed almost like twins. Both had enjoyed marvelous college careers; both entered the draft as happy heroes. But after nearly thirty years of scouting, coaching, and running football teams, Polian knew how some players' motivation could crumble in the face of tougher challenges. For quarterbacks especially, the opponents are fiercer; the training regimen more exhausting; the public scrutiny relentless. It was up to Polian to figure out ahead of time who might not be able to handle the load—and to tell that person: "No."

When did Polian know he had made the right pick? The answer probably came in late September 1998, five months after the NFL draft and a few weeks into the two quarterbacks' rookie seasons. Manning and Leaf each got clobbered in the worst losses they had ever suffered in organized football. After losing one game 44–6, Manning still saw himself as a leader who could regroup and accomplish something good the next week. As he told reporters, "It's not fun, not at all. You're not going to accept losing and you never want to get used to losing. But we have thirteen games left. All we can do is learn from it." By contrast, Leaf sounded eager for the safety and obscurity of a seat on the bench. "It kind of feels like someone ripped my heart out of me," he said at a press conference after a 34–16 loss. "I certainly wasn't helping us win the football game. Based on my performance this year, there's no reason for me to be the starting quarterback."

Five years after the 1998 draft, Manning was named the NFL's Most Valuable Player. Leaf no longer played in the pros.

At Stanford University's business school, there's an expert in everything. Kathryn Shaw happens to be the professor who studies talent. One of her landmark papers, "Reaching for the Stars," has become the definitive explanation of why video game companies are willing to pay more than $1 million a year in cash and stock options for the best game designers. In the paper, Shaw also explains why companies that can't afford to do so are probably doomed.

Partway through the research for this book, I visited one of Shaw's classes, called "Managing Talent." It was in an amphitheater-style classroom, with Shaw standing in the middle, almost like an orchestra conductor. She was ringed by about seventy MBA students, all of whom were eager to champion the cause of highly talented people who could demand—and win—seven-figure pay packages. Once these students graduated, after all, they would be chasing such deals themselves. Shaw didn't deny them their exuberance. She just wanted to share a cautionary message on that particular afternoon. And so she talked about Tom Cruise.

When Cruise made his acting breakthrough in 1983, with the film *Risky Business*, he was one of Hollywood's great bargains. It cost The Geffen Company and Warner Brothers just $75,000 to sign him for the role. The movie ended up grossing $65 million at the U.S. box office alone. Three years later, Cruise's bargaining power had improved to the point that he could fetch $2 million to appear in *Top Gun*. Within the business logic of Hollywood, he was still painfully underpaid. That movie grossed an estimated $345 million worldwide. Paramount, which produced the film, was able to land its star for less than 1 percent of the movie's box-office rewards. The studio could have paid Cruise five times as much and still done extraordinarily well.

Cruise and his backers weren't going to let such shameful exploitation continue for long. He began negotiating not just for more up-front money—but also for a meaningful slice of either the profits or the total revenue that a movie might generate. He earned $20 million that way for making *Jerry Maguire* with TriStar Pictures in 1996. He collected a remarkable $75 million from Paramount for starring in 2000's *Mission: Impossible II*. Both those movies (and many other Cruise films) were spectacular hits.

For a while, at least, Cruise and his managers held the upper hand. He was unique; the studios to some extent were interchangeable. He could press for the best possible terms from Paramount, the studio that produced most of his films. If executives didn't like it, all they could do was step aside and let someone else make movies with him. Becoming known as the nervous finance guy who was too cheap to sign Tom Cruise was not a good way to develop one's career. As long as Cruise's films kept being huge hits, he could remain known as the expensive star who was worth it.

What eventually happened? As Shaw pointed out to her class, people with extreme star power—like Tom Cruise—don't top out with 70 percent or even 90 percent of the economic value of their work. Their bargaining power seems so strong that for a brief while, they commandeer more than 100 percent of the juice. Hiring them becomes a losing proposition, even though they reliably produce bestsellers. They're simply too expensive.

That's what happened in the movie business, where Cruise's payout rates kept climbing, even as his box office appeal dimmed a bit. In the *Mission: Impossible* series, the third film, released in 2006, was Paramount's most expensive, with Cruise's pay pushing up costs, yet it did the worst at the box office. Sumner Redstone, chairman of Paramount's parent company, Viacom, abruptly cut off ties between Paramount and Cruise in 2006 over a variety of issues, including money. In a *Vanity Fair* interview soon afterward, Redstone said he hoped his decision "sent a message to the rest of the world that the time of the big star getting all this money is over."

A few years later, Paramount and Cruise decided they could work together, after all. But Redstone's outburst wasn't in vain. When Paramount got to work on the next *Mission: Impossible* film, Cruise's pay was scaled back down to $12.5 million. He was still one of

America's top-earning actors; he just wasn't earning so much that it made no economic sense to hire him.

Hollywood isn't the only arena where bosses can trap themselves into overpaying for proven talent. Bill Cosby's foray into book writing is a cautionary tale in the publishing industry that still attracts notice two decades later. Everything started well in 1985, with Doubleday editor Paul Bresnick signing up Cosby to write a short book that became *Fatherhood*. That book's gentle mix of advice and wisecracks captivated America. Readers snapped up more than 2.5 million hardcover copies, creating millions of dollars of profits for Doubleday and making its author's advance of $850,000 seem like a bargain.

Doubleday briskly signed up Cosby for another book, this time on what it's like to get old. The publishers paid $3 million for the rights to *Time Flies*, which had strong but not spectacular sales. Everyone decided to try a third time. This time Doubleday paid $3.5 million for *Love and Marriage*, which ran into serious buyer resistance. Of the 850,000 hardcover copies printed, journalist Gayle Feldman reported, barely one third had been sold a year after the book's debut. This latest project was at risk of sticking Doubleday with losses of $1 million or more. Ordinary business logic would suggest that Doubleday stop publishing Cosby's books, or at least stop paying so much for them.

Even so, Doubleday nearly ended up publishing Cosby's next book, *Childhood*, for another hefty advance before tensions between publisher and author caused *Childhood* to be published by a different house. Feldman, who summarized the economic rise and fall of Cosby's titles in a *New York Times* feature, declared that such follies are just part of the way publishing works. In her words, "famous authors' advances frequently rise in inverse proportion to the sales of their books." The main reason, she contended, is that authors press for more and their publishers capitulate, fearful of seeing a major author go elsewhere.

For the last word on acquiring talent at sensible prices—and avoiding catastrophic overpayments—the right expert is football's Bill Polian. "In any given year," he says, "there are exceedingly overpriced areas of the talent market. That's most common with free agents, and it's usually recognizable." Other teams battle to sign the players everyone wants; Polian seldom does.

"You get confident over time about breaking from the pack," he says. In his pre-NFL jobs, his budgets were so tight that he had no choice but to look for low-cost ways of filling his roster with the overlooked or underappreciated. Now he remains thrifty by choice. "You need to be as efficient as you can about solving the problem," he says. "You don't take things for granted. You analyze the solution. You find a solution. There is always a solution."

11: Picking the Boss

Randy Street wants to hear your story. He can meet in whatever city works best for you. If you are traveling through the southeastern United States, consider the Delta Sky Club at Concourse A in the Atlanta airport. The coffee is good there. Randy knows the staff. He can book a quiet conference room and bring in some bagels or a fruit platter. You will be able to recognize him just fine. He's the cheery, fresh-faced consultant with the neatly combed black hair. He looks a lot like the actor Tobey Maguire. Even if you're nervous about this hastily put-together meeting, you will find Randy to be surprisingly likable. It's not just that he's a gracious host. It's the fact that he listens.

He really listens.

For four hours, Randy will sit cater-corner from you at the conference table, taking notes on his Toshiba laptop. He will want to hear about each "chapter" of your career. Nobody else in the world may care about your first real job as an adult, but Randy does. He wants to know what you did, and how it worked out. He wants to know who your boss was, and what you thought of him or her. He wants to hear about your on-the-job triumphs and your setbacks. This won't be like the harsh questioning of a legal deposition, or the free-form ramblings of a self-help group. Randy is a former executive himself.

If you run a business or aspire to do so, Randy knows your world. You can talk about budgets, "deliverables," and "strategic plans." He won't yawn. He won't look at his watch. He will welcome your memories and anecdotes.

Expect a barrage of follow-up questions.

For all his gentle ways, Randy has an agenda. In the course of your 240 minutes together, he wants to march through your career with the millimeter-by-millimeter precision of a CAT scanner creating images of your internal organs. Each story you tell isn't just a trip down memory lane. It is a glimpse of how you operate. On his laptop is a detailed list of what needs to get done in the job, as well as thirty categories that define executive excellence. He will press you, gently but incessantly, for extra details that will help him rate you. Soon after your meeting is over, Randy and his consultant colleagues at ghSMART & Company will pick through a transcript of your remarks, looking to see what each anecdote reveals. Are you efficient? Flexible? Organized? Do you set high standards? Are you open to criticism? Randy's goal is to finish the interview with five hundred data points that will be used to fill out your scorecard.

In some ways, Randy Street's routine brings us back to familiar territory. His interviews amount to a richly detailed audition for CEOs, akin to the routines showcased in chapter 1 and chapter 5. This neatly dressed consultant resembles those Army Special Forces examiners, standing off to the side in the sandy pinelands of North Carolina, taking notes on soldiers' gaze and carriage in the midst of a long march. He is a kindred spirit to the basketball coaches at the big Nike tournament, watching players' body language during time-outs to get a sense of who is coachable and who isn't. Like them, Randy Street is a detail guy who can draw big conclusions from many small observations.

All the same, there's something startling about the way this newcomer has injected himself into the process of picking a CEO. If you end up being hired, that four-hour session with Randy Street will change your life. But you probably won't ever see him again. He won't be one of your directors, shareholders, or key lieutenants. While you redefine yourself in the job of a lifetime, Street will continue to travel from conference room to conference room. Every few days, he will open up his laptop and start typing as a new CEO candidate starts telling his or her story. The side table will be stocked with the same brands of coffee and bagels. This is Street's calling: to travel across America in a never-ending quest to get the right people into the right jobs.

Ten or twenty years ago, such a dispassionate approach to picking the boss would have seemed unthinkable. Organizations of all sizes—ranging from giant corporations to local school boards—treated leadership searches as highly charged courtships. The best candidates were supposed to make everyone's pulse race a little quicker. I saw this dynamic up close when I reconstructed Hewlett-Packard's 1999 search for a new CEO, as part of the book *Perfect Enough*. HP's climactic meetings were worthy of a Jane Austen novel, with talk of a reluctant director suddenly being "dazzled," or "hooked." Rendezvous were held in clandestine locations like Chicago's Gaslight Lounge. Excitement and hope filled the air. The company's decision came from the heart, at least as much as from the head.

Many of these impetuous decisions have turned out badly. That's what has created a climate for change. Hewlett-Packard, for example, brought in a charismatic outsider, Carly Fiorina, as CEO in 1999, only to see her leave in 2005 amid deteriorating relations with the board. Similar missteps at Harvard and Albertsons were chronicled in the last chapter. A recent study by business professors James S. Ang and Gregory L. Nagel, looking at nearly seven thousand CEOs' fates since 1985, found that bosses brought in from outside performed significantly worse than internal hires.

Writing some years ago about the foibles of how we hire people, *The New Yorker*'s Malcolm Gladwell took aim at the romantic subtext of such decisions. "For most of us," he wrote, "the job interview functions as a desexualized version of a date. We are looking for someone with whom we have a certain chemistry, even if the coupling that results ends in tears and the pursuer and the pursued turn out to have nothing in common. We want the unlimited promise of a love affair."

At last, those old dynamics are starting to change. A new class of investor/directors—personified by the big Wall Street takeover barons such as Blackstone Group, Carlyle Group, and Kohlberg Kravis Roberts—views CEOs more dispassionately. These firms aren't looking for new buddies. They just want CEOs whose operating savvy will help jack up the stock price. Such deal-minded owners feel quite comfortable asking for clinical-grade advice on picking the next boss.

Meanwhile, a new breed of outside assessment experts is getting better at winning boardroom credibility. Old-time stereotypes of odd-looking psychologists in tweed jackets have succumbed to the arrival of polished assessors with MBAs and big-league experience at Bain, McKinsey, and other strategic consulting shops. These interlocutors know how executives think and act; some are so accomplished that they could sit on either side of the table. In turn, directors have sobered up. Aware of the hit-and-miss results that come from falling in love with candidates, board members are much more amenable to formal screening methods instead. Highly structured interviews may not be as fun as a couple rounds of drinks at a speakeasy. But if a carefully scripted approach produces better results, it's hard to argue against it.

There's a parallel here with Major League Baseball, where laptop-carrying data crunchers have had a huge impact on the talent market. As chronicled in Michael Lewis's book *Moneyball*, the numbers geeks proved that major-league teams had been paying far too much for flashy home run hitters, and not enough for scrappy ballplayers who kept reaching base by drawing walks. The teams with practically unlimited budgets could chase whatever form of talent they wanted. But the smaller-market teams needed to be more careful with their dollars. The Oakland Athletics' general manager, Billy Beane, bought into that idea wholeheartedly. In the late 1990s, he started producing some of baseball's most winning teams on a surprisingly skimpy budget.

What delighted the Moneyball crowd—and infuriated traditional scouts—was the humdrum nature of their hunt. (No fan ever leaps to his or her feet shouting: "Did you see that walk!?") These analysts had found a formula for winning more games that was hidden in plain sight. The key to success had been in front of everyone the whole time. Traditional scouts had been too busy gasping at home runs to notice.

Could something similar be true in hunting for executive talent? It's still early days. The ingredients for a successful CEO are far more complicated than the elements that define an All-Star baseball player. But it's intriguing to see where dispassionate assessors are focusing their attention. Spotlights are centered on everyday virtues—such as efficiency, self-reliance, and an ability to "read the room" when people with different interests are crammed together for a meeting or a negotiation. Such skills are the equivalent of baseball's walks. They aren't nearly as thrilling as the excitement of a CEO's brilliant speech or high-stakes strategic thrust. Over time, though, it's the little stuff that may add up to lasting success.

Spotting clues about a CEO candidate's everyday capabilities can come down to something as simple as having the nerve to ask "the third question," says Thomas J. Friel, former chairman of the executive search firm of Heidrick & Struggles. As Friel points out, most boardroom discussions start at a high level of abstraction and generalities. It's hard to tell much from the first question-and-answer exchange on any topic. Even the initial follow-up question may do no more than scratch the surface. Only when a questioner has the temerity to ask a third question do problems come out into the open. Likewise, it's the third question that clarifies the exact nature of success and its contributors.

"It's hard for directors to ask that third question," Friel says. "Everything in the boardroom is set up so that one person isn't supposed to monopolize the conversation." If everyone talks a little bit, and no one presses too far on any key issue, breakthroughs are rare. An hour-long meeting with a candidate can become not much more than a festival of "hellos" and minor social bonding.

Friel's persistent style helps him answer highly nuanced questions such as: Is this CEO candidate "intelligent enough"? That standard is both humbler and more powerful than hunting for *Jeopardy!*-caliber genius. He needs candidates with the wisdom to think through the consequences of their decisions. If a company raises prices or sues a slow-paying customer, what is likely to happen next? CEOs need to make a lot of decisions in the face of uncertainty. The good ones manage risks well. Bumblers keep creating crises that didn't need to happen. Clues are evident in candidates' work history; it just takes a lot of careful probing by people like Friel to find them.

Every leadership expert uses a slightly different list of key traits to define executive success. Each list is valuable, at least in the right settings. After all, being CEO is an extremely complex job, with lots of competing priorities. Bosses need to be clear thinkers, decisive actors, powerful builders of teams, and morally sound leaders. Business gurus constantly expand and refine those basic ideas in a beautiful swirl of conceptual pageantry. Insights abound. The hard part is being able to tell, ahead of time, how candidates stack up against any of these ideals.

When directors and trustees go outside their ranks for advice on picking leaders, what they crave is someone with the skills and nerve to be an "aggressive listener." Typically, listening is regarded as a weakling's trait, defined by passivity. Listeners are anonymous spectators in the auditorium seats, sitting passively in the dark. All the glory belongs to the speakers on brightly lit stages, projecting their ideas and energy into an audience full of acolytes. Start seeing the world that way, and new encounters become tinged by an unhelpful desire to dominate the conversation.

By contrast, aggressive listeners gain authority by being incredibly attentive to other people. These experts catch the gestures, pauses, and inflections that hint at something beyond the words being said at the time. "Watch their hands, watch their eyes," explained Lyndon Johnson, one of the finest aggressive listeners Washington has ever seen. "The most important thing a man has to tell you is what he's not telling you." According to biographer Robert Caro, when Johnson was Senate majority leader in the 1950s, the great Texas politician regularly augmented his power through intense one-on-one conversations with rival politicians. These chats wouldn't end until Johnson unearthed someone else's secret.

Aggressive listeners know these techniques, even if few are as relentless as LBJ. They are persistent, patient, and polite as they keep probing for hidden insights. They keep command, even if they say very little. In the boardroom, such skills seem as rare and mysterious as an ability to speak with the dead. Little wonder that directors feel more comfortable asking outsiders to help, rather than trying to master these dark arts themselves.

In truth, anyone who wants to become an effective listener can do so. Dean Stamoulis, an assessment expert at the executive-search firm of Russell Reynolds, is often in the position of trying to figure out whether a CEO candidate has an admirable commitment to accuracy—or tends to play a bit loose with the facts, creating beautiful first impressions that don't hold up under scrutiny.

To ferret out clues, Stamoulis looks for executives who edit themselves in mid-conversation, making quick adjustments to correct a minor detail. That's a rare habit—and a good sign, he says. When executives talk about a trend "throughout Asia," and then amend their remarks a moment later to say, "or at least in what I've seen of India and China," that impresses him.

In Boston, executive recruiter John Isaacson looks for three key traits, which he calls "hunger, speed, and weight." Hunger is the eagerness to master new challenges. Speed is the ability to do so. And "weight" refers to a leader's judicious use of the power within each job. "Weight is the most essential part of the job, and also the most elusive," Isaacson says. It speaks to the question: Why would anyone follow you?

To get the answers, Isaacson says, "I immerse myself in the history of the person. I want to see, over the course of their adult life, the kinds of tasks they take on and what they excel at. I provide the framework. They fill it in." He's ready to hear about all kinds of approaches. Some leaders succeed by inspiring people. Others function more like shrewd political ward bosses, trading favors to get what they need. Isaacson isn't judgmental. He just wants to know how each leader operates, so that the universities and nonprofits that hire him to run their searches can then make a measured decision about whether this is the right next leader for them.

Can aggressive listening reveal new insights into executives' general problem-solving skills, too? Justin Menkes, a Southern California psychologist, is betting that the answer is "Yes." As part of his Ph.D. dissertation at Claremont Graduate University in 2002, Menkes asked about seventy UCLA business-school students how they would resolve workplace scenarios involving demoralized employees, missed deadlines, or hostile colleagues. Each student offered ideas in a private, videotaped session. Then Menkes picked apart their approaches to see who possessed what he dubbed "executive intelligence."

The results surprised him. A confident, well-dressed man put forth the most vapid ideas. An awkward woman in a rumpled blouse dissected the problems beautifully and explained how to solve them. His two-minute scenarios weren't just reinforcing existing impressions of which candidates were strongest. As Menkes saw it, he was unearthing new, hard-to-get insights about candidates' critical thinking skills. Those findings, he believed, could be a crucial new tool in sizing up leaders.

After earning his Ph.D., Menkes started running critical-thinking tests for corporate clients. He wrote a book about his approach called *Executive Intelligence.* He teamed up with a Canadian business executive, Robert Stark, and formed a small consulting firm, Menkes Stark, that specialized in evaluating what it called "this evasive stuff called executive smarts." Proud of their methods, Menkes and Stark could seem boastful at times. As their Web site proclaimed, "No one more accurately assesses executive talent. We've proven it."

Before long, Stark realized that the little consulting firm would fare a lot better with a big, established partner who could help connect the consultants to boardrooms more gracefully. That partner turned out to be Spencer Stuart, a leading executive-recruiting firm. The two firms started working together in 2003, helping size up internal executive talent for clients such as Interbrew, a big European beer maker. More shared work followed, culminating with Spencer Stuart's acquisition of Menkes Stark in 2007.

"I could see clients' eyes lighting up when Executive Intelligence was being described to them," one of Spencer Stuart's top Silicon Valley partners, Cathy Anterasian, told me. "There's a simplicity to it that resonates with them." She and an Austrian colleague, Gerhard Resch-Fingerlos, took charge of introducing what was now called the "ExI product" to Spencer Stuart clients around the world. Thanks to their guidance, ExI could now be presented with understated confidence instead of braggadocio.

"We just want to see whether leaders can handle themselves well around other people," Resch-Fingerlos told me. That pared-down explanation resonated well with top bosses. A critical test came at one point in New York, when Spencer Stuart presented the ExI approach to its CEO advisory council, which consists largely of retired executives from some of the world's biggest companies. At the end of the demonstration, former Exxon Mobil CEO Lee Raymond declared: "That's the job of a CEO. You're doing it."

By the time I met Menkes in 2010, he and Spencer Stuart had turned these scenarios into a global business line that involved thousands of senior executive assessments worldwide. Menkes's scenarios were positioned as a low-stress way of finding out who could sort through the nasty stuff on the job. Could potential bosses defuse conflict? Could they tell jerks to back off, in ways that were both clear and appropriate? This was perilous territory for corporate directors to explore when top jobs were up for grabs. But the message from within Spencer Stuart was that their scenarios could extract the truth in clear, engaging ways. Candidates might actually like taking the test.

Spencer Stuart clearly had big ambitions for this new approach. It was time to test it on an eager volunteer who hadn't ever managed more than seven people. In other words . . . me.

"I'm going to throw you into a tough situation," Menkes warned me, as he sketched out one of his scenarios. We were sitting in a sleek modern conference room in Spencer Stuart's Los Angeles office. Working from notes on his laptop, Menkes sketched out a business encounter that was about to go horribly wrong. I could see trouble unfolding. There wasn't any obvious way to stop it. What did I want to do about it?

This is just awful, my inner voice said. Menkes had stopped talking. He was staring at me, waiting for my answer. "My reputation is at stake," I began. "I'm scrambling . . . it's too late to stop the meeting . . . there's no sense in having a screaming match." After a few moments of awkward meandering, I hit on a solution that would extricate me from trouble while making only a half-hearted attempt to fix everyone else's problems. As I wrapped up what amounted to a ninety-second answer, I noticed my heart was pounding. Racing to answer these scenarios was surprisingly exciting—and scary.

Once I stopped talking, Menkes adopted the patient voice of a high-school teacher awarding partial credit for a somewhat flawed answer. I got high marks for ethics. He liked my understanding of the risks involved in all directions. Beyond that, nothing about my approach was very impressive. At least I wasn't making the situation worse. Before I could catch my breath, Menkes came at me with an alternative approach that sounded insane. What did I think?

It's hopeless, I said. "You create a firestorm. You need to pick your spots."

Menkes nodded. Then he offered a radically different approach. It was brief, lucid—and way better than my idea.

Gulp. "I like that," I blurted out. "If I think about my original answer, that's an approach that's worth incorporating." I babbled on for a bit, trying to decide whether I should just plain capitulate, or whether it was wiser to look for a way to salvage part of my original approach and create some sort of new, blended alternative. Menkes didn't give me any guidance. He was quite content to let me stumble around the issue for a bit, waiting to see how I sorted it out. He was learning a lot more about my problem-solving skills—or lack of them—than I had expected.

A few minutes later, the demonstration was over. Everything returned to normal. We were just two guys with business cards and laptops having a pleasant conversation in a nice conference room. But the power of Menkes's demonstration remained.

Spencer Stuart had developed a simple, socially acceptable way to see what happens when a corporate leader is hurled into dangerous terrain. Ordinary job interviews don't dare go there. It feels rude, or bullying, to probe for details about the genuine showdowns in an executive's life. Even if interviewers have the nerve to try, most candidates answer guardedly. Such moments feel too personal and too emotional to be shared freely. By conjuring up these scenarios, however, Spencer Stuart had found a way to coax out much more candid answers. In fact, the process didn't even seem to require much coaxing. Once a scenario was in place, I could see, candidates would jump at the chance to "solve" it. Simply by marching through such scenarios (with all their spring-loaded traps), Spencer Stuart's evaluators could explore a dimension of candidates' capabilities that otherwise would almost certainly stay hidden.

Having seen Spencer Stuart's system in action, it was time to find out how corporate clients regarded it. The answer turned out to be more complex than I expected. Instead of telling clients what they expected to hear, Spencer Stuart sometimes brought surprising news. Overlooked managers might fare unexpectedly well on the critical-thinking quizzes, while high-level executives might stumble repeatedly. Were CEOs prepared to act on such disruptive findings? The answers varied greatly.

Some CEOs saw the analysis as a wake-up call, spurring them to deal with talent issues that had been lingering for too long. Other bosses tended to disregard findings that didn't mesh with their long-held views of who could get the job done and who couldn't. Calling on outsiders to size up management talent could be both appealing and jarring. The scenario tests sometimes generated such intense, disruptive findings that executives wanted the right to back off at any time, for any reason. In Europe, Spencer Stuart's scenarios were welcomed as part of the next wave of executive assessment. In the United States, some regarded the experiment as more audacious than accepted.

By contrast, the inch-by-inch approach of ghSMART's marathon interviews has met much less hesitancy in boardrooms. The idea of assessing people on the basis of a close look at their performance to date has been a mainstay of Western culture since biblical times. The notion of asking one group of people to do the hard analytical work of sizing up the candidate's past—while another group explores the more delicate bridge-building possibilities of building a future together—makes intuitive sense. And the mechanics of conducting such interviews have been largely established already, lower down on the career ladder.

In Wadsworth, Illinois, a leafy Chicago suburb, psychologist Brad Smart has built a long career out of showing factory bosses, supermarket chains, and insurance companies how to size up their managers by taking ultra-detailed work histories in face-to-face interviews. He is a methodical, sometimes even dogmatic man. In his world, employees are either A players, B players, or C players. Hire him to size up your workforce, he says, and he will pinpoint the A's that you want to keep and the C's that you want to discharge.

Brad Smart calls his system "Topgrading," and has written a successful book about his methods with the same title. Detractors call his approach "rank and yank." The person with the most intriguing take on the original Smart system is Brad Smart's son, Geoff. A psychologist by training, the younger Smart has retooled his dad's work in a way that is very much akin to stepping into a Toyota factory—and figuring out how a mass-market Camry can be recast as a high-end Lexus.

In Geoff Smart's hands, the original Topgrading template becomes more free-flowing and flexible. Interviewers aren't as closely tied to a rigid checklist; they have a lot more discretion to pursue follow-up questions as they see fit. The list of traits being evaluated becomes more intricate, reflecting the greater complexity of CEOs' jobs. In the biggest switch, the whole process becomes friendlier. Topgrading is obligatory: the sort of program that happens within a company because the boss tells everyone to do it. At ghSMART & Company, Geoff Smart hand-sells his executive interviewing approach to directors and CEO candidates, one at a time. Warmth and polish are a vital part of the experience.

What's it like to be in the midst of a ghSMART interview? I'd rather battle Jared Sullinger for rebounds than pretend that my gypsylike writing career provides a legitimate basis for four hours of scrutiny into my "leadership methods." So instead of wiggling into the interviewee's chair with ghSMART, I pressed the consulting firm for glimpses of how real executives fared. Company founder Geoff Smart provided an overview; his number two executive, Randy Street, pulled back the curtain and showed me more.

The most intriguing examples involved two executives who made almost identical statements partway through their interviews. Each one declared that in a previous job, he had done good work building a sales organization. Each time, a ghSMART interviewer pressed for details. There wasn't anything sly or sophisticated about the follow-up questions. But each simple query required an answer. Each response invited more follow-up questions. Within a few minutes, two profoundly different pictures had emerged.

Street took me through the first example, reconstructed from his notes. "Here's someone who said he was proud of building up a leadership team," Street remarked. "So I asked him: 'How did it go?'"

"*So-so,*" he replied.

"Tell me more."

"*I hired ten people, and I had to let five of them go.*"

"How long did it take you to terminate the weak ones?"

"*Too long. I waited nearly a year.*"

"What did you do next?"

"*I hired five more.*"

"How did that work out?"

"*Better, but we still had some problems.*"

The genius of Street's catechism lay in its grade-school simplicity. There wasn't time for candidates to dress up answers with gentle boasts and mild evasions. Even though Street's tone was cheery and pleasant, the questions kept coming every thirty seconds or so. This wasn't at all like a free-wheeling boardroom conversation. It was a civil but relentless hunt for information. By the time ghSMART's postinterview workup was done, this contender was likely to get high marks for "respect." He wouldn't do nearly as well at "efficiency," "hiring top players," or "developing people." In the category "removes underperformers," his score would be outright poor.

In a ghSMART training video, another executive makes a nearly identical claim about building up a sales force—and then reveals an entirely different narrative. Once again, ghSMART used its blandest questions to elicit the most surprising answers.

"How did you get it done?"

"I fired the bums and hired stars."

"Wow! How did you get started?"

"I went to big clients we weren't doing business with. I went by myself and asked them why they weren't buying from us. This may sound obvious, but it was unorthodox for us. I got the facts and brought them back . . ."

"What did you find?"

"We had an arrogant sales force. We didn't do demos. We wanted clients to do business our way, instead of their way."

"What did you change?"

"I created a crisis. I rallied the troops and told people: These aren't my opinions; these are customers' opinions. Then I told people how much they could increase their income if the group got a bigger market share. And then I publicly hanged a few people."

"You let them go?"

"Yeah."

The entire exchange took only a few minutes. By the end of it, ghSMART's assessors knew they were hearing from a radically different sort of executive: someone who was efficient, decisive, and iron-willed. He had the nerve to try something unorthodox, and the foresight to rally support for his position ahead of time. He didn't flinch at getting rid of underperformers. His main deficit? A lack of respect for people who didn't meet his expectations. The two candidates were polar opposites. Each could thrive at the right sort of company. There wouldn't be a single enterprise on the planet that would regard them as interchangeable.

Could ghSMART's methods point to any universal virtues that help define effective leaders? Or is each boss's job so distinctive that a strength in one situation might be a deficit in another? In 2005, University of Chicago finance professor Steve Kaplan gained access to a decade's worth of ghSMART write-ups, which he then compared to later data concerning CEOs' on-the-job performance. Kaplan and two research colleagues, Mark Klebanov and Morten Sorensen, spent several years analyzing data on more than three hundred CEOs before submitting their findings to the *Journal of Finance,* which in 2010 accepted the paper for publication. Among the professors' conclusions: traits such as organization, aggressiveness, commitment, persistence, proactiveness, setting high standards, and holding people accountable were especially closely tied to later success in leading companies owned by private-equity firms. Meanwhile traits such as teamwork, flexibility, and being open to criticism were less valuable and in some cases might even be detrimental.

The types of ideal leaders that Kaplan and colleagues identified wouldn't always win a popularity contest. So be it. As Kaplan told a graduating group of business-school students in 2008, "CEOs who are persistent and proactive get things done. CEOs who are not, do not get things done, even if they are good listeners, team players, etc. And if you do not get things done, the people working for you get frustrated or even leave, particularly the better ones."

Running a company well requires a lot of hard-nosed resolve. The methods described in this chapter—as diverse as they are—all converge on a single goal: identifying leaders with the skills and resolve to succeed, rather than getting sidetracked by the short-lived allure of glittering resumes and charming personalities.

12: Fitting the Pieces Together

Near the beginning of the movie *Men in Black*, seven clean-cut recruits show up at a massive government building, looking for work. You may not think that a film about stopping space aliens' dastardly plots is also a parable about how to find talent. But that's the sly art of Hollywood's best screenwriters. They lampoon our everyday frailties in the midst of stories that seem like pure escapist entertainment. In this case, the drama-within-a-drama involves the unbearably asinine ways in which the grim-faced boss, Agent Zed, is trying to pick a new alien-fighter.

There is a written test. It goes on forever. Each candidate is stuck inside a weird, egg-shaped chair, without any desks nearby. Test takers end up in pretzel-like positions, struggling to balance test papers on knees or thighs. The vast, sterile exam room is lit like a prison, with harsh overhead bulbs casting ominous shadows. No one knows what's going on. The stress is excruciating but pointless.

Only one recruit dares to snicker: Edwards (played by actor Will Smith). His insouciance galls Agent Zed. Yet at the end, Edwards wins the job. The reason: the night before, Edwards aced the only test that matters. He chased down an alien, racing on foot across the streets of New York City. That is what other field agents admire. For the rest of the movie, Agent Edwards will be the hero.

We love such scenes because they puncture the arrogance of selection systems gone bad. We want Edwards, a hardworking city cop, to get a fair shot. We know that no matter what the line of work, lots of good people are out there, if only the cynics could see them. So when the eerie audition is transformed into a triumph of common sense, that's sweet vindication for us. Even in the movies, picking great talent doesn't need to be a contrived or bullying process. The information we need to make the correct choice is right there in front of us.

This book is meant as an infusion of common sense, too. As a society, we often make talent-picking too contrived and too complicated to be effective. It's time for a better approach. This book started with a young manager at Google, trying to identify the simple clues in people's lives that could signal greatness. The examples that followed have shown how mavericks in many other fields also clear out the clutter, so they can make better decisions. Now it is time to pull together all these examples and principles into a single, cohesive toolkit.

This concluding chapter will spell out three essential ways to put *The Rare Find*'s lessons to work in your own life. These are distilled from interviews with more than one hundred bosses, scouts, recruiters, casting agents, scholars, coaches, editors, venture capitalists, inventors, and surgeons. Not to mention several foundation executives, a Puzzle Master, and an assortment of generals, colonels, majors, and sergeants. Everyone uses different examples and imagery. Time and again, the experts converge on the same three principles.

Widen Your View of Talent

The best assessors in any field look at people differently. It doesn't matter whether the experts wear Army fatigues, business suits, or a surgeon's scrubs. These judges all have the courage to focus on candidates' underlying character and motivation, rather than sticking merely to classic measures of experience. Transcripts, credentials, and job history still matter, but they aren't the whole show anymore. Once some basic level of competency has been established, the key question stops being: "What can you do for us today?" Instead, it becomes: "What might you be able to do for us years from now?"

The payoff from this bolder, more forward-looking perspective can be huge. People early in their careers may still be trying to find the right path. Rather than insist on perfect pedigrees, make room for at least a few offbeat candidates who have shown great hunger for success in unexpected arenas. Over time, those newcomers could redirect their energies in ways that could bring astounding success in the fields that matter most to you. That's why experts like Todd Carlisle, a Ph. D. psychologist at Google, often read résumés "upside down." It is a way of looking for flickers of brilliance that may register first in off-the-job achievements.

Being willing to see people's potential is especially important in smaller, scrappier organizations. If you can't outspend your bigger competitors, it's all the more important to outsmart them. Spotting promise is the great equalizer. In fields such as music and publishing, some of the biggest discoveries have been made by some of the smallest houses. The little-known executives who bet on singer Taylor Swift or author J. K. Rowling succeed by taking small chances before it's fully clear how a newcomer will fare.

Compromise on experience; don't compromise on character. If this were a book about how to hire carefully in fields where basic competence is sufficient, then experience would be king. But we're in the midst of an enormous economic and technological upheaval that is redefining what it means to be enduringly successful. Long track records may be irrelevant or impossible to find in fields that are taking shape so fast that everyone is a newcomer. Competence alone isn't enough anymore. The difference between growth and stagnation comes down to finding people with bold, fresh approaches, who can create opportunities that no one else saw before. That's true not just in Silicon Valley, Hollywood, and Wall Street; it's the new norm in almost every field.

Look at the ways iconic organizations center their talent hunts on people with the right values, rather than a preset level of experience. Goldman Sachs wants strivers. Linear Technology wants tinkerers. The FBI wants "quiet professionals." Each organization has a unique sense of which character values are essential. Such self-awareness can provide a big edge in sizing up candidates whose track records to date look like a weird mix of promise and pitfalls. The more you know about your core values, the easier it will be to shrug off flaws that don't really matter—and to make the most of virtues that your competitors don't understand.

That's the key lesson to draw from the parts of the book that focused on "jagged résumé" candidates. Such people won't succeed everywhere. But if you know your own values well, you will be able to spot the ones who can succeed with you.

Seek out "talent that whispers." The world is full of overlooked people, shunned for reasons of geography, status, or background. Take time, every now and then, to ask what pools of people you aren't seeing—but should. Sometimes all that is required is a willingness to consider Kansas when everyone is fussing over the same limited pool of candidates on the Eastern Seaboard. Other times, looking in new places involves the courage to start hiring women on Wall Street when other firms aren't. It may feel safer to stick with the pack. But scouting the same way everyone else does amounts to paying a huge "conformity tax."

On the fringes of talent, ask: "What can go right?" Most conventional assessment is all about finding candidates' flaws. That's appropriate in the final stages of selection, when top-tier candidates have already established their allure. But if you're going to spot some promising long shots, you need different methods. The great unexpected discoveries happen only if assessors are willing to suspend their skepticism at first, so that the underdogs get a chance to show a spark of promise. On such expeditions, bring your open-mindedness, optimism, and curiosity. The scouts who fare best are the ones most willing to be surprised.

Take tiny chances—so you can take more of them. In some of the most speculative talent-hunting domains—such as art, popular music, and the outer edges of publishing, sports, and political campaigning—it's impossible to say for sure which long shots will succeed. All you can establish is what amounts to a portfolio of long shots. It's as if you bought a fistful of lottery tickets. Good instincts can improve your odds a bit. But it's just as important to make your misfires as painless as possible, so that you can be more daring.

There's a lesson in the publishing adventures of editors whose bestselling books were bought with advances of less than $5,000, because they were willing to speculate on authors who didn't catch anyone else's eye. There's another lesson in Facebook's use of automatically evaluated puzzles to start a low-cost conversation with crack programmers around the world. If you want to explore the long tail of talent, find ways to minimize the costs, distractions, and emotional fatigue associated with frequent mismatches. That way, you can take your boldest risks with your smallest dollars. Your prospecting can pay off even when yields seem meager.

Find Inspirations That Are Hidden in Plain Sight

The Rare Find is based on a belief that the talent-hunting principles are powerful and universal. That is why previous chapters have drawn examples from so many arenas. Patterns that may be difficult to see in one realm can be stunningly clear in others. This willingness to learn by analogy isn't just a hallmark of this book. It is how the experts themselves stay sharp. During the interviews that shaped each chapter, I discovered that one of the most clear-thinking Army officers liked to draw comparisons to baseball. Software companies knew a surprising amount about how great teachers are recognized. Venture capitalists found parallels to Hollywood. And an advertising executive couldn't stop talking about the military. Talent is a universal language that just happens to be spoken in many different dialects.

Draw out the "hidden truths" of each job. It's unnerving how many talent hunts go astray because no one ever makes a brave, clear-headed call about what the job really requires. Look at what happens when universities hire academia's most brilliant arguers to be their presidents, or when sports teams rely on stopwatches and radar guns to pick their next stars. Disappointment beckons. If quests are driven mostly by prestige or a desire to focus on traits that sound good and are easy to measure, trouble awaits. Only later do universities realize that they really wanted the careful diplomat; sports teams, the iron-willed competitor. Chapter 2 pointed out the importance of business strategist Peter Drucker's great maxim: "Think through the assignment." His advice sounds so obvious that many organizations don't bother with it. Their standards remain hazy or superficial. They are in too much of a hurry to get started with the drama of screening candidates, without ever fully knowing what the hunt is all about.

Slow down. Take stock of the hidden virtues that define success for your particular situation. Your results will be vastly better.

Be willing to use your own career is a template. One of the best talent recognition tools at our disposal is free of charge, doesn't require any special training, and often produces great results. Yet many leaders are loath to use it. They shy from invoking their own life experiences when looking for ways to evaluate candidates. That's because they feel trapped by a school of thought that calls for extreme neutrality in assessments—wiping away any trace of personal insight in the name of avoiding bias. Such anxieties are downright counterproductive. Without personal insight, all that is left is a civil service approach to filling positions by formula.

Sometimes you will want people who share your strengths. Think of admissions director James Weiss at Johns Hopkins Medicine, whose childhood ordeals made him into a very compassionate doctor. He is an expert, now, at spotting such compassion in premed applicants. But your opportunities go far beyond hiring "mini-me." Seek out people with strengths you never had—but always admired. One of the best recruiters in women's college basketball today is Amy Tucker, an associate coach at Stanford, who was a classic, post-up shooter in her younger days. Many of Tucker's best finds have been superb, ballhandling guards. They don't play the way she did. Instead, they are the players on the court who make it possible for the Amy Tuckers to succeed.

Harvest a wide range of insights from your own experience. Think about all the talents an organization needs to succeed. Look for winners in each dimension.

Rely on auditions to see *how* and *why* people achieve the results they do. In any field where public performance is part of the job—and that includes everything from sports and music to corporate leadership—there comes a time to see what candidates can do. Instead of relying strictly on the indirect insights that emerge from résumés, references, and interviews, it is time to ask the actor to step on stage; the pilot to crawl into the simulator; the educator to teach a class. With a well-run audition, it's possible to see right away who possesses the right stuff.

To learn the most from an audition, pay attention to more than the absolute caliber of the performance. Concentrate hardest on what you can learn about the candidate's character. Auditions provide a rare chance to see how a candidate achieves his or her results, not just what gets done. Pay attention to intensity of effort, teamwork, and resiliency. Conversely, watch carefully to see who cuts corners, who turns brittle under pressure, and who ultimately doesn't care. Some of the most intriguing clues may surface in a small gesture or a casual remark during a break. Take in everything. Whether you are dazzled or not is only a small part of what you can learn from an audition.

Master the art of aggressive listening. In most organizations, listening is regarded as passive and powerless. All the glory and excitement resides with the people who are up on the brightly lit stage, doing the talking. Listeners are the anonymous souls sitting in the darkness, absorbing someone else's message. But great talent scouts are great listeners—and there isn't anything passive about the way they size up other people. The best assessors are constantly posing tests and interjecting questions. They hear not just what is said, but why and how it is said, too. That's the lesson to take away from basketball scouts watching the many social cues of players' conduct during time-outs—or from casting agents looking for unexpected little quirks that could signal a gifted actor who needs to be trying out for different roles.

When you are an aggressive listener, you interview candidates differently. Once you get past the initial pleasantries, you don't ramble or try to make friends. You stay focused and intensely interested, but not "palsy." Zero in on the issues that matter most to you, which usually relate to candidates' core character. Ask a lot of follow-up questions. Keep digging. Your best queries may be as basic as "Why?" or "What happened next?" In the course of getting to know a candidate, don't settle for well-rehearsed stories. Look for ways to pull back the curtain on candidates' aspirations, frustrations, and lifelong habits, both good and bad.

Anyone can master these habits. Once you do so, you will see more, hear more, and know more. You will enjoy a new sense of control, and a deeper understanding of other people's potential.

Simplify Your Search for Talent

Be willing to pick one trait that matters more than anything. Often the ability to recover from setbacks is what separates people who surpass expectations from those who disappoint. Resilience is prized by Army Special Forces, by Teach For America, and by some leading hedge funds, as they look for portfolio managers who can think calmly in a market meltdown. Yet our societal attitudes toward resilience are as tangled as can be. When periods of crisis are long past, we celebrate resilience. Yet when life is playing out in real time, there's no room for even a whisper of anxiety about setbacks along the way.

American social norms call for job candidates to tell a story of uninterrupted success. Previous experiences are burnished until they all sound like triumphs. Traditional résumés are set up so that resilience becomes invisible. That's a horribly unfortunate distortion. At some point, fate slams all of us to the ground. What happens next determines who we become. Some people are so bitter or dispirited that they never fully recover. Others do whatever it takes to bounce back. The more you can learn about how people handle adversity, the more astutely you can judge them.

Be alert to other invisible virtues, too. Curiosity is also invisible on most résumés yet it is a remarkable talisman in many careers. One of the all-time greatest groupings of high-tech talent took place at the University of Utah in the late 1960s and early 1970s. A handful of graduate students there became the pioneers who led the creation of Pixar movie studios, early Apple Macintosh computers, the Netscape Internet browser company, and more. These innovators didn't have especially great grades in college or dazzling early work histories. But they were burning with desire to get to the frontiers of knowledge and to create something exciting. That gung-ho curiosity was the key to their later success.

Efficiency is another oft-overlooked virtue. Glance at someone's work for just a brief spell, and you can't tell much. Lots of people are working on interesting projects; it's hard to tell how fast any of them are moving. Know people over longer spans, and you can start to see enormous differences in people's output. Some people struggle to creep forward, or end up stumbling in circles. Others make every minute count; they are the Franz Joseph Haydns with 106 symphonies or the Thomas Edisons with 1,093 patents. If efficiency matters to you, take a tip from venture capitalists. Figure out a way to stretch out the getting-acquainted period so you can see your most interesting candidates in action for a month or two. The best ones will rip through their to-do lists, week after week. The inefficient ones will remain stuck on the same tasks as work keeps piling up.

Self-reliance rounds out the list. The farther people advance in life, the less guidance anyone else can provide about what to do next. That's the excitement—and the terror—in being at the front of the pack. People who can set their own agenda, wisely and productively, are invaluable. How do you find them? On paper, everyone is a self-starter, constantly "launching," "creating," or "spearheading" various initiatives. Move beyond the slogans, though, and it's easier to tell who can find the right path when none is obvious.

Insist on the right talent. Glistening résumés can get caught up in some of the bitterest leadership failures. A brilliant Cabinet secretary stumbles as a university president. An All-American college quarterback can't make it in the pros. A famous entrepreneur plunges his second start-up into bankruptcy. The key insight: the more prominent a talent hunt may be, the easier it is for selectors to lose track of what they really need. Candidates' prestige, social affinity, and other factors become huge distractions. It's easy to end up with someone who is spectacular, but also spectacularly wrong for the job. Assessors focus on what's easy or gratifying to evaluate, not what is important. Only afterward is it clear how much got overlooked in the stampede to make a decision that looked good.

Push your best candidates to grow even stronger. It's exciting to be scouting among candidates with "talent that shouts." It's also perilous. If top performers don't feel tied into the organization that hires them, all their marvelous potential may be useless. Their careers may be marked by quarrels, betrayals, squandered opportunities, and repeated job-hopping in moments of anger. In such situations, even the nicest perks and bonuses won't buy lasting loyalty if they aren't accompanied by the chance to do great work. There's a fine lesson in the way that talent-rich organizations such as Johns Hopkins Medicine, General Electric, and Pixar deal with their highest achievers.

Top talent wants to be challenged, not coddled. These racehorse personalities are driven by such an intense desire to make a mark in the world that it surpasses every other motivator. Play to that reality. Set audacious goals and run the hardest auditions. Develop legends within your organization that become models of how the most gifted achievers should carry themselves. Portray hardship and possible failure as selling points for your jobs, rather than as liabilities. Middle-of-the-pack candidates won't want any part of this. But for exceptionally talented souls, such heroic quests are thrilling and addictive. Winners will push themselves remarkably hard to stay on top. Candidates' potential for growth won't be a mystery anymore. Motivation will reveal itself as the selection process plays out. And successful candidates will form competitive friendships with their peers, in ways that will drive everyone forward for years to come.

Become a citadel of achievement. Here's an example of what does not work. In the late 1990s, someone at Enron decided that it would be a fine idea to adorn its Houston headquarters with brightly colored banners affirming the company's values. So workmen were summoned and hoists were raised. Before long, anyone who walked into Enron's lobby could behold four giant words: RESPECT, INTEGRITY, COMMUNICATION, and EXCELLENCE. All are lovely terms. Anyone can put them on a lobby ceiling. But Enron's toxic corporate culture made a mockery of those adjectives. After Enron collapsed in scandal in late 2001, government investigators found the company's growth was built in large part by sharp-edged schemers. The values that actually defined Enron turned out to be contempt, rapaciousness, dissembling, and fraud.

By contrast, the most dedicated talent spotters aren't trying to win rhetoric contests. They simply make the right choices, day after day. They don't even see their own "Wow!" moments. To them, extraordinary effort is a way of life. If you really care about people, and you really care about your craft, why would you act in any other manner?

All through the research for this book, I kept coming across examples of decision makers putting so much effort into what seemed like minor parts of their job that it made me wonder: "Have they lost perspective? Are they teetering on the wrong side of the dividing line between dedicated and obsessive?" Special Forces sergeants patrolled roads at 2 A.M. in the North Carolina pinelands. Emily Lewis-Lamonica kept cold-calling influential professors at college campuses, trying to drum up more interest in Teach For America, even though her program was already oversubscribed ten-fold. John Cameron put his scalpel away on weekends but he couldn't stay away from the hospital. At 8 A.M. each Sunday he invited the rawest interns to join him for an hour of informal chat about surgery—passing along whatever pointers and lore he thought might help them.

"Does it really matter that much?" I wondered.

The answer is: Yes it does. People with great reputations for attracting and developing talent regard the search for brilliance as their calling. They see themselves as discoverers, protectors, and builders of an entire discipline. They don't just hope to get lucky for a few years, create a fancy reputation for themselves—and then wait lazily for more good candidates to show up. They are cultivating a garden, not running a toll booth. No matter how long they have been sizing up people, there are moments when they act as if it's still their first year on the job, and they are just starting to explore the outer bounds of what they can accomplish.

If you choose to champion great talent, you will be picking one of the most altruistic things a person can do. Making the most of the next generation of achievers is akin to parenting, except on a larger scale. The benefits to society are likely to be much greater than the personal gain. In any given year, quick-hit operators may make more money and win more recognition, at least briefly. Over time, though, that dynamic reverses. The greatest builders of talent—people like Harvard's late-nineteenth-century president Charles Eliot, for example—come to be appreciated on an ever greater scale after their time in office. That is when we realize the vastness and the durability of what they have done.

13: Becoming a Rare Find

Shortly after the hardcover edition of this book was published, a group of entrepreneurs and young professionals convened a networking event in Southern California under the banner "Embracing the Jagged Résumé." Attendees arrived with more than hiring on their minds. This was a union of like-minded strivers, all seeking validation of the unusual career paths they had followed. One of this book's central concepts was taking on a second life as a personal badge of pride for America's unusual achievers.

In Washington, Daniel H. Pink, the enormously popular motivation and work-practices guru, told his readers that he was particularly intrigued by the concept of the jagged résumé because it struck a chord in his life, too. By the late 1990s, he had earned a law degree from Yale but hadn't ever practiced the profession. He had worked on the losing side of several political campaigns. He had ended up as a political speechwriter because of what he ruefully described as "my lack of aptitude for anything else." After a stint working for Vice President Al Gore, Pink was out of work and not sure where to turn. Yet he was on the brink of creating a powerful career for himself, jagged résumé and all. Within a few years, Pink became renowned as the champion of "Free Agent Nation" and a series of other powerful business ideas.

The core ideas of this book—listening for talent that whispers, making room for the jagged résumé, valuing character markers such as resilience, and so on—turn out to be crucial in unexpected ways. Each tenet's significance extends beyond business leadership and the creation of high-impact organizations. There is a personal dimension to these principles as well. They point the way for anyone looking to avoid professional stagnation and instead to make the most of his or her career.

So in this final chapter, it's time to turn our perspective 180 degrees. We've seen what the world looks like from the vantage point of the sergeant on the hill, the coach on the sidelines, or the editor at her desk. Dispassionate assessors of talent have already enjoyed their turn as the book's protagonists. Now they fade into the background so that attention can focus on people hoping to become tomorrow's world-class achievers.

Future stars don't rest in a gazebo, immobilized, waiting for someone to notice them. They hone their craft. They set their goals. What's more, they move into the spotlight so that when the big-league talent-spotters do arrive, the odds of being recognized aren't hopeless. In short, it's possible to improve the odds of becoming a rare find.

Inklings of these opportunities have been imbedded in many of the stories told so far. Evan Priestley didn't wait for one of Facebook's California recruiters to find him in faraway Maine; he took his chances on a difficult programming test that was open to all comers. J.K. Rowling didn't let elite publishers' disdain deter her from pursuing a career as a novelist; she signed on with a smaller house that had something to prove, too. And the best young surgeons-in-training at Johns Hopkins didn't rest on their past achievements; during their first few months as interns they won their mentor's respect by establishing how much they wanted to keep improving.

If you are reading this chapter because leading employers seem dismissive and impenetrable, don't assume that your job searches must be restricted by their barriers. New techniques are creating exciting ways to run a job hunt on your terms. Yes, it may take luck for everything to work out, but to a surprising extent you can control your own luck.

Build a plan of action that starts bringing you closer to your goal, and you greatly increase the chances that serendipity can help you prevail. If you have something special to offer the working world, there ought to be some way to stand out. That's true even if you're coming to market with a jagged résumé in which your greatest strengths might be masked by some supposed flaws. You can succeed even if you didn't graduate from the perfect school, earn perfect grades, or log time in the perfect summer internships.

If you are a natural project manager, then develop a project plan. If you like marketing, build a marketing campaign that centers on reasons why employers should want you. If you prefer detective work, make your job search a scavenger hunt of monumental proportions. Whatever approach you settle on—and no matter what job you want—you will get a better chance to show your mettle. In particular:

- You will escape the clutter of job-posting stampedes, where the odds of winning even a barista's job can be slimmer than the chances of getting into Harvard.
- You will start finding jobs through the "hidden market," even as you discover the value of small companies with big ambitions.
- You will brand yourself as an ultravaluable "quick learner."
- Finally, you will learn to construct a social media profile that becomes a beacon to great employers looking for talent. The payoff: in many cases, they will find you.

Escaping the Clutter

Right now, much of the job market is a crowded, frustrating mess. Leading online job boards such as Monster.com and CareerBuilder routinely list at least one million openings in the United States. Job fairs and government postings appear to offer equally rich pickings. Scroll through those listings, and it can seem as if the whole world is waiting to hire you, regardless of how fastidious you might be about careers and locations. Interested in being a dental hygienist in Florida? Monster has fourteen jobs available. Would you rather try Java development in Seattle? CareerBuilder can point you toward 230 openings. The chances to imagine "what if" are endless.

Yet that early euphoria vanishes when candidates discover what happens next. Each listing, on average, will attract more than one hundred applicants. Really good jobs may attract five hundred or more seekers. Hiring managers shudder when the digital résumés start arriving in their e-mail inboxes. In their eyes, they've been pelted with a terrifying spray of solicitations from strangers across the country, including many who lack the skills, experience, or interest to be serious candidates. The only way to stay sane is to kick out 90 percent or more of those candidates as fast as possible—and then focus a bit more intently on the last few survivors.

Picture a hiring manager, stuck at a desk at 6:45 P.M., unable to go home until he or she clicks "Delete" on ninety résumés. Each application is likely to get no more than a five-second scan, with a finger hovering over the DEL key all the while. Limited industry experience? DEL! Slow to graduate? DEL! Currently unemployed? DEL! Typo on the cover letter? DEL! Silly-sounding e-mail address? DEL! DEL! DEL!

When the purges are finished, candidates can't guess why they got cut. As Wharton management professor Peter Cappelli observes,

"There is virtually no feedback. Applicants feel helpless. They don't know what it means not to hear back. If they are rejected, they don't know why. It can easily seem random."

Similar disappointments await candidates seeking work by answering newspaper job ads or by mailing résumés to human resources departments without helpful allies talking up their candidacies. By some estimates, as many as forty million unsolicited résumés are floating around the HR departments of U.S. companies, waiting for somebody—anybody!—to review them. Most submissions won't get a glance. At best, a candidate's résumé may be run through automated screening software to see if it includes enough of the right keywords to warrant a closer look.

No wonder Richard Bolles, author of the bestseller *What Color Is Your Parachute?*, dismisses online job boards, career fairs, and unsponsored résumé mailings as three of the most frustrating ways of seeking work. As he points out, an unmanageable rush of candidates turns such situations into "an elimination game." Employers stop looking for reasons to like you. They devote their early energy to coming up with reasons *not* to hire you. The process is swift, arbitrary, and pretty much impossible to appeal.

Throwing huge numbers of candidates through harsh and superficial sorting isn't just bad for you; it's tiresome and disappointing for employers as well. Companies don't like wading through mismatched résumés. Deep down, they know their five-second assessments are woefully imprecise in sizing up candidates. Creating a dumpster full of failed résumés is hardly ideal for them, either. Employers would much rather pursue hiring methods that are more personal, more in-depth—and more visibly influenced by the delicate art of personal judgment. In fact, most do so by using what's called the hidden job market.

Karen Siwak, a job-search strategist with Résumé Confidential, estimates that more than 60 percent of all jobs are filled quietly, without a formal announcement or job posting. How do employers do it? They ask their employees for referrals. They scout the competition. And, most important, they drop hints to all sorts of trusted people in their ecosystem—customers, suppliers, lawyers, accountants, ad agencies, and the like. The message: "If you know someone good who might want to work for us, let us know."

Add up these channels, and you have the hidden market. If you're thinking, "This sounds like the way people got hired 150 years ago," you're right. Reflect on it a bit more, and you'll realize there's only one reason such an old-fashioned hiring system can still be going strong.

It works.

Careful referrals remain the best way of sizing up someone's performance and character in detail. Employers prize insight from someone who has seen firsthand, over long spans, how candidates behave at their best (and worst). These are the people who know how eager you are to improve, how you handle criticism, whether you're more comfortable being a leader or a follower, and so on. So much of successful hiring is defined by figuring out who will thrive in a new culture over time. Sheer competence is the essential prerequisite, of course. But the difference between great hires—and ones that blow up—often comes down to questions of "fit."

If you already have a fine referral network, then the hidden market can start working its magic for you. But most people haven't focused on building such networks and aren't sure how to proceed. You need a way to engage the hidden market's decision makers.

Cracking the Hidden Market

Let's start with an analogy. Suppose you want a nice apartment that will become your home for the next few years. Perhaps you're moving to a big city such as New York, Chicago, or Seattle. Maybe you're opting for a college community such as Madison, Chapel Hill, or

Austin. Either way, you've got a dream outcome in mind. Maybe you and a friend want two bedrooms, hardwood floors, and a lakeside view. Or possibly you're looking for a quiet street, a short walk to downtown, and a modern kitchen with skylights.

Can you succeed with a hunting strategy that's purely reactive? Let's see what happens. First, you burn up time waiting for someone else to start the process. You're constantly on the prowl for online listings or fresh ads in the local paper. Once you see a listing, you race into action, hoping your belated energy will make up for your late start. You phone strangers, set up appointments, and race off to see one disappointment after another.

Just about all the listings involve flawed apartments. They're too old, too expensive, too noisy, too dark, or too likely to be in an unpleasant part of town. On the rare occasion when a great apartment does come on the market, you try to shove your way past twenty or more people who all want to rent it, too. You're constantly competing and never winning. After a few months of this, you start to notice something spooky. The best apartments in town are never listed. They don't need to be. Somehow they keep getting filled through a back-channel process that's invisible to you.

Sound familiar?

Now consider a totally different strategy, favored by journalist and health care expert David Whelan. (He happens to know a lot about the housing market and even more about finding jobs.) Here's what David recommends:

"Stop looking at classifieds. Instead, find five buildings in the city that meet your criteria. Introduce yourself to the owner of the buildings, the superintendent, the property manager, and the broker who does the listings. You might get lucky right away and find out about an opening that hasn't yet been advertised. Or, at the very least, you have the opportunity to make a good impression with these people. Now there's a chance they will think of you, right away, when a tenant gets ready to move out."

Hunt for a great job, and the same concept is even more powerful. The best job opportunities seldom are posted for public scrutiny. They will quietly be claimed by people who play one step ahead of everyone else in the hidden job market. There are lots of ways to put that principle into action, but they all center on a basic truism: *Get to know the landlord.*

Early in his career, Whelan was working as a reporter for the *Contra Costa Times*, a relatively small California newspaper serving the eastern suburbs of San Francisco. It was a decent place to start, but he had bigger ambitions. "I was desperate to move into a job at a top business publication," he recalls. "I knocked really hard on the doors of *Fortune, The Wall Street Journal, Forbes,* and *BusinessWeek,*" hoping for something in their San Francisco bureaus.

Whelan's breakthrough came when he made a crucial connection with Quentin Hardy, *Forbes*'s San Francisco bureau chief at the time. Some early banter led to lunch meetings every month or two. Whelan pitched new story ideas each time. After a while, Hardy suggested meeting *Forbes*'s editor in chief, Bill Baldwin. So Whelan created a New York stopover on a family trip and stopped in to see the big boss at *Forbes*.

"Bill showed up ninety minutes late because he had forgotten about the meeting," Whelan recalls. "But when he finally arrived, we had a great conversation about stock buybacks and other topics. And within two months, I had a job at *Forbes*—even though there was officially a hiring freeze at the time."

Need another illustration? Fast-forward a few years to Whelan's next career stage, when he was pursuing an advanced degree in health administration at the University of Iowa. Each winter, students constantly scan the department's internal Web site waiting to see what summer internship opportunities will be posted. Then dozens of them compete for those three or four spots.

Whelan, of course, opted for a different plan. He wanted an internship at Children's Hospital of Philadelphia, one of the nation's most renowned treatment centers. CHOP wasn't seeking applicants from Iowa. But Whelan introduced himself to the hospital's chief executive anyway. Then, as Whelan puts it, "I followed up repeatedly with him until he understood how much I admired his organization." Within a few months, Whelan had the Philadelphia internship he wanted.

As you pursue these sorts of openings, remember the three Ps—be persistent, patient, and polite. You will need to do a lot of prospecting; not every appealing opportunity will bear fruit. But if you start by figuring out what neighborhood you want to live in, you will be off to a good start. Then figure out how to get noticed by decision makers or the people who influence them.

In the publicly posted job market—with all its frustrations, overcrowding, and slim chances—openings either exist or they don't. You aren't expected to knock on companies' doors unbidden. They will tell you when they are ready to hire. The rules are clear, yet they camouflage a different system that works much better.

In the hidden market, job opportunities arise quietly and gradually. Bosses watch for interesting candidates, expecting to match people, projects, and jobs as the future takes shape. A classic example in American history involves Army General George Marshall's efforts to get to know his officer corps in detail during the late 1930s. He could tell that war in Europe was coming. He would need to build army leadership to a huge degree once the fighting started. Some of his top officers weren't capable of leading major parts of the war effort. Some of their subordinates were. So Marshall took it upon himself to visit countless military outposts and form a detailed opinion of each officer's potential. When war did arrive, he could rapidly promote his highest-potential officers to jobs of great power, while sliding aside others whose seniority masked mediocrity.

Even in everyday commerce—where the stakes aren't nearly so momentous—the best bosses and hiring managers think like George Marshall. They know that anticipating change is a huge part of their jobs. So even if they aren't hiring today, they want to meet bright people who could help their business in the future. There's more room than you would expect to get a conversation started.

What are you going to talk about? Your first visit can be a classic "informational interview." You aren't looking for a job (yet). All you want is to learn a bit about what a career in this field would be like. If you ask politely and show some fascination with the field, you will be surprised how many people are willing to clear out a few minutes on the phone or over coffee to share some stories and insights with you. Your odds improve even more if you seek a briefing from someone who grew up in your hometown or attended your college. Even a minor point of shared identity is enough to break the ice.

As careers expert Alexandra Levit points out, briefers are friendliest if they can regard you as a modern-day version of who they used to be, years ago.

Don't rush to turn these early conversations into a "Hire me!" pitch. There's a ritual to these exchanges, and it starts by establishing that you're an engaging, helpful person. Provide some benefit to the people you're speaking with, says California recruiting expert John Sumser, and you earn the right to ask favors from them.

How good is your network of contacts? Your first assessment may be far too modest. No, you don't have the private cell phone number of every U.S. senator, and you haven't played golf at Pebble Beach with CEOs of America's largest companies. But you don't need such glittering connections to have a strong network in your own right.

Start with college alumni—particularly people with whom you might share a tie to a campus club, sports team, fraternity, sorority, or undergraduate major. LinkedIn can be your ally, too. Pick a few companies that intrigue you, and then use www.linkedin.com/alumni to find people who got their start at your university. Next, follow up with an e-mail or phone call. Your entry point is good enough to create rapport, even if you and your potential ally haven't ever met.

Now consider people you might know through church, civic work, summer jobs, ROTC, or military reserves. Many high achievers guard their calendars against pursuers craving a work favor. But these leaders can be surprisingly generous with their time if your point of entry involves a shared connection outside the office. Groups as diverse as Amnesty International, the World Wildlife Fund and the National Rifle Association have been networking havens over the years.

Naturally you shouldn't fake an interest in a civic group that appeals to you only as a career ladder. It won't take long for other people to become suspicious about your motives to the point that they will frown on your efforts and tell others to steer clear of you, too. But if it's a cause that rings true to you, keep your mind open to the possibility that other volunteers on that canned food drive just might care about your career hopes, too.

Bring some energy to this quest! Once people sense that you're an engaged, optimistic person, you will be surprised how generous they can be with tips and contacts. If you're shy or unsure of yourself at times, striking up these conversations can seem a little odd and uncomfortable. Those doubts will vanish fast if you keep faith in what you're selling: the chance to hire you. Give your inner skeptic some time off. Draw on whatever motivational techniques have helped you achieve in the past. Remind yourself that you only need one contact to pay off for the whole exercise to be worth it.

Make special room in your contact list, too, for people with rambling, on-the-go jobs that bring them in constant contact with the decision makers you care about. You're looking for the equivalent of the FedEx driver who calls on elite hedge funds in Greenwich, Connecticut. (In fact, if you want to start as a receptionist or tech support person at a hedge fund, you *do* want to be talking to the FedEx guy.) If you're interested in a career in fine dining, it wouldn't hurt to chat with a local restaurant inspector about which owners and chefs impress him and which ones don't. Odds are his gleanings over the years can alert you to hidden-market opportunities long before any job openings are posted.

Here's one more surprise about your network. It's not your closest friends who are most likely to guide you into a great job. Their networks typically are too similar to yours. That vast overlap of friends makes you feel comfortable being around them. But it also means that they aren't likely to arrange introductions that never would have occurred to you.

Instead, the people you know only slightly may be able to do you the biggest favors. Stanford University sociologist Mark Granovetter documented this in the 1970s when he tracked the contacts most important in helping people find new jobs. He found that 55 percent of referrals came from people whom subjects saw only occasionally, while another 28 percent came from people they saw even less often. Author Malcolm Gladwell featured this finding in his first book, *The Tipping Point,* and it has been a topic of conversation ever since.

Not only do your casual acquaintances enjoy more diverse networks, they may also spend less time stressing about whether a new job prospect is exactly right for you. Sometimes too much knowledge can be stifling. Suppose someone knows you well enough to compile a detailed mental list of all your job preferences (short commute, five weeks of vacation, no overly stern bosses, etc.). That good friend may never spot an ideal job for you. Casual acquaintances are more likely to send recommendations your way, without worrying about whether a match is perfect.

Sharon Jones, an author and former associate director of

UNC–Chapel Hill's career services office, says that in her experience, fourth- and fifth-stage contacts tend to be the most common ways that people find their first few jobs. Now we're talking about reconnecting with your freshman-year roommate (stage one) whose older sister (stage two) works at a great company where the hiring manager (stage three) would be willing to introduce you to the design team boss (stage four) who needs three new graphic artists in a hurry.

Each link is a bit of jump into the unknown, but you don't need everything to line up perfectly ahead of time for such chains to work. As long as you get started, there's likely to be an interesting prospect down the road.

I Can Learn It Quickly

Start a career in sports, music, or movies—and you will be judged at first by how much you might improve. Professional scouts in those fields know greatness often roars out of nowhere. They look beyond your current efforts, envisioning who you might become. That soaking wet actress who lost her script may turn out to be the next Julia Roberts. That skinny Panamanian pitcher throwing on a backyard field could be another Mariano Rivera. That unknown teen singer with her parents in tow might be a new Taylor Swift. In such fields, raw promise is enough to start finding work, as long as breakthroughs might lie ahead.

In the mainstream corporate job market, the hunt for potential ought to be just as important. Companies thrive by finding people like Alex Ivlev: a Siberian immigrant in his mid-twenties who joined IGN Entertainment as a software developer after an unlikely journey into high tech. He brought the skills, focus, and desire to become a long-term winner, even though his patchy résumé included two years of community college and a stint as a restaurant manager at Fat Daddy's café in Ocean City, Maryland. San Francisco–based IGN took a chance on him for two reasons: he demonstrated strong coding skills on his application, and he wrote persuasively of his hard work to win a better life. Before hiring him full-time, IGN offered him a six-week summer tryout under an offbeat recruiting program known as Code Foo. That provided bosses with a relaxed, safe way of sizing up dozens of intriguing but unproven candidates—and figuring out which ones would be wise permanent hires.

More often, companies struggle to balance potential and pickiness. Top management may be fascinated by unproven potential. But your immediate boss is likely to be frazzled, demanding, and worried about your Day One productivity. Line managers don't enjoy the luxury of imagining how good everything could be in five years. They are constantly judged by this week's challenges. Life is all about getting something into production, shipped, and sold. Defect rates matter. In this world, a single day's blunder can be career ending.

If there's no way to get hired without winning the support of a stressed-out line manager with a short time horizon, what can you do?

Turn this predicament to your advantage. Reframe the conversation so you can meet the manager's anxieties while redirecting attention to your strengths. Showcase your ability to master new challenges, especially if you're early enough in your career that your work history is sparse. You already have figured out how to live independently. You have tried out various part-time or summer jobs. You have plunged into new areas of academic study on short notice; you've probably traveled to unfamiliar places and helped build some clubs, teams, or activities where you started out as a stranger and became a valued member of the group. You are at your best when you are thrown into a new situation, even if the only advice you get is: "Figure it out, quickly!"

In short, potential bosses should see you as a quick learner.

Have you heard the saying, "Hire for attitude; train for skill"? It's the title of a legendary article that *Fast Company* magazine ran in 1996 and republished in 2007. It explains why innovative companies like Southwest Airlines and DoubleTree Hotels cherish quick learners, even if these hires don't have much direct experience related to their new jobs. The *Fast Company* article also explains how employers classify candidates. That's useful knowledge: it can help you explain your merits in language that resonates with the interviewer across the table.

Consider how Californian John Duckett set out to become a high-end winemaker. That's a hard field to break into. It's a bit like screenwriting, fashion design, travel photography, or sports announcing. In these glamorous arenas a few superstars become world famous. Meanwhile another few thousand professionals earn a good living in these fields and win their peers' recognition. After that, no end of people dream of getting into these fields, but never get past the ranks of frustrated dreamers.

A few years into his quest, Duckett was still on the fringe. He had studied enology in college and spent three summers as a low-paid intern at California wineries. That was a decent start, but it didn't rocket him past thousands of other people, all chasing a few openings at elite vineyards. He needed more experience to win the full-time job he wanted. There wasn't much to gain by staying at home and mailing out résumés.

So in the midst of the U.S. winter, Duckett traveled halfway around the world. After a seven-thousand-mile flight, he arrived in New Zealand, ready to work a third internship, this time at Delegat's Wine Estate, maker of some of the world's most renowned chardonnays and sauvignon blancs. The southern hemisphere's harvest season was under way, and Delegat's needed an extra pair of hands. Much of his work was menial. Working as many as twelve hours a day, Duckett moved barrels, operated machinery, and kept everything sanitary. He also got a chance to mingle with the savvy winemakers who produced Delegat's Oyster Bay wines, learning everything he could about their craft.

When Duckett finished his stint in New Zealand, he no longer was indistinguishable from thousands of college-trained wannabes knocking on winemakers' doors. He had shown a deeper commitment to the field. He had gained valuable overseas training. He quickly found work as a lab technician at Jordan Vineyard & Winery in California's Alexander Valley. By the end of the year, Jordan had promoted him into its wine-making ranks, as an enologist.

Could you share a version of that New Zealand wine cellar story to a different employer? Think carefully. It worked for Duckett for two reasons. It spoke to his determination to make it as an enologist, even if it meant paying his dues far from home. It also allowed him to train with the best. Among wine aficionados, a New Zealand tour of duty wins admiration. His willingness to do sweaty chores on the way up was totally appropriate; winemaking is one of many crafts in which success involves a blend of physical labor and exquisite judgment.

Try telling a similar story to a global investment bank, though, and your candidacy will collapse within seconds. Bankers don't do physical labor, except to press the yellow Go button on a Bloomberg Terminal. They're looking for brainpower and breeding. An office internship in London or Hong Kong may impress them; spending time scrubbing floors at bank branches in New Zealand won't.

The key insight: find stories from your life that speak to the skills most prized by the organization you want to join. Expect your interviewers to be willing to stretch a little to see how your story relates—but not to draw giant inductive leaps. If your quick-learning triumphs seem irrelevant to the job at hand, sharing them won't improve your candidacy. In fact, such mismatches may signal that you have targeted the wrong field.

Bringing your career dreams to a small, ambitious organization can be the most effective way of entering the fast track. Yes, friends who work for giant enterprises will let you know that they have corporate American Express cards, free gym memberships, and lots of other perks that you lack. But don't think you're getting the short straw. Small, growing organizations will provide far more room to run. Bureaucracy will be scarcer. Instead of sitting in meetings all day, you will be on the front lines of change. The opportunities to build out your ideas, or to win new customers and allies, will be endless.

Big companies' name recognition gives them a constant glut of résumés. But, as recruiting expert John Sumser points out, big companies account for probably no more than 15 percent of the jobs offered each year to college graduates. They just don't hire that aggressively. His advice: "When you get out of college, expect to work for a company you've never heard of before."

Remember, too, that even the most famous companies were tiny and unknown once. If you end up at a little-known but fast-growing organization, you may find yourself swept upward by success. Silicon Valley's startups catch most of the public attention here. The allure of being tomorrow's equivalent of Facebook employee no. 12 keeps people dashing into startups. Even in government, academia, and nonprofits, small players may be en route to becoming big-time actors—especially if you're willing to help get them there.

Short-term trial assignments provide another path into great jobs. "The old paradigm of a job for life with a single employer has faded into history," the McKinsey Global Institute declared in a 2011 report on the future of work. Employers want a more flexible workforce, bringing people on and off the payroll as particular projects evolve.

Entrenched workers may regard this trend as menacing, but for newcomers, workforce flexibility is a boon. Within a two-year span, there are far more opportunities to try out different careers, cities, or employers. A six-month engagement on one project can become a stepping-stone that leads to a bigger role on a related engagement immediately afterward. Even a short-lived, part-time job can be a way of getting to know an organization, demonstrating rapid learning—and gaining entry to the hidden job market.

Consider the way movies get made. Studios no longer sign a pool of actors and off-camera specialists to long-term contracts. Instead, film producers and studios prefer project-by-project engagements with whatever superspecialists are needed to handle each of the many tasks for that particular movie. That creates an abundance of work—project after project—for costume designers, special effects gurus, composers, musicians, voice-over specialists, and the like.

Mainstream businesses may be headed that way, too. In fields ranging from creating Web content to reviewing patent applications, companies increasingly prefer to hire outsiders on a project-by-project basis, rather than trying to manage a big in-house staff in the face of uncertain demand. You can turn your nose up at such interim arrangements—or you can seize the opportunities that they present.

Help Them Find You

Remember Zack Canfield, the ad-agency executive in chapter 6 who was constantly hunting for offbeat recruits in unexpected places? One of his big finds was a champion college debater who turned out to be a first-rate researcher for Canfield's firm of Goodby, Silverstein & Partners. The debater, Ralph Paone, hadn't ever applied to Goodby. In fact, Paone had no intention of making a career in advertising. But as Canfield wandered through the Internet, he took a liking to Paone's well-informed, friendly videos about debating strategy.

In Canfield's world, everything worked better if the employer did the early prospecting, trying to find insanely great candidates who weren't expecting a job offer. Canfield was willing to endure the hard work and periodic disappointments of wooing strangers. His thinking: if the very best candidates were left to their own resources, they might not ever enter his corner of the job market. But they could be spotted—and won over—by anyone astute enough to find traces of their brilliance on the Internet.

Such role reversals aren't eccentric rarities any more. They are rapidly becoming a major way that high-prestige companies do their hiring. Instead of waiting for resumes to arrive and making candidates do all the early work, diligent sleuths within these companies go looking for people whose blog posts, online comments, and other Web content reveals something extraordinary. This latest twist in the hidden market's workings provides you with ideal opportunities to be seen as a rare find. Put signs of your best work on display, and you can leap ahead of other job-seekers pursuing traditional paths. You can become the prize candidate that big-name companies pursue on their own.

Consider how Ian Sefferman ended up as a software engineer at Amazon.com straight out of college. Sefferman never mailed in a resume to Amazon. Instead, he caught the company's attention because he founded a popular e-mail marketing group on the Orkut social network while he was still an undergraduate at the University of Chicago. His constant posts and updates on that group caught the eye of Amazon engineers in charge of the company's huge e-mail systems. They were impressed enough to offer Sefferman a summer internship at Amazon's Seattle headquarters, followed by a full-time job.

Practically every big social media site, in fact, is catching intrigued glances from employers eager to learn which job candidates might have the right stuff. LinkedIn is the first stop for many recruiters, who can shuffle through more than 160 million members' job histories, looking for a few extraordinary candidates. Facebook, Quora, Pinterest and even YouTube attract intermittent attention along the same lines. New companies such as TalentBin, BranchOut, and Reppify are springing up, providing employers with ways of crawling through people's Twitter feeds and Facebook postings in search of standout prospects. It's increasingly easy for employers to devise lists of top-twenty candidates without ever announcing a job opening.

As a job hunter, you have two choices. You can absorb this transformation passively, making no special effort to improve your chances of being found for a great job. Or you can harness this revolution to your advantage.

To seize these new opportunities, start by thinking of your online presence as the "zeroth impression" that you make on employers. Even before the classic first impression—where you walk into a room and radiate clues about your poise, hygiene, cheeriness, and demeanor—your online presence is sending powerful signals about what kind of person you are.

Ideally, what you do on Twitter, Facebook, and other Web sites should score high in five dimensions: you should establish yourself as bright, well-informed in your field, conscientious, creative, and likeable. Excel across the board, and you will welcome employers stumbling across your name. Your Internet presence will shout "Hire me!" without ever needing to beg for a job.

Li Pi is a case in point. As a junior at the University of California, San Diego, he was one of hundreds of computer science majors. But he stood out from the crowd by posting frequently on Quora, a popular knowledge-sharing site. Some of Pi's posts, such as a primer on the technical features of Java, showed detailed technical knowledge. That won ninety-four endorsements, including some from engineers nearly twice his age. Another post sized up the relative merits of three obscure computing languages (Haskell, Erlang, and OCaml). In it, Pi blended sassy opinion with shrewd insight, creating a write-up akin to a film critic's verdict. That post won sixty-eight endorsements.

Occasionally Pi was just plain silly, sharing advice on how to arrange a one-day rental of a baby elephant. (Guaranteed to liven up any party!) That playful post wasn't his main reason for being on Quora, but it helped show that he might be fun to have around the office, too.

Before long, Pi engaged the attention of a senior engineer at Cloudera, a Silicon Valley startup with ambitious plans for data storage and processing. Cloudera started a dialogue with Pi, arranging job interviews and inviting him to join the company as a summer intern. The internship worked out so well that Pi won a full-time job as well as feelers from other Silicon Valley startups wanting to know if they could hire him instead.

If you're a job hunter with a jagged résumé, building your online presence can be especially fruitful. Potential employers will get to know you entirely on the basis of what you do best. They will discover what earned you an A-plus in your favorite class rather than seeing you through a blended transcript that includes some Cs in classes that never held your interest.

If your desired career involves any form of public performance—from sales to theater, news broadcasting, teaching, or mechanical engineering—think about showing off on YouTube. A three-minute video of you in full mastery of your craft is a powerful way of capturing an employer's attention. You don't need a $5,000 video production team to create something engaging, eye-catching, and unique. Get a friend to film you. Make sure the sound and lighting aren't so hopelessly mangled that no one will know what you're doing. Then share a little bit of yourself with the world.

Drake Martinet did exactly that after college when he traveled through Chile, filming what he hoped would become a full-fledged documentary about indigenous peoples. The documentary never quite came together. But some short clips became a vital part of his application for graduate journalism school. As he tells it, he got into Stanford in large part because the admissions committee wanted someone who didn't just want to learn about video journalism—but who already was practicing it.

If you're a designer, a graphic artist, or someone interested in any field where great work can be visualized, think of Pinterest as your new best friend. Create a board with samples of your finest work, as well as a thoughtful reprise of other projects you admire. In architecture, for example, your conversation starter can be a well-curated review of what John Roebling did right (and wrong) in building the Brooklyn Bridge. Your diligence and insights will be on display to a wide range of visitors, including potential employers who you otherwise might not know about. They can linger over your work samples, too, taking time to decide whether it's worth contacting you.

Until recently, career counselors regarded job seekers' online presence mainly as a source of potential embarrassment. "Take down any Facebook pictures of partying or drinking" was the standard advice. Fair enough. But that's akin to telling résumé writers to proofread their work or to avoid mailing documents to potential employers in goofy envelopes with bunnies on the front. Getting a great job requires much more than dodging blunders. Your online strategy should involve spending no more than 25 percent of your time getting rid of the bad stuff. The bulk of your energy should go into making the most of your strengths.

After all, the Internet lets employers whiz past a stream of potential candidates faster than ever. You want to create a reason why your future boss might suddenly stop at something you have created and say: "Wow!"

How you build your professional networks is rapidly evolving, too. A generation ago any answer would have involved allusions to cliques, clubs, business contacts, and "pull." Now the term of art is the "social graph." Imagine a vast map of all the people in the world, with each of us represented by a tiny circle. Lines radiate from our circles to all the people we know. Thin lines represent casual acquaintances. Thick lines represent our best friends and immediate family. Hermits have hardly any connections on this social graph. Powerfully networked people radiate contacts in all directions, touching many thousands of other lives.

We've all been building and reshaping our social graphs since the days when we first shared a toy with another toddler in a sandbox. (Or seized some other child's toy, as the case may be.) Usually this evolution happens gradually, one contact at a time. But there are a handful of life transitions when our social graphs become radically redefined. Among them: joining the workforce or switching jobs.

The more you can build your social graph to support your next career move, the happier and more productive you will be. A lot of new ties can—and should—be formed by old-fashioned, face-to-face meetings. But when you're gazing into what seems like an ocean of strangers, one of the best ways to get started is by using the online world to start connecting with people that will become part of your new tribe.

Alyssa Henry, a communications major at Syracuse University, hit the jackpot during her senior year. She was on stage at a campus conference, talking about the future of social media. Behind her, a large screen displayed attendees' Twitter posts as the conference was taking place. In the midst of her remarks, people started applauding for no obvious reason. She turned around—and there was a tweet from an ad-agency executive with ties to a giant Fortune 100 corporation. His comment: "She's great—someone in my network ought to hire her."

Such happy developments don't happen by accident. For nearly a year she had been building a three-part Twitter strategy that did wonders for her social graph—and is a model for anyone else, too.

Henry started by creating a career-focused Twitter account that was meant as a way of connecting with a wider circle of people, mostly off campus, who might one day become her professional colleagues. That meant all her postings would be at least loosely related to work. There wouldn't be any updates about dorm food, runny noses, or campus humor (unless it was really funny).

Then she started following practitioners in her field who were active on Twitter and two or three steps ahead of her on the career ladder. By and large, she didn't burn up energy trying to follow business celebrities who didn't really want to talk with their fans. Instead, she was aiming to get connected with less famous but still successful people who might reciprocate—and follow her back.

As she began to build an audience, she posted steady updates about her field, drawing on three pools of content. Sometimes she tweeted about interesting articles in mainstream media. (These could include sites such as WSJ.com and NYTimes.com, as well as specialty news sites focused on her field.) Then she added campus updates involving books she was reading, speakers who were coming to her classes, and lively comments from lectures. Finally she shared content from other bloggers and tweeters, building up a spirit of mutual support. In each case, she looked for way to make her posts sparkle by adding an intriguing question or a pithy quote related to the topic.

Once Henry's readership grew, she earned the right to connect with more decision makers in her field. Her social graph was spreading. Now friends of friends of friends started to become her acquaintances, too. She wasn't just an inconsequential spectator in the cheap seats—she was starting to become a voice worth noticing.

The result: when she finally got her chance to speak at the campus conference, she was well positioned to succeed. Rather than being dependent on the support of any one contact, she had built at least thin-line connections to hundreds of potentially helpful people on her social graph.

Remember that even on the Internet, where everything goes

faster, it can take you at least six months—and probably longer—to become known as a thoughtful voice worth noticing. The "three Ps" of traditional networking (being patient, persistent, and polite) still matter online. So does the importance of providing value in return. Strangers won't warm up if you come across as nothing more than a digital panhandler, expecting favors simply because you are needy. But if people see you as a helpful ally and an engaging person, you will enjoy all the benefits of a soaring social graph.

Process matters. As this chapter has shown, there's a step-by-step progression that will improve your chances of being seen as a rare find. Escape the clutter. Get to know the hidden job market. Reach out to people who are just thinking about hiring. Learn to harness the power of weak ties. Tell stories that showcase what you can do uniquely well. Don't be afraid of starting your career at a small, ambitious outfit. Take trial assignments.

If there's one overarching message, it's the importance of taking charge of your own career. Many of the best job opportunities in the next decade are likely to involve careers that don't exist yet. These paths don't open up because an older generation guides newcomers into safe jobs. The big opportunities take shape without a master plan, simply because pioneers find that demand for their offerings is far greater than anyone expected.

One of the most intriguing conversations I had in researching this book was with Marcie Kirk-Holland, a career counselor at the University of California's Davis campus. There's little smugness or sense of entitlement as seniors head toward graduation, she told me. "Students know the economy has been through hard times," she says. "They're better prepared. They've read up more." Even liberal arts majors have boned up on skills such as accounting and Web design that can help them find jobs. Her only hesitation is that current entrants to the job market may be too pessimistic about their chances.

If she could change anything, she says, she would inject her seniors with some extra self-confidence.

Fortunately, this is a great time to be launching a career. After three years of high unemployment, the U.S. economy may finally be on the mend. Banks are lending again. Businesses are expanding. Job creation is fitful, but pockets of encouraging news are undeniable.

There's enormous room for new products, new ideas, and fresh innovators in the United States. Start setting your sights on the areas where you can make a mark. Don't be afraid to break from the pack to pursue opportunities that are uniquely right for you. The paths to success that paid off for Alex Ivlev, Li Pi, Alyssa Henry, and many others can work for you, too.

Notes

Introduction

pg. 1 **Carlisle began an experiment:** This account is based on an in-person interview March 2, 2011, with Todd Carlisle, a follow-up phone interview with Carlisle in April 2011, and coverage of Google's talent quests in *The New York Times,* Jan. 3, 2007.

2 **tinkering with a Commodore 64:** Ken Auletta, *Googled: The End of the World as We Know It,* p. xx (New York: The Penguin Press, 2009).

3 **focusing inordinately on candidates' education:** Steven Levy, *In the Plex: How Google Thinks, Works, and Shapes Our Lives* (New York: Simon & Schuster, 2011), p. 140.

4 **75,000 résumés a week:** Bloomberg.com, Feb. 3, 2011.

6 **business strategist Marc Effron:** "2010 State of Talent Management," p. 12, published by the New Talent Management Network, http://newtmn .com/ResourceCategories.aspx.

6 **208,000 full-time recruiters:** Bureau of Labor Statistics, November 2009 Monthly Labor Review, Table 1.2. http://www.bls.gov/emp/ep_table _102.htm. The BLS data groups together "employment, recruitment and placement specialists."

12 **The military tested more than 10 million people:** At least nine million people took the Army General Classification Test in World War II, while an estimated three million participated in the Navy General Classification Test, according to government records. http://aad.archives.gov/ aad/series-list.jsp?cat=WR26.

12 **psychologists such as K. Anders Ericsson:** His landmark publication is the 901-page *Cambridge Handbook of Expertise and Expert Performance* (Cambridge: Cambridge University Press, 2006), edited by K. Anders Ericsson, Neil Charness, Paul Feltovich, and Robert Hoffman.

274

12 **This is known as "deliberate practice":** The case for this is made quite vigorously in Geoff Colvin, *Talent Is Overrated: What Really Separates World-Class Performers from Everybody Else* (New York: Portfolio, 2008).

1: Sand, Sweat—and Character

15 **trailer 2K9395:** Its current condition is based on firsthand observation at Camp Mackall, North Carolina, in September 2010. Historical records on the trailer's use were summarized to me in an e-mail from Army major David Butler.

16 **The encounter begins:** Firsthand observation at Camp Mackall, North Carolina, in September 2010.

24 **Special Forces' history and identity:** Helpful resources here included: Anna Simons, *The Company They Keep: Life Inside the U.S. Army Special Forces* (New York: Free Press, 1997); Dick Couch, *Chosen Soldier: The Making of a Special Forces Warrior* (New York: Crown, 2007); Derek Leebaert, *To Dare and to Conquer: Special Operations and the Destiny of Nations* (Boston: Back Bay Books, 2007); Mike Guardia, *American Guerrilla: The Forgotten Heroics of Russell W. Volckmann* (Havertown, Pa.: Casemate, 2010); and Aaron Bank, *From OSS to Green Berets* (New York: Pocket, 1987).

25 **"deal confidently with the unknown":** Simons, *The Company They Keep,* p. 63.

25 **Dick Couch:** Couch, *Chosen Soldier,* p. 5.

26 **"Come see for yourself":** In-person interview with Don King, September 6, 2010.

30 **Log Drill:** Extended personal observation throughout September 2010 at Camp Mackall.

33 **"There is no shortcut":** In-person interview with Bennet Sacolick, September 9, 2010.

34 **King went through:** In-person interview with Don King, September 19, 2010.

36 **"We may think":** ibid.

2: The Talent Problem

37 **"What is wind?":** Wendy Kopp, *One Day, All Children: The Unlikely Triumph of Teach For America and What I Learned Along the Way* (New York: Public Affairs, 2001), p. 35. In her book, Kopp writes: "Looking back, I have to laugh at the thought of our recruiters asking this question of every applicant."

37 **students at elite schools clamored:** A flurry of newspaper and magazine articles in the early 1990s documented college students' eagerness to

join Teach For America. These included pieces in the *Los Angeles Times*, March 27, 1992, the *Christian Science Monitor*, July 21, 1992, and the *San Jose Mercury News*, August 21, 1993. The *Los Angeles Times* piece hailed a "growing receptivity to volunteerism on campuses."

38 **Others faltered grievously:** A January 7, 1996, article in *The New York Times* chronicled Teach For America's "growing pains," including the account of one new TFA teacher who quit after nine weeks. That teacher described the New Orleans school she was placed in as a "trash can."

39 **"Nobody knows anything":** William Goldman, *Adventures in the Screen Trade* (New York: Warner Books, 1983), p. 39.

39 **"symmetrical ignorance":** Richard E. Caves, *Creative Industries: Contracts Between Art and Commerce* (Cambridge, Mass.: Harvard University Press, 2000), p. 3.

40 **"Mistakes get made":** *Sports Illustrated*, May 23, 2010.

40 *"Think through the assignment":* Peter F. Drucker, *The Essential Drucker* (New York: HarperCollins, 2001), p. 141.

41 **Like an airplane pilot:** Dan Ariely, *Predictably Irrational: The Hidden Forces That Shape Our Decisions* (New York: HarperCollins, 2008), p. 3.

42 **The Knicks placed:** David J. Berri and Martin J. Schmidt: *Stumbling on Wins: Two Economists Expose the Pitfalls on the Road to Victory in Professional Sports* (Upper Saddle River, N.J.: FT Press, 2010), pp. 13–32.

43 **"a great foundation":** *New York Post,* March 12, 2007.

43 **Data loses its power:** Jim Collins, *How the Mighty Fall: And Why Some Companies Never Give In* (New York: HarperCollins, 2009), pp. 77–79.

43 **how many golf balls:** *Boston Globe,* July 4, 2004.

45 **"in constant flux":** Boris Groysberg, *Chasing Stars: The Myth of Talent and the Portability of Performance* (Princeton, N.J.: Princeton University Press, 2010), p. 100.

46 **"young, energetic white men":** Bryan Burrough, *Public Enemies: America's Greatest Crime Wave and the Birth of the FBI, 1933–34* (New York: Penguin, 2009), p. 11.

46 **J. Edgar Hoover's views:** Details abound in biographies of Hoover published after his death. Notable ones include: Curt Gentry, *J. Edgar Hoover: The Man and the Secrets* (New York: W. W. Norton, 1991), as well as Richard Gid Powers, *Secrecy and Power: The Life of J. Edgar Hoover* (New York: Free Press, 1988), and Ronald Kessler, *The Bureau: The Secret History of the FBI* (New York: St. Martin's Press, 2002).

47 **hat size:** Joseph L. Schott, *No Left Turns: The FBI in Peace and War* (New York: Praeger, 1975), p. 42.

48 **class-action suits:** *New York Times,* April 22, 1992. The *Times* reported that the FBI "said it would allow outside consultants to review its promotion system and would accept fundamental changes in how it selected, groomed and evaluated employees for advancement to the senior managerial ranks."

48 **"I'm a pioneer":** In-person interview April 26, 2010, with Elizabeth Kolmstetter.

50 **"What I realized":** Kopp, *One Day, All Children*, p. 165.

51 **He wasn't dynamic:** Kopp, *One Day, All Children*, p. 166.

51 **kitchen timer:** Phone interview with Anthony Griffin, June 2011.

52 **he burst into tears:** "What Makes a Great Teacher," *The Atlantic,* January/February 2010.

52 **"reverse engineering":** Phone interviews with Josh Griggs in July and August 2009.

53 **people like Emily Lewis-Lamonica:** In-person interviews with Emily Lewis-Lamonica, August 28, 2009, and December 9, 2009. Her performances as a Brown University hurdler are documented on directathletics.com, a sports Web site: http://www.directathletics.com/athletes/track/80676.html.

54 **a simulated classroom:** The account is based on firsthand observation at Berkeley's Career Center on December 3, 2009.

3: Decoding the Jagged Résumé

59 **Alan Kay was:** His child prodigy achievements and University of Colorado meanderings were well chronicled in a *New York Times* profile, November 8, 1987. He shared additional details about his college transcript in a phone interview in June 2009.

59 **Ed Catmull spent:** Catmull's youth is sweetly described in a *Fortune* profile, November 15, 2004. In it, he cites "Pinocchio, Peter Pan, and Einstein as the cultural heroes of his youth." Catmull shared additional details about his dead-end days at Boeing in an in-person interview at Pixar headquarters, May 22, 2009.

59 **Jim Clark was thrown:** Michael Lewis, *The New, New Thing* (New York: W. W. Norton, 1999), pp. 28–29. Additional details are in a *BusinessWeek* profile, October 12, 1998.

60 **Evans is one:** Many basic elements appear in his obituary in *The New York Times,* October 12, 1998. Considerable additional detail was provided in phone interviews with seven University of Utah alumni in the spring of 2009: Ivan Sutherland, Alan Kay, Martin Newell, Chuck Seitz, Alan Erdahl, Gary Watkins, and Mike Milocheck.

61 **these specifications:** John A. Byrne, *The Headhunters* (New York: Macmillan, 1986), p. 131. Byrne refers to one recital of qualifications as "a long, seemingly never-ending list of superlatives, a list no living executive could possibly meet."

64 **Dennis's experiment:** Details of Richard Dennis's unorthodox search can be found in a September 5, 1989, *Wall Street Journal* article by Stanley Angrist; in Michael W. Covel, *The Complete TurtleTrader* (New York: HarperBusiness, 2007), and in Curtis Faith, *Way of the Turtle*

(New York: McGraw-Hill, 2007). The "turtles in Singapore" quote is from Angrist's article.

66   **a $200 million fortune:** *Chicago Sun-Times* profile of Richard Dennis, February 1, 1987.

66   **Dennis and Eckhardt:** Phone interview with Liz Cheval in April 2011; Covel, *The Complete TurtleTrader*, pp 34–35.

67   **the results bore out:** Covel, *The Complete TurtleTrader*, pp. 218–20.

68   **"ask the tough questions":** Phone interview with Ari Kiev in October 2009.

69   **"I was willing":** Phone interview with Jason Karp in October 2009.

70   **Tidrow had seen Lincecum:** Tidrow's return visit to the Washington campus is described in the *San Jose Mercury News*, July 14, 2008. Tidrow's upbeat comments on draft day were quoted on sfgate.com on June 7, 2006. Other Tidrow perspectives appear in "Just Go With It," a Lincecum profile in *ESPN The Magazine*, March 2010.

72   **Dobkin wants engineers:** In-person interview with Bob Dobkin, January 14, 2010.

73   **"like listening to Oscar Peterson":** In-person interview with Robert Reay in the spring of 2007. Other aspects of Linear's culture appear in a *Wall Street Journal* profile of the company, July 10, 2007.

75   **When Evans arrived:** Details about David C. Evans's salary, working conditions, strategy, etc., are contained in an extensive collection of his working papers at the J. Willard Marriott Library at the University of Utah. I reviewed these in May 2009.

4: Where Insights Are Born

81   **about 42,000 college students:** Medical School Admissions Requirements, (Washington, D. C.: Association of American Medical Colleges, 2011.) p. 55–56.

83   **"When I was a senior":** In-person interview with James Weiss, September 30, 2009.

83   **everything clicked:** Weiss holds a named-chair professorship at Hopkins; his accomplishments are spelled out on the Johns Hopkins Web site: http://webapps.jhu.edu/namedprofessorships/professorshipdetail .cfm?professorshipID=124.

84   **Mary Schuler Cutler:** *Baltimore Sun*, January 4, 2004, and "A Kind of Calling" in *Hopkins Medicine*, Spring/Summer 2007.

87   **"Remain objective":** Lou Adler, *Hire with Your Head* (New York: Wiley, 2002).

89   **state licenses in Texas:** The Texas Department of Licensing alone covers twenty-nine occupations, from elevator operators to auctioneers, as specified on its Web site, http://www.license.state.tx.us/. The Texas

Department of State Health Services covers another twenty-three professions: http://www.dshs.state.tx.us/plc/default.shtm.

89 **personality tests:** Peter Cappelli, *Talent on Demand: Managing Talent in an Age of Uncertainty* (Cambridge, Mass.: Harvard Business Press, 2008), p. 52.

89 **Sherwin Rosen tallied:** Sherwin Rosen, "The Economics of Superstars," *American Economic Review*, December 1981.

91 **"I like young entrepreneurs":** In-person interview with Ram Shriram, January 26, 2009.

91 **Doerr by then:** The definitive profile of John Doerr's rise appeared in *The New Yorker*, September 8, 1997.

92 **"So many breadcrumbs":** VentureBeat, April 6, 2010.

93 **Sam Phillips, the founder:** Colin Escott and Martin Hawkins, *Good Rockin' Tonight: Sun Records and the Birth of Rock 'N' Roll* (New York: St. Martin's Press, 1991), p. 10.

95 **"a lusting enthusiasm":** Charles D. Ellis, *The Partnership: The Making of Goldman Sachs* (New York: Penguin, 2008), p. 84.

96 **"I had $50,000":** In-person interview with Nick Hanauer, December 1, 2009.

5: Auditions That Work

101 **Gibbons is the informal dean:** Useful profiles of Gibbons include "Analyst's Word Satisfies Demand for Data," *Kansas City Star*, November 10, 1991; "Gibbons Goes Fourth Watching Basketball," *Chicago Sun-Times*, July 4, 1994, and "Gibbons Built Career on Keen Observation," *Charlotte Observer*, July 7, 1995. I met with Gibbons on July 13, 2009.

107 **"I like quirky":** In-person interview with Susan Vash, September 1, 2009.

108 **"There may not be":** Phone interview with Doug Smuin, May 2010.

108 **"I'd speak a lot":** In-person interview with Heidi Roizen, January 28, 2009.

110 **assaulted three buildings:** *Washington Post*, March 11, 1977.

111 **Coulson and his aides:** Danny O. Coulson and Elaine Shannon, *No Heroes: Inside the FBI's Secret Counter-Terror Force* (New York: Pocket Books, 1999), pp. 131–68.

112 **"a grueling, Darwinian process":** Henry M. Holden, *To Be an FBI Special Agent* (Minneapolis: Zenith Press, 2005), p. 118.

113 **"You'll see more":** The FBI demonstrations took place July 15, 2010.

114 **John Piser talked about:** In-person interview, July 14, 2010.

116 **Everything began to change:** The dark side of youth basketball's rise to prominence is well cataloged in Dan Wetzen and Don Yaeger, *Sole Influence: Basketball, Corporate Greed, and the Corruption of America's Youth* (New York: Warner Books, 2000). The NCAA's current recruiting rules, with allowances for a "summer evaluation period," are available at www.ncaa.org.

118 **"the guards excel early":** In-person interview with Tom Konchalski, July 13, 2009.

119 **"Jordan excelled":** Phone interview with Gibbons in August 2009.

6: Talent That Whispers

121 **top-gun programmers:** Facebook's early ambitions are well described in "Facebook's Mark Zuckerberg: Hacker. Dropout. CEO," *Fast Company*, May 2007, and in David Kirkpatrick, *The Facebook Effect: The Inside Story of the Company That Is Connecting the World* (New York: Simon & Schuster, 2010).

122 **Facebook couldn't wait:** In-person interview with Yishan Wong, April 8, 2011; e-mail exchange with Adam D'Angelo in April 2011.

123 **Evan Priestley chafed:** This account is based on several in-person interviews with Priestley in October and November 2008. I wrote a condensed version of his experiences as a question-and-answer interview that appeared on Facebook's Web site, http://www.facebook.com/careers/story.php?story=3.

125 **Jonathan Hsu:** In-person interviews with Hsu in December 2008 and on July 16, 2009, and February 10, 2011.

126 **"Breathalyzer":** The puzzle can be found online at http://www.facebook.com/careers/puzzles.php?puzzle_id=17.

126 **lowercase *f*:** This puzzle can be found online at the Puzzle Master's Facebook page: http://www.facebook.com/PuzzleMaster.

127 **More than two hundred submissions:** Statistics in this paragraph are from the February 10, 2011, interview with Hsu.

127 **"the long tail":** Chris Anderson, *The Long Tail: Why the Future of Business Is Selling Less of More* (New York: Hyperion, 2008).

129 **"Nobody wanted me":** The quotes in this paragraph are from "All-Star Christian," an interview on beliefnet.com, http://www.beliefnet.com/Entertainment/Celebrities/All-Star-Christian.aspx.

131 **world-renowned brands:** As cited on Goodby's Web site: www.goodbysilverstein.com/#/clients.

131 **Zach Canfield:** In-person interview, November 22, 2010, with Zach Canfield.

132 **his job involves hunting:** Useful published interviews with Canfield include "Why Goodby's Talent Director Goes Far Afield to Find Outstanding Hires," *Advertising Age*, June 19, 2009, and "Why I Think Zach Canfield's the Zen Master of Recruiting," *Advertising Age*, October 21, 2009.

133 **Paone showed a knack:** A fine sample is "Debating Nietzche on the Poverty Topic," a Web video in which Paone explains debating tactics, http://www.planetdebate.com/media/preview/Video154.

135 **investment expert Jack Rivkin:** Fuller details are in a Harvard Business School case study by Ashish Nanda, Boris Groysberg, and Lauren

Prusiner, *Lehman Brothers: Rise of the Equity Research Department* (Cambridge, Mass.: Harvard Business Publishing, 2006).

7: What Can Go Right?

139 **his Mercedes sedan skidded:** A full account of the accident is in Hubert Feichtlbauer, *Franz König: der Jahrhundert-Kardinal* (Vienna: Holzhausen, 2003). Briefer English-language accounts include "König at 94 Still Carrying Torch of Renewal," *National Catholic Reporter*, October 8, 1999, and an interview with König in Giuseppe Alberigo and Oscar Beozzo (eds.), *The Holy Russian Church and Western Christianity* (London: SCM Press, 1996) pp. 75–78.

140 **"a crucial watershed":** Franz König, *Open to God, Open to the World* (London: Burns & Oates, 2005), p. 38.

140 **celebrated mass in Warsaw:** *New York Times*, May 3, 1971.

140 **museum of atheism:** König, *Open to God, Open to the World*, p. 53.

141 **"like a boy playing on the seashore":** This quote appeared in a very early biography of the great English mathematician, Charles Brewster's *The Life of Sir Isaac Newton* (New York: Harper Brothers, 1831), pp. 300–301. Brewster offered the quote without attribution, though later historians believe Newton expressed such thoughts to his nephew (and valet), John Conduitt, who later helped guide them into prominence as part of the remarks at Newton's funeral. Regardless of the quote's murky origins, it is now as secure as calculus in Newton's legacy.

141 **As a young academic:** Useful accounts include Ellen Cole, et al., *Feminist Foremothers in Women's Studies, Psychology and Mental Health* (New York: Routledge, 1996), pp. 490–91; biographical remarks by Stimpson at Bryn Mawr's 2010 "Heritage and Hope" conference; and an in-person interview with Stimpson, January 8, 2009, as well as subsequent e-mail exchanges with Stimpson. A transcript of her Bryn Mawr remarks is at http://www.brynmawr.edu/125th/conference/proceedings.html.

142 **MacArthur program scanned:** Nancy Kriplen, *The Eccentric Billionaire* (New York: Amacom, 2008), p. 133.

142 **"the most civilized award":** Wuorinen was quoted in "After the MacArthur's Golden Touch," *The New York Times*, July 17, 1988.

142 **"decisive cultural moments":** Stimpson interview, January 8, 2009.

143 **Daniel Socolow:** "Venture Capital for Geniuses," *Forbes*, February 23, 1998. His brief stint as an animal-gland buyer came up in an in-person interview, January 12, 2010. "I picked up a very strange kind of Spanish by the time I was finished," Socolow remarked.

144 **"no pattern":** Phone interview with Socolow in February 2009.

144 **"marvelous bouquets":** In-person interview with John Seely Brown, March 17, 2009.

145 **"without the advice or consent":** Quoted in Hugh Hawkins, *Between Harvard and America: the Educational Leadership of Charles W. Eliot* (Oxford, UK: Oxford University Press, 1972), p. 62.

146 **"Bill immediately put on a hat":** David Packard, *The HP Way: How Bill Hewlett and I Built Our Company* (New York: Collins, 1995), p. 100.

146 **"maniacal attention":** Stephen Levy, *The Perfect Thing: How the iPod Shuffles Commerce, Culture, and Coolness* (New York: Simon & Schuster, 2007), p. 48.

147 **best known for leading:** Jun Xia described his work on the tower in an Asia Society lecture in New York on October 20, 2009. Video of that talk appears on the Asia Society's Web page: http://asiasociety.org/arts-culture/visual-arts/genslers-shanghai-tower.

147 **McCurdy was blown away:** Phone interview with Phil McCurdy in March 2009.

148 **"foreign words on tins":** König, *Open to God, Open to the World*, p. 95.

148 **König studied:** Helpful books included König, *Open to God, Open to the World*; Feichtlbauer, *der Jahrhundert-Kardinal*; and Alberigo and Beozzo (eds.), *The Holy Russian Church and Western Christianity*. A useful Web biography appears in *The Cardinals of the Holy Roman Church*, Salvador Miranda, http://www2.fiu.edu/~mirandas/cardinals.htm. Pertinent newspaper articles include König obituaries in *The New York Times*, March 15, 2004; *National Catholic Reporter*, March 26, 2004; and *The Guardian*, March 16, 2004.

149 **The cardinals' conclave:** Detailed accounts of the October 1978 conclave and earlier contacts between Cardinals König and Wojtyla appear in George Weigel, *Witness to Hope: The Biography of John Paul II* (New York: HarperCollins, 1999); Jonathan Kwitny, *Man of the Century: The Life and Times of Pope John Paul II* (New York: Henry Holt, 1997), and Carl Bernstein and Marco Politi, *His Holiness: John Paul II and the Hidden History of Our Time* (New York: Doubleday, 1996).

149 **"a state of spiritual shock":** Weigel, *Witness to Hope*, p. 252.

152 **a one-man theater festival:** *Harvard Crimson*, June 7, 1984.

153 **"Kronauer Group":** E-mail exchange with Ted Osius in June 2009, as well as a phone interview with Bill Rauch, May 2011.

153 **Cornerstone Theater Company:** Phone interviews in February 2009 with Bill Rauch and Cornerstone alumna Alison Carey provided many details. Also helpful was Sonja Kuftinec, *Staging America: Cornerstone and Community-Based Theater* (Carbondale: Southern Illinois University Press, 2003), and *Cornerstone Theater Company: Community Collaboration Handbook*, a 130-page troupe history and manual prepared by consultant Ferdinand Lewis in 2006. Cornerstone's own Web site, www.cornerstonetheatre.org, provided additional background material. National media coverage included "If This Is Kansas, Toto, Why Are Those

Farmers Doing Tartuffe?" *People*, February 8, 1988, and "Road Movie: A New Documentary Recounts Cornerstone's Quixotic National Tour," *Back Stage West*, August 19, 1999.

154 *Hamlet* **on the Great Plains:** Phone interviews in February 2009 with Rauch and Carey provided the Cornerstone perspective. Phone interviews with Marmarth natives Patti Perry, Jim Carroll, Merle Clark, and Dan Flor provided other details and views. Useful media coverage in North Dakota included "Hamlet on the Prairie," *Bismarck Tribune*, October 19, 1986.

157 **"It's sick. Really wild":** Firsthand observation of Rauch directing, January 20, 2010.

158 **"a show that makes compulsive sense":** *Wall Street Journal*, June 18, 2010.

8: Lottery Tickets

159 **When Scott Borchetta founded:** In-person interview with Scott Borchetta, Feb. 5, 2009.

160 **Garth Brooks rattled around:** Bruce Feiler, *Dreaming Out Loud: Garth Brooks, Wynonna Judd, Wade Hayes, and the Changing Face of Nashville* (New York: William Morrow, 1998), p. 109.

161 **the cover of** *Rolling Stone*: "The Very Pink, Very Perfect Life of Taylor Swift," *Rolling Stone*, March 5, 2009.

162 **fans on Facebook:** On April 24, 2011, allfacebook.com, which keeps track of such matters, listed Taylor Swift with 19.9 million fans on Facebook. Barack Obama had 19.5 million, the Beatles had 16.9 million.

164 **promptly signed Rivera:** Cited on baseball-reference.com.

164 **when I chatted:** Phone interview with Herb Raybourn in December 2010.

168 **"consumer tastes":** "The Greatest Mystery: Making a Best Seller," *The New York Times*, May 13, 2007.

168 **Knopf's internal memos:** The Sylvia Plath and John Barth examples are quoted in "Publication Is Not Recommended: From the Knopf Archives," *The Missouri Review*, Number 3, 2000. The Anne Frank example was cited in "No Thanks, Mr. Nabokov," *The New York Times*, September 9, 2007.

168 **a few such missteps:** Speer Morgan's introduction to "Publication Is Not Recommended," *The Missouri Review*, Number 3, 2000.

169 **Trying to predict:** The Taliban and Oprah examples are cited in John B. Thompson, *Merchants of Culture: The Publishing Business in the Twenty-First Century* (Cambridge, UK: Polity, 2010), p. 185.

170 **samizdat literature:** Malcolm evoked the image in a series of e-mail exchanges in March 2011.

171 *Washington Post*: *The Washington Post*, July 28, 2005.

172 **"All hits are flukes":** William T. Bielby and Denise D. Bielby, "All Hits Are Flukes," *American Journal of Sociology*, March 1994.

173 **Carly Hennessy:** *The Wall Street Journal*, February 26, 2002.

173 **The younger Borchetta:** In-person interview with Scott Borchetta, February 5, 2009; follow-up e-mail exchange in February 2009. Trisha Yearwood in a phone interview in February 2009 confirmed the receptionist story.

9: Talent That Shouts

180 **John Cameron's voice:** An invaluable source here is *Letters of the Halsted Residents to Dr. John L. Cameron M.D.*, a bound collection of tributes and reminiscences from seventy-two of his former residents, presented to Dr. Cameron when he retired as surgery department chair in 2003. Multiple contributors spoke of hearing his voice years later. The specific admonitions are all cited (sometimes repeatedly) in the letters or in phone interviews with former residents. In an in-person interview, September 29, 2009, Dr. Cameron confirmed his use of the "elevator shaft" analogy. ("That was when I was younger and didn't have as much good sense," Dr. Cameron observed.) Having listened to Dr. Cameron's rhetorical buildups firsthand, I could easily see why his former trainees never forget the sound.

182 **"Here's your second opinion":** *Letters of the Halsted Residents*, an appendix titled "Classic Lines from Dr. Cameron and Others."

182n. **another side to Halsted:** Gerald Imber, *Genius on the Edge: The Bizarre Double Life of Dr. William Stewart Halsted* (New York: Kaplan Publishing, 2010), pp. 58, 80, 142, etc.

183 **"not at the bedside":** Phone interview with Rob Udelsman in September 2009; John Cameron confirms the anecdote.

183 **Halsted Resident:** Phone interview with Rob Udelsman in September 2009; John Cameron recalled the conversation, said he didn't specifically remember the visit to the Halsted room but had no reason to doubt Dr. Udelsman's account.

188 **Growing up in Oregon:** *Los Angeles Times*, October 31, 2004; "Innovation Lessons from Pixar," *McKinsey Quarterly*, April 2008; *Animation World Network*, June 30, 2009; Sheerly Avni and Michael Snegow, *Cinema by the Bay* (Skywalker Ranch, Calif.: George Lucas Books, 2006), pp. 166–67.

188 *Iron Giant*: as tallied by imdb.com, an online film industry database.

189 **"He has no patience":** *USA Today*, September 24, 2009.

189 **"grossed $624 million":** That total and the top-fifty status are as tallied by imdb.com.

190 **"just trying to live":** collider.com, June 25, 2007, http://collider.com/entertainment/interviews/article.asp/aid/4739/tcid/1.

191 **"you will get less sleep":** Couch, *Chosen Soldier*, p. 179.

191 **"They didn't expect me":** In-person interview with Dazerell Fleming, September 7, 2010.

192 **At General Electric:** Phone interview with Peter Mondani in October 2009; phone interview with GE alumnus Gary Wendt in November 2009; "How to Pick Winning Finance Execs," cfo.com, April 15, 2005, and "School for CFOs," *CFO* magazine, December 1, 2000.

195 **"the eyes of the world":** The ebullient language is from "What You Can Do for Your Country," a 1961 Peace Corps recruiting brochure. Broader context comes primarily from Scott Stossel, *Sarge: The Life and Times of Sargent Shriver* (Washington: Smithsonian Books, 2004).

195 **"pure ideals and pure publicity":** Stossel, *Sarge*.

196 **"bedside to bedside":** Interview with John Cameron, September 29, 2009.

196 **the Whipple procedure:** "Old School, New Vision," *Baltimore Sun*, August 14, 2006; "Goodbye to All That," *Hopkins Medical News*, Winter 2003.

197 **Dexterity didn't matter:** As Cameron phrased it in his September 29, 2009, interview: "When we interview a medical student, we don't say: 'Here are some pick-up sticks. Let's see how you can do.'"

197 **"the toughest surgeon":** *Letters of the Halsted Residents,* Kenneth Kern to John Cameron, February 17, 2003.

10: When to Say No

200 **charismatic new bosses:** Rakesh Khurana, *Searching for a Corporate Savior: The Irrational Quest for Charismatic CEOs* (Princeton, N.J.: Princeton University Press, 2002).

202 **"It's the right time":** *Wall Street Journal*, April 24, 2001.

202 **Johnston was:** "Bagging Profits," *The Chief Executive*, April 2002; "Albertsons Announces ex-GE Exec as New CEO," *The Idaho Statesman*, April 25, 2001; *Wall Street Journal*, April 24, 2001.

202 **"not building the space shuttle":** *Wall Street Journal*, May 15, 2003.

202 **Jack Welch:** Jack Welch, *Jack: Straight from the Gut* (New York: Warner Business Books, 2001).

204 **talk less and listen more:** *Wall Street Journal*, May 15, 2003.

205 **"the GE glow":** *New York Times*, January 4, 2007.

205 **Harvard's priorities:** *Harvard Crimson*, April 14, 2006.

206 **three finalists:** *New York Times*, March 11, 2001.

206 **Lawrence Summers:** "A Worldly Professor," *Harvard Magazine*, May–June 2001; "Potential Gains from Trade in Dirty Industries: Revisiting Larry Summers' Memo," *Cato Journal*, Fall 2007.

206 **"like being run over by a tank":** "Can Larry Summers Save the Economy?" *Time*, January 29, 2009.

207 **"one of the most respected scholars":** *New York Times*, March 12, 2001.

207 **First Summers:** "Renaissance Man," *The Guardian*, October 5, 2004; "Summers' Remarks on Women Draw Fire," *Boston Globe*, January 17, 2005; "At Harvard, the Bigger Concern of the Faculty Is the President's Management Style," *New York Times*, January 26, 2005; "Harvard's 'Faceless' Board Gets Heat on Summers and Its Rules," Bloomberg.com, March 10, 2005; "What Harvard Taught Larry Summers," *Time*, February 26, 2006.

208 **Summers resigned:** *New York Times*, February 22, 2006.

209 **Nicholas Lemann:** *Time*, February 26, 2006.

209 **Donald A. Norman:** Donald A. Norman, *The Design of Everyday Things* (New York: Basic Books, 2002).

210 **Ryan Leaf:** *Los Angeles Times*, August 11, 1998; *Chicago Sun-Times*, September 21, 1998; *New York Times*, November 7, 1999.

210–211 **"If I had got that wrong":** In-person interview with Bill Polian, June 15, 2010.

211 **"Did we overanalyze?"** "The Toughest Job in Sports," *Sports Illustrated*, August 17, 1998. Polian told me that Colts coaches and executives watched each player's college passes a total of four times. The Wonderlic scores are as reported by Mac Mirabile, an economic analyst who runs a Wonderlic-score Web site (http://www.unc.edu/~mirabile/Wonderlic.htm).

211 **In the weirdest:** Details are in "The Toughest Job in Sports," *Sports Illustrated*, August 17, 1998. Polian acknowledged to me a "ceiling" in Manning's arm strength but said he didn't think it was meaningful.

212 **Leaf's motivation:** *Seattle Post-Intelligencer*, February 9, 1998; *New York Times*, April 12, 1998; *Chicago Tribune*, April 27, 2007.

214 **When Cruise made:** As reported by imdb.com.

216 **Bill Cosby's foray:** "The Best-Seller Blues: Hard Lessons from a Cosby Book," *New York Times*, June 10, 1990, as well as a phone interview with Paul Bresnick, May 2011.

217 **"In any given year":** Polian interview, June 15, 2010.

11: Picking the Boss

218 **Randy Street wants:** Phone interviews with Randy Street in March 2010 and March 2011; Geoff Smart and Randy Street, *Who: The A Method for Hiring* (New York: Ballantine Books, 2008).

220 **HP's climactic meetings:** George Anders, *Perfect Enough: Carly Fiorina and the Reinvention of Hewlett-Packard* (New York: Portfolio, 2003).

220 **bosses brought in from outside:** James S. Ang and Gregory L. Nagel, "Outside and Inside Hired CEOs: A Performance Surprise," (November 6, 2009). Available at SSRN: http://ssrn.com/abstract=1501024.

221 **Malcolm Gladwell:** Malcolm Gladwell, "The New Boy Network," *The New Yorker*, May 29, 2000.

221 **the numbers geeks:** Michael Lewis, *Moneyball: The Art of Winning an Unfair Game* (New York: W. W. Norton, 2003).

222 **"the third question":** In-person interview with Thomas J. Friel, April 11, 2011.

224 **"Watch their hands":** Robert Caro, *Master of the Senate: The Years of Lyndon Johnson* (New York: Knopf, 2002), p. 136.

224 **executives who edit:** Phone interview with Dean Stamoulis, April 2010.

225 **"hunger, speed, and weight":** Phone interview with John Isaacson, April 2011.

225 **Justin Menkes:** Justin Menkes, "What Do Structured Interviews Actually Measure: A Construct Validity Study," Ph.D. dissertation, Claremont Graduate University, 2002.

226 **The results surprised him:** In-person interview with Justin Menkes, June 6, 2010.

226 **He wrote a book:** Justin Menkes, *Executive Intelligence: What All Great Leaders Have* (New York: HarperBusiness, 2005).

226 **"eyes lighting up":** In-person interview June 18, 2010 with Cathy Anterasian.

227 **"We just want":** Phone interview in July 2010 with Gerhard Resch-Fingerlos.

227 **Lee Raymond declared:** Told to me by Justin Menkes in June 6, 2005, interview; confirmed May 2011 in an e-mail exchange with Claudia Radford, an assistant to Raymond.

227 **"a tough situation":** In-person interview June 29, 2010, with Justin Menkes.

231 **Street took me through:** Phone interview with Randy Street, March 2011.

233 **Kaplan gained access:** Phone interviews with Steve Kaplan and Geoff Street, March 2011.

233 **Kaplan and two:** Steven N. Kaplan, Mark M. Klebanov and Morten Sorensen, "Which CEO Characteristics and Abilities Matter Most," *Journal of Finance*, listed May 15, 2011 as a forthcoming article, www.afajof.org/journal/forth_abstract.asp?ref=646.

233 **"CEOs who are persistent":** Steve Kaplan, "A PEP Talk: What Can You Learn From Successful CEOs?" Convocation speech, University of Chicago Graduate School of Business, June 15, 2008.

12: Fitting the Pieces Together

241 **Tucker's best finds:** In-person interview with Amy Tucker, May 27, 2009.

246 **Enron's lobby:** Mimi Swartz and Sherron Watkins, *Power Failure: The Inside Story of the Collapse of Enron* (New York: Doubleday, 2003), p. 5.

13: Becoming a Rare Find

248   **struck a chord:** In an interview for Pink's "Office Hours" blog in October 2011, Pink remarked: "I was especially intrigued by your idea of the "jagged résumé" in part because I realized that I, myself, sort had one of these way back when." http://www.danpink.com/archives/2011/10/how-to-find-great-talent-4-questions-for-bloomberg-views-george-anders. Pink recounts his own career zigzags in detail in Daniel H. Pink, *Free Agent Nation: The Future of Working for Yourself*, pp. 2–3 (New York: Warner Books, 2001).

252   **"virtually no feedback":** Capelli is quoted in "Why the Job Search is like 'Throwing Paper Airplanes Into the Galaxy,'" http://knowledge.wharton.upenn.edu/article.cfm?articleid=2947.

252   **Bolles dismisses:** Richard Bolles, *What Color Is Your Parachute? 2012: A Practical Manual for Job-Hunters and Career Changers*, pp. 16–17 (New York: Ten Speed Press/Random House, 2012).

254   **"Stop looking at classifieds":** This and subsequent details are from e-mail exchanges with David Whelan in February and March 2012.

259   **People you know only slightly:** Mark S. Granovetter, "The Strength of Weak Ties," *American Journal of Sociology*, Volume 78, Issue 6 (May 1973), pp. 1360–1380.

260   **Fourth-stage contacts:** E-mail exchanges with Sharon Jones, February and March 2012.

260   **Ivlev's journey:** In-person interviews with Alex Ivlev, Feb. 13, 2012 and Feb. 21, 2012.

262   **Duckett's journey:** In-person interview with John Duckett, Feb. 15, 2012.

264   **Big companies' role:** Phone interview with John Sumser, editor of *HRExaminer* and principal analyst at HRxAnalysts, February 2012.

264   **No more jobs for life:** James Manyika, et al. "An economy that works: Job creation and America's future," McKinsey Global Institute, 2011, p. 45.

266   **Sefferman's journey:** Phone interview with Ian Sefferman, April 2012. He now runs a Seattle company called AppStoreHQ.

267   **Pi's journey:** Pi in 2011 provided a detailed account on Quora.com of his route to Cloudera: http://www.quora.com/Recruiting/Has-anyone-been-offered-a-job-because-of-their-Quora-participation. Pi confirmed his Quora post and added details in a series of private e-mail messages.

268   **Martinet's journey:** Phone interview with Drake Martinet, February 2012. Some of his footage of Chile's indigenous people can be seen on Vimeo: http://vimeo.com/5904507.

270   **Henry's journey:** Phone interview with Alyssa Henry, February 2012; e-mail exchange with Henry in March 2012.

272   **"Little smugness":** In-person interview with Marcie Kirk-Holland, February 15, 2012.

Acknowledgments

This book's origins go back a long way. My parents, Joan and Edward Anders, loved to create mosaics of ideas during family mealtimes. They were ambitious immigrants whose curiosity about all things American never stopped. When I was growing up in the 1970s, they drew me into discussions about everything from a scientist's rise to a politician's fall. Several passages in this book flow directly from those long-ago chats. So does the book's overall tone of spirited inquiry.

Editors at the *Wall Street Journal* and *Fast Company* magazine allowed me to travel around America with a notepad from the 1980s onward. Those rambles gradually led me to focus on talent hunts in all walks of life. I'm particularly grateful to Norm Pearlstine, Dan Hertzberg, John Brecher, Bill Taylor, Alan Webber, and Mike Miller for their guidance, encouragement, and high standards.

More recently various friends, scholars, and professional acquaintances have sharpened my thinking about how we find great people. Beyond the experts who are quoted in the book, I'm indebted to Kevin Helliker, Gregg Zachary, Michael Schrage, Sarah Noble, Elaine Pulakos, David Schiman, Abigail Johnson, Kevin Bousquette, Quentin Hardy, Rob Guth, and Charles Fishman.

Within specific subject areas, many people have gone out of their way to help me meet the right characters and learn the subtleties of each new discipline. In sports, I'm thankful to Bruce Anderson, Brian Gray, Dana O'Neil, Dave Telep, and Joanna Hunter. In theater and acting, Amy Richards, Marsha Robertson, Debra Zane, and Sonja Kuftinec made my journey easier. In the worlds of high tech, finance, and commerce, John Hamburger, Bob Hirth, Ben Machtiger, and Marshall Kiev opened doors. Andy Grove pointed me toward Utah. In the civic-minded professions (teaching, medicine, and philanthropy),

Joan Abrahamson, Diane Coutu, and Kathleen Loughlin stood out. Ann Todd got me into an FBI helicopter and out of the Shooting Room. Tom Ricks suggested spending time with Army Special Forces; Major Dave Butler and Sergeant Marshall Pesta were sure-handed guides once I arrived.

Melissia Heape transcribed countless interviews with good cheer and precision. Ray Brayer and Lisa Werner got me started in a fine office. John Saba made my stay at "Lorton Labs" even better. Memorable friends of the book included Lamar Graham, Laura Heberton, Alan Hunter, Cathy Panagoulias, Robert Spector, Joe Sweeney, Casey Wardynski, and Helen Whelan. Tim O'Brien deserves a special shout-out for giving me a chance in March 2009 to try out the book's early themes in a Sunday *New York Times* feature.

I'm also thankful to many friends at Odyssey School, both for their moral support and for the intense, hands-on learning that we shared during my time on the school's board of trustees. Special thanks to Jan Pickering, Kay McGough, Keri Satterwhite, Linda Blum, Daniel Popplewell, Steve Smuin, and Hiroshi Imase.

My agent, Kim Witherspoon, provided wise advice at every stage, as did her colleagues, Richard Pine and Michael Carlisle. As draft chapters took shape, Brian Eule, Jack Corcoran, Carol Hymowitz, Paul Carroll, Amy Reece, Bernie Wysocki, and Kevin Salwen demonstrated "aggressive listening" at its best. Their close reading of chapters was invaluable. Our oldest son, Matthew, joined the readers' brigade and captured his first awkward adjective within minutes. Younger brother Peter regularly asked "How's the book going, Dad?" with just the right blend of optimism and impatience to keep me on task.

Portfolio's editing team provided everything an author could hope for. Adrian Zackheim becomes more powerful each time I see him, but he still likes authors despite our many foibles, and I'm grateful. Courtney Young knew exactly when to cheer and when to kick back a chapter for improvements. Her unerring judgment helped make this a better book. She also writes some of the funniest notes in the margins that I've ever seen. Eric Meyers kept everything moving; Will Weisser, Michael Burke, Jennifer Tait, Angela Hayes, and Amanda Pritzker worked their magic, too.

Every book needs a good genie to protect it and my wife, Elizabeth Corcoran, played that role brilliantly. She read countless drafts at the strangest hours of day and night, pointing out ways to make each one better. She became my in-house expert on everything from Catholic doctrine to Netscape's history. She also created the Vancouver Island Symposium at a crucial moment in the book's evolution, arranging for one of the happiest and most productive weekends in my life. Without her, this book would not have been possible.

Index

acting, 105, 106–7, 110
Adler, Lou, 87
advertising industry, 131–34
aggressive listening, 224–25, 242
Akers, John, 151
Albertsons Inc., 201–5, 220
Algorithmic Image, The (Rivlin), 80
Alves, David, 137
Amazon, 10, 91, 95–97, 128, 266
Amnesty International, 258
Anderson, Chris, 128
Andreessen, Marc, 78
Ang, James S., 220
Angrist, Stanley, 65
animation, 44, 80, 188–90
Anterasian, Cathy, 226
Apple, 10, 77, 87, 92, 146–47, 243
architecture industry, 147
Ariely, Dan, 41
Army, U.S., Special Forces (Green Berets),
     6, 7, 15–36, 105, 109, 187, 190–91, 219,
     239, 246
auditions, 62–63, 100–120, 219–20, 241–42, 192
Austen, Jane, 168
aviation, 107–8, 165

"Bad Weather Reroute," 107–8
Baker, Kathy, 107
Baldwin, Bill, 255
Bancroft, Andrew, 132, 134
Bank, Aaron, 24–25
baseball, 6–7, 40, 70–71, 86, 128–29, 163–65,
     221–22, 239
     see also specific players and teams
basketball:
     high school, 7, 50–51, 63, 100–104, 116–20,
     166, 219
     see also New York Knicks
Beane, Billy, 222

Beck, Teresa, 202
Berri, David J., 42
Bezos, Jeff, 95–97
Bielby, William and Denise, 172
Big Machine Records, 160–62, 176, 178–79
Bird, Brad, 188–90
Blankfein, Lloyd, 95
Bolles, Richard, 252
Bollinger, Lee, 206
Borchetta, Mike, 173
Borchetta, Scott, 159–63, 173–79
Boss, Shira, 168
Branch Davidians, 112
BranchOut, 266
"Breathalyzer" puzzle, 126
Brin, Sergey, 2–3, 91, 93
"broken arrows," 82–84
Brooks, Garth, 160
Brown, John Seely, 144
Buehrle, Mark, 129
Buffett, Warren, 63–64
Burke, James, 151
Burrough, Bryan, 46

Cadell, Thomas, 168
calmness, 31, 51, 63, 84, 103, 108
Cameron, John, 10, 180–85, 187, 196–98, 246
candidates:
     internal vs. outside, 220
     late bloomers, 82–83
     "maybes," 61–62
     overlooked, 4, 13, 21–22, 40, 69, 99,
     121–38, 140, 160–62, 174, 238–39
     pools of, 33, 40, 47, 49, 57, 94
     successful choices of, 11, 13, 62–63, 72,
     127–28, 244
     superstar, 13, 90, 162, 180–217
     unconventional, 3–4, 13, 59, 64, 76–80,
     94–95, 99, 123–25, 143–44, 243

candidates *(cont.)*
  unlikely, 7, 13, 21, 31–32, 69, 99, 123, 132, 238
  unrecognized genius in, 59–80, 131
  as versions of assessor, 42–43, 46–47, 241
  wrong people as, 200, 203–9
Canfield, Zach, 131–34, 265
Cappelli, Peter, 89, 251
CareerBuilder, 251
Carey, Alison, 153, 158
Carlisle, Todd, 1–4, 237
Caro, Robert, 224
Carroll, Jim, 155
Carter, Jimmy, 151
Catmull, Ed, 59–60, 78, 80
Caves, Richard, 39
Chamberlain, Wilt, 116
character, 24, 29, 52, 63, 71, 89, 97–98, 101
  experience vs., 62, 237–38
  nine FBI traits for assessment of, 114–15
  as revealed through auditions, 105–20, 241–42
  see also temperament
charisma, pitfalls of, 38, 50, 200–201, 205, 220–22, 234
Chasing Stars (Groysberg), 45
Cheval, Liz, 66, 67
Chicago, University of, 145, 205, 233
chief executive officers (CEOs), 7, 63, 106, 187, 200–205, 218–34
"chief talent officers," 12–13
Chosen Soldier (Couch), 25
Clark, Jim, 59, 78–79
Clark, Merle, 154
classroom simulation assessment session, 54–57
Cloudera, 268
Coleman, Van, 166
college admissions, 93–94
Collins, Jim, 43, 71
Company They Keep, The (Simons), 25
Complete Turtle Trader, The (Covel), 67
Compton, Calif., 50–51, 56
computer science, 11, 21, 43–44, 60, 72–81, 85, 91–93, 108, 121–27, 145–47, 191–92, 226
Condos, Rick, 134
confidence, 25, 31–32, 63, 103
Conine, Jeff, 129
Corddry, Paul, 202–3
Cornell, Ezra, 145
Cornerstone Theater Company, 153–56
Cosby, Bill, 216
Couch, Dick, 25–26, 190–91
Coulson, Danny, 110–11
Covel, Michael W., 67
Craft, Aaron, 102–4
Creative Industries (Caves), 39
creativity, 14, 19, 20, 26, 35, 141–44
Cruise, Tom, 214–16
Cunningham, Barry, 169–70

curiosity, 243
Cutler, Mary Schuler, 84–85, 87
Cyrus, Miley, 178

D'Angelo, Adam, 122–27
Delegat's Wine Estate, 262–63
"deliberate practice," 12
Dennis, Richard, 64–68, 86
Design of Everyday Things, The (Norman), 209
DiMaria, Jim, 67
Disney, 188–89
Dobkin, Bob, 72–74, 86–87
Doerr, John, 91–92
Dolan, James, 43
Donohue, Dan, 157
dot-com boom, 8, 92, 110
DoubleTree Hotels, 262
dropouts, 20, 28–29, 32–33, 65
Drucker, Peter, 40–41, 49, 240
DuBois, Greg, 26–27
Duckett, John, 262–63

Eastern Europe, 139–40, 148, 150
Eckhardt, Bill, 64–68
efficiency, 243–344
Effron, Marc, 6
Eitel, Nick, 97
Eliot, Charles William, 145, 207, 247
Enoch, Phillip, 31–32
Enron, 245–46
entrepreneurship, 108–9
Ericsson, K. Anders, 12
Esquivel, Josie, 136
Evans, David C., 60, 75–81, 85–87
Evans, Peter, 78
"executive intelligence" (ExI), 225–29
Executive Intelligence (Menkes), 226

Facebook, 44, 121–27, 136–38, 187, 191, 192, 239, 264, 266–67, 269
Fagan, Dan, 15–20
Farr, Steven, 51–52
Fast Company, 262
Federal Bureau of Investigation (FBI), 10, 238
  Hostage Rescue Team (HRT) of, 10, 110–16
  outdated assessment procedures of, 46–49
  retooling selection systems of, 47–49
  women and minorities in, 46, 48–49
Feldman, Gayle, 216
Fineberg, Harvey, 206
Fiorina, Carly, 220
five-to-one productivity standard, 10–11, 13
Fleming, Dazerell, 191
flight simulators, 75, 80, 107–8
Flor, Dan, 154
football, 40, 134–35, 210–13
Forbes, 255
f puzzle, 126–27
Fraenkel, Fred, 135

Frankfurt, Harry, 170–72
Freeh, Louis, 48
Friel, Thomas J., 222–23

Garzarelli, Elaine, 136
Gatekeepers, The (Steinberg), 93
General Electric, 187, 202–5, 245
    Corporate Audit Staff program of, 22–23,
        192–94
"genius awards," MacArthur, 141–44, 153, 167
geniuses:
    in computer science, 76–80
    creative, 141–44
    unrecognized, 59–80, 131
Gerstner, Lou, 151
ghSMART & Company, 219, 229–33
Giamatti, Paul, 107
Gibbons, Bob, 100–104, 119–20, 166
Gladwell, Malcolm, 221, 259
Goldman, William, 39
Goldman Sachs, 94–95, 136, 238
Goleman, Daniel, 98
Goodby, Silverstein & Partners, 131–34
Good to Great (Collins), 71
Google, 1–5, 10, 90–93, 124, 237
Graham, Martha, 186
Granovetter, Mark, 259
Gray, Kevin, 103, 104
Great Depression, 150
Griffin, Anthony, 51
Griggs, Josh, 52, 58
Groysberg, Boris, 45
Guidry, Ron, 86

hackathons, 191–92
Halsted, William S., 182, 187
Halsted Residents, 183–84
Hamlet, Rauch productions of, 154–58
Hanauer, Nick, 95–97
Hardy, Quentin, 255
Harper, William Rainey, 145
Harry Potter series, 7, 169–70
Hart, John, 173
Harvard University, 145, 205–9, 220, 247
Hennessy, Carly, 172–73
Henry, Alyssa, 270–71, 273
Herlong, H. Franklin, 84
Hewlett, Bill, 146
"hidden job market," 250, 252–53, 255–56,
        259, 265–66, 272
Hire with Your Head (Adler), 87
Hoover, Herbert, 150
Hoover, J. Edgar, 46–48
Hopkins, Nancy, 208
How the Mighty Fall (Collins), 43
Hsu, Jonathan, 125–27, 136–38
"hunger, speed, and weight," 225

Ibañez, Raúl, 129
IGN Entertainment, 260–61

Incredibles, The, 189–90
Indianapolis Colts, 134, 210–13
Ingram, Jack, 175–76
International Business Machines (IBM), 151
interviews, 47, 49, 104, 219, 221, 229–33
investing, 8, 45, 63–69, 72, 86, 94, 135–36,
        221, 238
    see also venture capitalists
Iron Giant, The, 188
Isaacson, John, 225
Ivlev, Alex, 260, 273

"jagged résumés," 13, 59–85, 94, 104, 123,
        201, 248–50, 268
Jennings, Brandon, 51
JetBlue, 133–34
Jobs, Steve, 92–93, 146–47
John Paul I, Pope, 149
John Paul II, Pope (Wojtyla, Karol), 140,
        148–50
Johns Hopkins School of Medicine, 10,
        82–84, 87, 94, 99, 180–85, 195–97, 241,
        245, 249
Johnson, Lyndon B., 224
Johnston, Larry, 202–4, 209
Jones, Allison, 179
Jones, Sharon, 259
Jordan, Bill, 171
Jordan, David Starr, 145
Jordan Vineyard & Winery, 263
Jordon, Michael, 119–20
Judson, Rob, 118–19
Jun Xia, 147

Kahl, Milt, 188
Kaplan, Steve, 233
Karp, Jason, 69
Kay, Alan, 59–60, 76–77, 123
Kelley, Clarence, 47
Kern, Kenneth, 197
Khurana, Rakesh, 200–201
Kiev, Ari, 68
King, Don, 26, 34–36
Kirk-Holland, Marcie, 272
Klebanov, Mark, 233
Kolmstetter, Elizabeth, 48–49
Konchalski, Tom, 118, 166
König, Franz, 139–40, 148–50
Kopp, Wendy, 38–39, 50–51
Kriplen, Nancy, 142n
Krol, John, 149
Kwiatkowski, Marc, 124

Land Nav test, 26–28
Lasorda, Tommy, 129
leadership, 16–19, 31–32, 114
Leaf, Ryan, 210–13
LeCompte, Elizabeth, 143
Lehman Brothers, 135–36
Lemann, Nicholas, 209

Leszczenski, James, 126, 137
Levit, Alexandra, 257
Levy, Marv, 135
Levy, Steven, 146
Lewis, Michael, 221
Lewis-Lamonica, Emily, 53–57, 246
licensing, history of, 88–89
Lincecum, Tim, 69–71, 87–88
Lincoln, Abraham, 6
LinkedIn, 258, 266
Linear Technology, 72–74, 238
Log Drill, 30
Lombardi, Vince, 6
Long Tail, The (Anderson), 128
long tail of talent, 127, 134, 239
"lottery tickets," 159–79, 239
   see also talent spotting, taking chances in
Lublin, Joann, 202

MacArthur, John D., 142
MacArthur, Rod, 142n
MacArthur Fellowship program,
   141–44, 167
McCurdy, Phil, 147
McKinsey Global Institute, 264
McNulty, John, 95
Malcolm, Ian, 170–72
"Managing Talent" course, 213
Manning, Peyton, 210–13
march/endurance test, 31–32
Marshall, George, 6, 256–57
Martinet, Drake, 268
Mayerson, Mark, 44
medicine, 9, 10, 72, 81–85, 88, 180–85
Menkes, Justin, 225–28
Menkes Stark, 226
Merchants of Culture (Thompson), 169
Michael, Gary, 201, 205
Microsoft, 43, 96, 124
Milocheck, Mike, 79
mistakes, failures, 14, 39–40, 44, 152, 153,
   154–55, 165, 187, 190, 245–46
   expensive, 42, 44, 165, 173, 201
   fear of, 5–6, 11
   fickle public taste in, 172–77
   hazy sense of job context in, 40–41,
      44–46, 49
   in hiring, 199–217
   learning from, 18, 68–69, 125, 199
   as motivation, 190–93
   of narrowness and superficiality, 41–44
   of outdated approaches, 46–49
   placing blame in, 209–10
   in publishing, 168–69
   of wrong priorities, 205–9
Mondani, Peter, 193
Moneyball (Lewis), 7, 221–22
Monster.com, 251
Mora, Jim, 212
Morgan, Speer, 168

Moritz, Michael, 91–92
motivation, 13, 22, 24, 36, 79, 87, 129, 212–13
   challenge as, 190–93, 245
   idealism as, 194–98
   mistakes as, 190–93
   teamwork as, 194–98
music industry, 6–7, 50, 93, 105, 159–63,
   172–79

Nagel, Gregory L., 220
Nardelli, Robert, 204
Nashville, 159–62, 173–74, 177–78
National Basketball Association (NBA),
   42, 51
National Football League (NFL), 134, 210–13
National Rifle Association, 258
National Institutes of Health, 184–85
Netscape Communications, 78, 87, 91, 92, 243
Newton, Isaac, 141
New York Knicks, 42
New York Yankees, 163–65
No Child Left Behind Act (2001), 51
No Heroes: Inside the FBI's Secret
   Counter-Terror Force (Coulson), 111
Noriega, Manuel, 25
Norman, Donald A., 209

On Bullshit (Frankfurt), 170–72
One Day, All Children (Kopp), 50
O'Neill, Pat, 82
Operation Iron Cross, 24–25
Ordoñez, Jennifer, 173
Oregon Shakespeare Festival (OSF), 152, 156
Orkut, 266
Osius, Ted, 153

Page, Larry, 91, 93
Paone, Ralph, 133–34, 265
papacy, 140, 148–50
Parker, Jerry, 67
Paul VI, Pope, 149
Peace Corps, 37, 194–95
Peck, Danielle, 176–77
Perfect Enough (Anders), 220
Perfect Thing, The (Jobs), 146
performing arts, 69, 105, 131, 172, 241
   see also specific categories
perseverance, 12, 24, 52–53, 58, 108–9,
   114, 191
personal insights, 62, 81–99, 240–41
Phillips, Sam, 93
philosophy, 170–72
Photoshop, 60, 78
Pi, Li, 267, 273
Piazza, Mike, 129–31
Pierce, Charles, 113–14, 116
Piet (computer language), 126–27
Pinterest, 266, 268
Piser, John, 114–15
Pink, Daniel H., 248

Pixar Studios, 60, 78, 80, 87, 187–89, 243, 245
Polian, Bill, 134–35, 210–13, 217
Posnanski, Joe, 39–40
Predictably Irrational (Ariely), 41
presidential elections, 150–51
Pride and Prejudice (Austen), 168
Priestley, Evan, 123–25, 130–31, 249
Princeton University Press (PUP), 170
Public Enemies (Burrough), 46
publishing industry, 168–72, 216, 239
Puzzle Master, 126–27, 130, 136–37, 166
puzzles:
    as faulty selection tools, 43–44
    programming, 122–27, 136–38, 239

Quora, 266–68

Rabar, Paul, 67
Rauch, Bill, 152–58
Raybourn, Herb, 163
Raymond, Lee, 227
"Reaching for the Stars" (Shaw), 213–14
Reagan, Ronald, 151
Reay, Robert, 73
Redstone, Sumner, 215
Repify, 266
Resch-Fingerlos, Gerhard, 226–27
resilience, 13–14, 21, 52–58, 105, 110, 187, 241–43
résumés, 3, 104, 243
    "upside-down" evaluation of, 4, 7, 82, 187–88, 237
    see also "jagged résumés"
Rich, Adrienne, 143
Rivera, Mariano, 40, 163–65, 169, 260
Rivers, Austin, 117–18
Rivers, Glenn "Doc," 117
Rivkin, Jack, 135–36
Rivlin, Robert, 80
Roberts, Julia, 260
Rockefeller, John D., 145
Roebling, John, 269
Roizen, Heidi, 108–9
Roman Catholic Church, 139–40, 148–50
Roosevelt, Franklin D., 150
Rose, Liz, 177
Rosen, Sherwin, 89–90
Rowling, J. K., 7, 40, 169, 237, 249
Russell Reynolds, 224

SAC Capital, 68–69
Sacolick, Bennet, 33
Salomon Brothers, 45, 136
San Francisco Giants, 70–71, 87
Schmidt, Martin J., 42
Schott, Joseph, 47
Seago, Howie, 157
Searching for a Corporate Savior (Khurana), 200

Sefferman, Ian, 266
Seidler, Howard, 67
self-reliance, 244
Sellars, Peter, 153
Sessions, William, 48
Shanahan, Brian, 29–30
Shanks, Tom, 67
Shaw, Kathryn, 213–15
Shooting House (FBI), 112–13
Shriram, Ram, 91
Silicon Graphics, 78
Simons, Anna, 25
Siwak, Karen, 252–53
Sketchpad, 76–77
Smart, Brad, 230
Smart, Geoff, 230–31
Smuin, Doug, 108
Socolow, Daniel, 143–44, 167
social graph, 269–71
Sorenson, Morten, 233
Southwest Airlines, 262
Spencer Stuart, 202, 226–30
Spivey, Junior, 129
sports, 6, 9, 10, 41–43, 69, 105
    scouting in, 100–104, 116–20, 134–35, 163–67
    see also specific sports
Stamoulis, Dean, 224–25
Stanford, Leland, 145
Stanford University, 145, 213
Stark, Robert, 226
Steinberg, Jacques, 93
Stepinac, Alojzije, 139
Stewart, Susan, 143
"stiff ratio," 172
Still, Ray, 83
Stimpson, Catharine, 141–43
Stone, Robert, 207
Street, Randy, 218–20, 231
Stumbling on Wins (Berri and Schmidt), 42
Sullinger, Jared, 101–4, 231
Summers, Lawrence, 206–9
"Sunday School," 197
Sun Microsystems, 92
Sun records, 93
surgeons, 180–85
Susmer, John, 257, 264
Sutherland, Ivan, 76, 80
Swift, Taylor, 6–7, 161, 177–79, 237, 260

Talbott, Strobe, 206
talent, 12, 13, 74
    challenges to, 186–87, 190–93, 245
    defining of, 8, 11, 39
    difficult aspects of, 188–90, 199–217
    early assessment of, 12, 166
    first encounters with, 162–63
    fostering of, 180–84, 194–98, 244–45
    great vs. right, 187, 200, 203–4, 244
    inability to tap into, 44, 45

talent (cont.)
    overpayment for, 214–17
    potential, 10, 31–32, 71, 87, 90, 106–7,
        151–53, 166, 237
    predictions of, 3, 5, 6, 7, 11, 74–75, 103, 159
    self-taught, 136–37
    widening view of, 236–39
"talent conglomerates," 45–46
"talent differential," 44
Talent on Demand (Cappelli), 89
talent spotting:
    applying lessons in, 235–47
    assessor's life experience in, 62, 81–99,
        240–41
    attention to details in, 21–22, 62, 98, 219
    contemporary failures in, 5–6
    explorer's spirit in, 85–87, 139–58, 246
    finding new ground in, 130, 132
    as frozen in time, 41, 46–49, 50
    going beyond immediate task in, 107
    hazy sense of job context in, 40–41,
        44–46, 49, 240
    historical view of, 6, 9, 11–13
    optimistic outlook in, 130, 139–58, 238–39
    retooling selection systems for, 37–39,
        47–49, 50–58, 109–10
    simplifying search in, 242–47
    strategies for finding unlikely prospects
        in, 130–31
    taking chances in, 7, 10–11, 13, 131, 153,
        159–79, 199, 237, 239
    as too narrow or superficial, 41–44, 50
    traditional, 5–6, 12, 14, 47, 61, 87–88
    universal qualities of, 9, 23, 233, 239–42
    see also auditions; candidates
"talent that shouts," 13, 123, 180–98, 201
    see also candidates, superstar
"talent that whispers," 13, 22, 121–38, 201, 238
    see also candidates, overlooked
TalentBin, 266
teachers, teaching, 9, 37–39, 51
    see also Teach for America
Teach For America (TFA), 21, 105, 187,
    195, 246
    retooling of selection system for, 37–39,
        50–58, 109–10
    West Coast recruiting session for, 54–57
Teachout, Terry, 157–58
team-building, teamwork, 16–19, 28, 31–32,
    35, 111–12, 115, 120, 194–98, 241
temperament, 63–68, 212–13
tenacity, 28–31, 35
tests, in selection process, 12, 15–36, 43–44,
    89, 112, 211, 227
test scores, 3, 51, 81–84, 89
Texas, education reform in, 51
theater, 63, 152–58
    see also acting
"third question," 222–23
Thomas, Bill, 168

Thomas, Isiah, 42–43
Thompson, John, 169
"three Ps," 256, 272
Tidrow, Dick, 70–71, 86, 87
'Til Death, 106
tinkering, 73–74, 86
The Tipping Point (Gladwell), 259
Topgrading, 230
Toy Story series, 189–90
Trading Places, 66n
Trahan, Bob, 192
trailer-pushing task, 15–21
Tucker, Amy, 241
"Turtles" experiment, 64–68
Twitter, 267, 270–71

Udelsman, Rob, 182–85, 198
universities, founding of, 144–45
Utah, University of, 75–80, 85–86, 87, 243

Valory Music, 179
Vash, Susan, 106–7
venture capitalists, 9, 10, 90–93, 108–9,
    110, 244
Vietnam War, 15, 25, 109
Vital Lies, Simple Truths (Goleman), 98
Volckmann, Russell, 24–25

Walker, Daniel, 146
Warnock, John, 77–78
Webster, William, 48
Weigel, George, 149
Weinberg, Sidney, 94
Weiss, James, 82–85, 98–99, 241
Welch, Jack, 202–3
Wendt, Gary, 204
West, Cornel, 207
"What can go right?," 130, 139–58, 170,
    238–39
What Color Is Your Parachute?, (Bolles), 251
"What is wind?" test, 37–38, 44, 56
Whelan, David, 254–56
Whipple procedure, 196, 198
Wilhelm, Hoyt, 164
Winn, Luke, 103
"winner's curse," 201–2
Witness to Hope (Weigel), 149
Wojtyla, Karol (Pope John Paul II), 140,
    149–50
women, 46, 48–49, 135–36, 208, 238, 241
Wonderlic exam, 211
Wong, Yishan, 122, 125
work ethic, 71–72
World War II, 6, 24–25, 85, 89, 109
World Wildlife Fund, 258
"Wow!" factor, 4, 105, 163, 246
Wuorinen, Charles, 142

Yearwood, Trisha, 174
YouTube, 266, 268